Praise for
Hervie Haufler's
Codebreakers' Victory

"Makes the provocative argument that codebreakers were the decisive factor in the Allied victory—more important than any MacArthur or Eisenhower or Nimitz . . . an accessible account [of] unsung heroes gagged by secrecy orders who are finding recognition only at the end of their lives."

—*The Baltimore Sun*

"A fascinating account of codebreaking in history in both Europe and the Pacific/Far East theaters of WWII, as well as the Cold War."

—SHAEF Communiqué

THE SPIES WHO NEVER WERE

THE TRUE STORY OF THE NAZI SPIES WHO WERE ACTUALLY ALLIED DOUBLE AGENTS

HERVIE HAUFLER

NAL
CALIBER

NAL Caliber
Published by New American Library, a division of
Penguin Group (USA) Inc., 375 Hudson Street,
New York, New York 10014, USA
Penguin Group (Canada), 90 Eglinton Avenue East, Suite 700, Toronto,
Ontario M4P 2Y3, Canada (a division of Pearson Penguin Canada Inc.)
Penguin Books Ltd., 80 Strand, London WC2R 0RL, England
Penguin Ireland, 25 St. Stephen's Green, Dublin 2,
Ireland (a division of Penguin Books Ltd.)
Penguin Group (Australia), 250 Camberwell Road, Camberwell, Victoria 3124,
Australia (a division of Pearson Australia Group Pty. Ltd.)
Penguin Books India Pvt. Ltd., 11 Community Centre, Panchsheel Park,
New Delhi - 110 017, India
Penguin Group (NZ), cnr Airborne and Rosedale Roads, Albany,
Auckland 1310, New Zealand (a division of Pearson New Zealand Ltd.)
Penguin Books (South Africa) (Pty.) Ltd., 24 Sturdee Avenue,
Rosebank, Johannesburg 2196, South Africa

Penguin Books Ltd., Registered Offices:
80 Strand, London WC2R 0RL, England

First published by NAL Caliber, an imprint of New American Library,
a division of Penguin Group (USA) Inc.

First Printing, January 2006
10 9 8 7 6 5 4 3 2 1

NAL CALIBER and the "C" logo are trademarks of Penguin Group (USA) Inc.

LIBRARY OF CONGRESS CATALOGING-IN-PUBLICATION DATA:

Haufler, Hervie.
    The spies who never were: the true story of the Nazi spies who were actually Allied
double agents/Hervie Haufler.
        p. cm.
    ISBN 0-451-21751-9 (trade pbk.)
    1. World War, 1939–1945—Secret service—Germany. 2. World War, 1939–1945—Secret
service—Great Britain. 3. Espionage—Germany—History—20th century. 4. Espionage—
Great Britain—History—20th century.   I. Title.
    D810.S7H37 2006
    940.54'86'092243—dc22   2005022622

Set in Adobe Garamond
Designed by Ginger Legato

Printed in the United States of America

Dedicated to the memory of friends
William Bowling, Harold Etler,
Mel Feinberg, Stanley Hardin,
Carl Peterson and Eugene Tinnell,
who were killed fighting a war that
we believed in, that was civilization saving
and that was non-preemptive

CONTENTS

CHAPTER ONE

THE MOST DELICIOUS IRONY

As the 1930s unfolded, Nazi Germany's chancellor, Adolf Hitler, discounted any thought of another war between Germany and Great Britain. He saw the British as an Aryan-blooded superior people whose rulers were descendants of German royalty. They should, therefore, be sympathetic to his ethnic policies. As a capitalist country, Britain should also be supportive of his animus toward the Communists of the Soviet Union. Instead of making war against him, the British might at least protect his back while the German war machine, the Wehrmacht, was wiping out the detested, ethnically inferior Bolsheviks.

In these beliefs, Hitler was encouraged by members of the British upper classes who expressed admiration for him, his regime and his ideas. It must have seemed to the German chancellor that much of the British aristocracy was on his side. Among those he could count on for support were the Duke of Westminster, the Duke of Hamilton, the Duke of Wellington, the Marquess of Graham and Baron Redesdale, father of the Mitford sisters, two of whom became such ardent pro-Nazis that the eldest, Diana, married Oswald Mosley, founder of the British Union of Fascists. The marriage took place in Joseph Goebbels' drawing room in Berlin with Hitler as one of six guest witnesses. Topping off this pantheon of Hitler enthusiasts was Britain's former king, the Duke of Windsor, who was feted by the Nazis and spoke glowingly of their merits.

Subsequently, the pro-Hitler British coterie so entranced Deputy

Fuehrer Rudolf Hess, whose blind, doglike devotion had begun to pall on Hitler, that he tried to regain his master's favor by making his mad solo flight to Scotland, where he hoped to enlist the aid of the Duke of Hamilton in negotiating a separate peace between the "Aryan blood brothers" of Britain and Germany.

With all this to sway him, Hitler was understandably loath to see this promising relationship soured by the possible unmasking of German secret agents operating in Britain. So as not to offend the British, in the summer of 1935 he ordered the Abwehr, the German defense and security intelligence organization, not to establish any spy network in Great Britain. Even when the Germans invaded Poland as a necessary prelude to their war against the Soviets and drove Britain to join with France in declaring war against Germany, Hitler persisted in believing that the British would come to terms and collaborate rather than continue to fight.

Only in mid-1940, when Britain refused to negotiate for peace after the fall of France, did Hitler change his mind. He gave up his hopes for a rapprochement with the stubborn British and accepted the idea that his forces might have to invade and neutralize the threat on his western flank before he could launch his planned attack against the Soviets. It was then that he ordered the Abwehr to carry out Operation Lena, his program for playing catch-up in the spy game.

His secret service was forced to build upon slim prewar beginnings. One reliable agent in their fold was Arthur George Owens, whose anger against the British was fueled by his ardent Welsh nationalist beliefs. Owens was an electrical engineer, chemist and inventor working for a high-technology firm with business interests in Germany. His special abilities in battery technology opened doors for him on the Continent. On his trips during the thirties, he let his German contacts know of his bitter anti-British feelings. Approached by the Abwehr, he agreed to serve the Germans as an informer who could supply useful information about the Royal Navy. To the delight of his controllers in Hamburg, Owens was willing to do more than rely on only his own observations. He began recruiting other dissidents to serve as his subagents reporting from vantage points around the British Isles.

When the war began and the Germans seized and occupied Jersey, one of Britain's Channel Islands, the Abwehr found another willing agent in

Eddie Chapman, a professional safecracker whom the British had embittered by capturing him and imprisoning him on the island. His German controllers saw in him and his criminal expertise the makings of an ideal saboteur. They released him from prison, code-named him Fritzchen and brought him to Germany for demolition training before parachuting him back into England.

In one of their own prisons, the Germans held a Polish Army Air Force officer, Roman Garby-Czerniawski. After the Wehrmacht had crushed Poland in 1939, he had escaped to France and, when France was conquered, become the leader of a Polish-French resistance group. He and some sixty of his followers had been captured by the Germans and faced execution. A smart Abwehr officer, however, recognized that Garby-Czerniawski had the intelligence and cool courage to become a first-rate spy. After interviewing the Pole, the officer offered him a deal: Become an agent in Britain for the Abwehr, and instead of executing the members of Garby-Czerniawski's resistance group, the Germans would treat them as prisoners of war. Garby-Czerniawski at first rejected the offer, but when the German armies began to roll up major victories against the Soviets, he reconsidered. He now saw that Russia, not Germany, was Poland's real enemy. By means of a prearranged "escape" to Britain, he became one of the Abwehr's most valued agents.

A Spaniard, Juan Pujol, sought out the Germans and volunteered to become a spy for them. Approaching the German consulate in Madrid, he asserted his willingness to undertake this dangerous duty because of the hatred of Communism he had formed during the Spanish Civil War. In July 1941 the Germans equipped him with a questionnaire, secret ink, money and an address to which he could mail his findings, code-named him Arabel and sent him to England. He began immediately sending back letters filled with acute observations. In addition, like Owens, he began to line up subagents to work with him, reporting from advantageous sites throughout England. His flow of information became so copious and valuable that in time, with his spymaster's approval, he began radio transmissions.

Dusko Popov was the scion of a wealthy Yugoslav family. Through his family's business interests and his own personal charm he moved comfortably in the elevated social circles of many countries. Once he had been chosen to introduce Britain's yacht-minded Duke of York to the Belgrade sailing club during the duke's visit to Yugoslavia. Before the war, Popov had gone to seek his doctorate in law at Germany's Freiberg University— an experience that had made him familiar with the regime of Adolf Hitler. Five months after the war began, and while he was practicing law in Belgrade, he was approached by two members of the Abwehr. Together they laid out a proposition to Popov. The Germans had agents in Britain, they told him, but none who was capable of operating at a high enough social level to secure top-drawer political, economic and military information. The Abwehr wanted Popov to go to England, under the cover of his business interests, and open the doors that would provide him, and the Germans, with information available in no other way. The proposal appealed to Popov's adventurous nature. In addition, he was pleased by the generous financing the Abwehr promised him. Code-named Ivan by his German spymasters, he went to England and made himself an acute observer of British leaders throughout the war.

Lily Sergueiew hated the Russian Communists: they had driven her family out of their homeland during a purge of suspected czarist supporters. Transplanted in France at the war's outset, she volunteered to serve as a spy for Germany. Her ability to handle Morse code radio messages interested the Abwehr officers in Paris. She was sent to England and was soon sending back to her spymaster as many as three reports per day detailing the Allied forces preparing for the invasion of northern France.

Conducting Operation Lena, the Abwehr sought out adventure-minded young men they could train as spies. One of these was Wulf Schmidt, the son of a Danish mother and a German father who had served in the German air force in its early days. The family lived in Germany until the start of the First World War. Then his mother took Wulf back to Denmark. He was, however, a German citizen, and when the Nazis came to power he became excited by a reading of Hitler's *Mein Kampf*. He left off his law studies at Lübeck University and joined the Nazi Party in Denmark. His zeal also prompted him to volunteer to be a spy for the Germans. After completing his training in Morse code, radio transmission, code work and parachute jumping, he was designated agent V-3725, a serial number indicating both the Abwehr station running him and his position on their list of agents. On the night of September 19, 1940, he landed in England, clutching his transmitter. During the war he sent more than a thousand messages back to Germany and became so trusted that, as we shall see, he became the Abwehr's paymaster to other agents.

In 1941 the Abwehr recruited two Norwegian lads, Helge Moe and Tor Glad, and trained them to be saboteurs. Landed by rubber dinghy on a Scottish beach along with demolition equipment and a two-way radio set, they succeeded in such missions as destroying a food storage dump and an electricity generating station. While their radio equipment was meant to be used to report their sabotage efforts, they also became keen observers of Allied military moves in Scotland and northern England.

The Abwehr's spy network was not limited to the United Kingdom. In Cairo, as an example, they had recruited a very productive agent named Paul Nicossof, an anti-British resident willing to keep the Germans informed on Britain's forces in the Middle East.

With these and some other lesser agents in place and submitting reams of valuable information, the Germans were confident that their needs for special intelligence were being met and they could slack off in extending their spy network.

For the Allies, the most delicious irony of the war was that not one of these agents was what he or she purported to be. The entire network of individuals seeming to work as spies for the Germans was actually under British control. It may seem incredible that every spy the Germans thought they had stationed in Britain was a double agent reporting back to his or her spymaster only what British case officers permitted them to report, but it is true. Those messages did contain carefully selected true information of some value, but increasingly they also included an edge of misinformation calculated to deceive the Germans and lead them to self-damaging decisions. As an official report expressed it: "By means of the double-agent system, we actually ran and controlled the German espionage system in this country."

Recognition that this claim was true took time to be accepted. Those in charge of the double-agent system ruefully admitted later that "opportunities were lost and chances missed by a pardonable excess of caution." Although they could not readily acknowledge that their control was complete, the British saw that they could build on the agents they *were* managing.

True, Arthur Owens, code-named Snow by the British as a partial anagram of his name, was Welsh, but any anti-British resentment he may have felt was not strong enough to make him serve the Nazis once the war began. Always rather a slick opportunist, Owens saw the chance, prewar, to use his business trips to Germany to collect items of interest to British intelligence while also passing on bits of information considered of value by the Abwehr. As war approached, however, he declared his real allegiance to Britain and agreed to his double-agent role. As for the band of subagents he had supposedly recruited in Britain, they were all figments of his imagination. To have Snow's network of spies reporting from different points in the UK was fully as much an advantage to his British controllers as it was perceived to be by his German spymasters.

Eddie Chapman's explanation of why he was ready to serve the Nazis was also a pose rather than a reality. Whatever anger he felt toward Britain for sticking him in stir was far from being a powerful enough motivation to make him betray his country.

Chapman was a nervy character who convinced the German command on Jersey to believe in his desire for vengeance against his captors, release him from prison and send him to the Continent to hone his skills with explosives. Trained by the Germans to be a demolition expert, he was parachuted back onto British soil, where he promptly gave himself up, received the British code name ZigZag and was helped to conduct sabotage efforts that were convincing when photographed by German reconnaissance planes without doing real damage to the facilities supposedly blown up.

Garby-Czerniawski's expressed belief that Germany was Poland's best hope for the future was only a ruse. From the first moment he made his deal with the Germans, he had betrayal in mind. Reaching England in July 1942, he soon declared himself to British military intelligence. It was arranged that he would join the staff of the Polish military in exile and serve as their liaison with the Royal Air Force—a position that would, in the Germans' eyes, make him a valuable source of information about Allied air force plans. Originally giving himself the code name of Armand, he became Armand Walenty when he operated his resistance group in

France and Hubert when he agreed to be a spy for Germany. He made his final transition to the British code name of Brutus, derived from his first name, Roman, and became a highly respected agent for the Nazis even though he was doing his best to deceive them.

The antipathy toward Communism that Juan Pujol gave as his reason for serving the Germans was more than overmatched by his detestation of Nazi Fascism. He entered the spy game simply because he wanted to do what he could to bring down the Hitler regime. Code-named Garbo by the British because he matched the film star Greta Garbo's ability to adapt to many different roles, Pujol, with his cast of imagined subagents, became the most highly regarded of the Germans' spies while also reigning as the star of the British show. The thousands of messages he dispatched to his Abwehr controller in Madrid contained enough fact to sustain the approval of the Germans and enough fiction to satisfy his English guides.

When Dusko Popov was courted by the Germans in Belgrade, he slipped away to check with the British embassy there. Yes, he was told, go along with the Germans while actually working for us. Popov did go to Britain as a very well-off Yugoslav businessman. His controllers there saw to it that he mingled with the governmental and social leaders from whom, as the Nazis hoped, he could secure indiscreetly revealed information of great value to the Germans. The British gave him the code name Tricycle because he soon lined up two subagents to form a triumvirate of deceit in Britain.

Lily Sergueiew's hatred for the Bolsheviks was only a pose. Her real animus was against the Nazis. She conned the Abwehr into taking her on as a spy in England who could send back reports both by secret-ink letters and by radio. She arranged for her true role by acquainting the British with her intentions even before her arrival in London. A temperamental woman given to instant rages, she nevertheless became a highly valued double agent with the code name Treasure. Her early letters relied heavily on material supplied by the British. But with the approach of D-Day, she began a heavy schedule of radio transmissions whose content was enriched by her romance with an American officer in England. Treasure made herself a prime figure in misleading the Germans to expect an attack accross the Channel from southeastern England rather than in Normandy.

As for Germany's own assigned agents, the hurried training they received left them vulnerable to gaffes that quickly gave them away. One made the mistake of trying to use his forged ration book to pay for a meal in a restaurant. Another thought that when he was billed two and six, he should pay two pounds and six shillings, not two shillings and sixpence. Still another tried to enter a pub at nine a.m., not realizing that the law forbade pubs to open before ten. And none of them could know that their faked identity papers contained easy-to-spot errors that had been placed there when, in preparing the documents, the Germans had sought the advice of Arthur Owens.

The prospect of a German invasion of Britain in 1940 forced the Abwehr to mount a desperate effort to make up for lost time and infiltrate spies into England. Of the twenty-one agents they landed on British soil, all but one were either captured or gave themselves up. The exception committed suicide. Faced with the choice of cooperating or being hanged, a number opted for survival. Wulf Schmidt was one of these. Code-named Tate for reasons explained later, he gradually underwent a most welcome conversion, rejecting the Nazi tyranny and embracing the democratic lifestyle of the British. He developed into one of the most trusted and useful of the double agents.

As soon as they could manage after their landing in Scotland, Helge Moe and Tor Glad surrendered to local police and were turned over to British counterintelligence. The Norwegians were there to commit sabotage, right? Very well, the same sort of British tricksters who were to aid Eddie Chapman went to work for their new double agents, whom they code-named Mutt and Jeff from the names of two American cartoon characters. The deception experts staged blowups that the successful pair could describe in their transmissions. Their reports, together with outraged accounts in the British press, made gratifying news for their German controllers. Subsequently, the duo figured prominently in one of the main deceptions supporting the D-Day landings.

As for the Cairo agent Paul Nicossof, he was what the British came to speak of as an entirely "notional"—that is, imaginary—spy. With the connivance of British intelligence in Cairo, he had been established there by an Italian Jew, Renato Levi, code-named Cheese, perhaps because he was the bait to catch the Axis mice. Levi had approached the German intelligence chiefs in Rome with the proposal that he go to Egypt, line up an agent there and return to handle the Italian end of the informational link. Using scripts prepared by the British and a British noncom as his radio operator, the notional Nicossof transmitted enough truth to affirm his bona fides before beginning deceptions important to the Middle East command.

While these were the main players in the double agents' drama, there was a large supporting cast. In all, some 120 individuals became double agents, many for only short periods, others until the end of the war. The files bristle with code names such as Balloon, Careless, Gelatine, Hamlet, Lipstick, Snark, Mullet, Puppet and Treasure. The humans beyond the code names varied from a successful English businessman too old for active service but wanting to do his bit, to a Yugoslav domestic servant working in England and recruited by the Abwehr to report on food prices, urban morale and whatever useful gossip she could pick up.

The British in charge of the double agents delighted in the success stories of captured would-be agents who were "turned." But they also realized that some of these captives had to be executed, for either of two reasons. One was that when a spy was captured not quietly by intelligence forces but very publicly by local police, press accounts were more than likely to reach the Germans. If no action was taken, the enemy's suspicions might be aroused. The other reason was that some publicized executions had to take place in order to protect those who were turned and working under British control. To have all their agents land without any being detected would, again, have raised questions in the minds of Abwehr officials.

In the end, the British wasted no time in gloating over the irony of having an enemy's entire espionage system under their thumbs. British leaders recognized theirs as an unprecedented but most fragile advantage, one that deserved the immediate and undistracted attention of the most gifted minds that could be assembled. Fortunately for the history of our times, those individuals did come together to create the system that made the most of that advantage without ever committing a blunder that would have negated it. Their task was huge: to supply superior brainpower to make up for Britain's inferiority in arms and numbers of fighting men.

CHAPTER TWO

MASTERMINDS OF THE DOUBLE CROSS

When the leaders of British military intelligence realized the potential benefits of controlling the German espionage program in the United Kingdom, they faced a hard decision: how to organize the management of the pseudo-spies. Wisely it was decided that this was an operation that should be outside the purview of Britain's existing intelligence agencies MI5 and MI6. With the one focusing on internal security and the other on espionage and counterespionage outside Britain, their responsibilities were too broad, varied and demanding to allow them to devote the kind of concentrated attention required by the running of a group of double agents. From that point on, it may seem to today's observer that the authorities went a bit overboard in their organizing zeal. They set up one group whose sole function was to coordinate the interests of MI5 and MI6 in managing the agents. That group, the Wireless Board, will be mentioned this once for accuracy's sake and will not appear again. Since that board did not concern itself with the day-to-day activities of the double-cross system, this task was assigned to a subcommittee, labelled B1A. And since B1A's charter was a broad one, extending to the care and feeding of the double agents as well as the assignment and direction of their case officers, the highly specialized challenge of creating and controlling the messages transmitted by the double agents was given to still another subcommittee, the Twenty Committee.

To head up B1A, the choice was a canny Scotsman, Colonel Thomas

A. Robertson, known as "Tar" for the way he initialed documents. And under him, to take charge of the Twenty Committee, the authorities selected an Oxford don, John Cecil Masterman, who had become proficient in German while a prisoner of war for four years during World War I.

Most of those associated with the Twenty Committee considered Masterman an inspired choice. Not content with writing only academic texts, he was the author of a well-received mystery, *An Oxford Tragedy*, and a family memoir, *Fate Cannot Harm Her*. Ewen Montagu, the Royal Navy's representative on the Committee, said of him that he "was not only a wise man, full of common sense, but also extremely tactful." Now, as his wartime duty, Masterman turned his agile mind to overseeing the preparation of texts of the messages that Britain's double agents sent to their controllers.

It was a finicky proposition. The reports transmitted by Garbo, Tate, Brutus and the others had to include enough accurate and revealing information to satisfy Abwehr controllers and confirm the agents' credibility, yet they could never disclose anything that might prove overly harmful to Britain's war effort. Also, for the work of the double agents to have a favorable long-term payoff for the British, some of the messages must eventually begin to include a subtle leavening of misinformation— and not random bits of untruth but seeming facts that, when put together by the Germans, would lead their commanders to false estimates and wrong decisions. It was considered important that the Germans must work hard to reach their conclusions, like fitting together the pieces of a complex jigsaw puzzle. The principle applied was that intelligence too easily obtained is intelligence too readily suspected.

The challenge was one that appealed to the antic, fey aspect of many British intellectuals. Reading notes left by Committee members such as Montagu, one senses the Oxbridgian gusto in playing this game of clever artifice. There was a fierce glee in putting one over on the stolid Germans, who, Hugh Trevor-Roper noted, "did not have imagination." Montagu put it more strongly: "In our penetration of their activities, we were helped immensely by the stupidity of the Germans." Probably a fairer judgment is that expressed by Whitney Bendeck in her study *The Art of Deception;* the British success "was not the result of German incompetence, but was due to the superior quality of the British system."

It should be noted that the very name of the Committee reflected that sportive edge of the British spirit: the Roman numerals XX amount to a double cross.

Committee members included representatives from the War Office, Foreign Office, the Home Defense Executive and the Home Forces as well as from the intelligence arms of the Royal Navy and the Air Ministry. Later, when the United States became an ally, representatives from U.S. services were added.

Masterman's Twenty Committee had its first meeting on January 2, 1941, and met every Wednesday thereafter until May 10, 1945, a total of 226 sessions. He liked to claim that his most important decision as the Committee's chairman was to arrange, despite the severe rationing of those early days, to provide tea and buns at every meeting—certainly one good reason for the Committee's nearly perfect attendance record.

Masterman was wise enough to see that the Committee must, in its early going, emphasize the need for passing true information before beginning to add in misleading material. The Committee, he wrote in his postwar summation, was "required to pass as much accurate information as possible for as many agents as possible, with a view to building them up for later deception."

An ironclad rule of the Committee, however, was that no message should ever go to the enemy whose contents had not been approved by the appropriate authority. There were discouraging times when carefully wrought scripts had to be scrapped because of a turndown from above. Overall, however, a reading of the messages that *were* approved shows the authorities stretching in order to cooperate. As Masterman wrote in his postwar analysis: "Only the most strenuous efforts, together with a great deal of goodwill and desire to assist on all sides, enabled us to keep up a sufficient flow of traffic to maintain and build up the cases which we desired to keep alive."

To read the questions asked of their supposed agents by the German controllers is to wonder how any assembly of minds, no matter how clever, could have devised answers that seemed to meet the demands without giving away information which would be detrimental. To cite one example: in February 1941, Tricycle was asked: "Do Vickers Armstrong possess factories at Brighton and Haward to the west of the aerodrome? Have the buildings which were near the aerodrome and which were used for Army purposes now been taken over by Vickers for manufacturing? How many Wellingtons [bombers] do Armstrong make each month? Where else are Wellingtons or parts for Wellingtons made? We want sketches showing sites for Vickers at Weybridge and Vickers near Crayford."

The answers approved for Tricycle in replying to these demands are spread over a number of his subsequent messages. A succinct example of questions and response is this exchange between Brutus and his spymaster in March 1944:

Q: What is the special task of the 13th Fighter Group of the RAF? Is there a 9th and 19th Air Support Command in the 9th American air force?
A: The 13th Fighter Group is at Inverness and is used for the defense of the north of Scotland area. I have heard nothing of any special task. With regard to the Ninth USA Air Force, Commander-in-Chief is General Brereton, Deputy Commander General Joyce; composition, Ninth Bomber Command, Ninth and Nineteenth Air Support Command and Ninth Troop Carrier Command. The Ninth Air Force arrived in England at the end of last year. It will play the same part with regard to the American army as the Tactical Air Force plays with regard to the British army. At first it was obliged to cooperate with the strategic bombing forces of the Eighth Air Force but this phase is now past and it is concentrated in the region of operations. The Ninth Bomber Command will continue to occupy the aerodromes north of the Thames Estuary. The Ninth Air Support Command is concentrated in the neighbourhood of the American units in the south and southeast. The 9th Air Support group is concentrated in the Kent area, which is to be its theatre of operations, on aerodromes between Ashford and Tunbridge.

To fashion responses such as this to daily barrages of spymasters' questions required both great ingenuity by the Committee's members and, as shown by Brutus's answers, great leniency on the part of their reviewing authorities.

One glimpse into how the challenge was met is given by Montagu: "It was so important to deception work to be able to put oneself completely in the mind of the enemy, to think as *they* would think on *their* information and decide what *they* would do—ignoring what you knew yourself and what you would do."

Committee members were constantly aware of their enterprise's vulnerability—always in their minds was an awareness of how this lacy structure could be demolished by one blow, one egregious error, one blown agent. The Committee served as a clearinghouse where the work of the various agents could be compared and kept consistent. Masterman and his colleagues made a cautious start. They must, they felt, be very guarded about mixing in misinformation until they could assure themselves that all the German agents in Britain really were in their hands.

Confidence in that assumption was slow in coming. Masterman wrote that "we could not bring ourselves to believe that we did in fact control the German system." The only sensible course seemed to be to accept that the Germans did have independent agents of whom the British had no knowledge and that the enemy would use these spies to check the reports of the double agents. "Beyond question," he added, "opportunities were wasted and chances missed by a pardonable excess of caution. Had we realised from the start that the Germans did *not* draw from other sources in this country we could have acted more boldly and offered a better service than we did, particularly in the sphere of deception."

It was all a cautious learning experience. Early on, the British tried to *create* double agents. They selected men for this role who should have been enticing to the Germans—an individual, say, who in time of peace had been attached to a British Fascist organization but who, in wartime, had discarded the affiliation and remained loyal to Britain. Such prospects were placed in neutral countries, hoping that the Germans would recruit them. No go. As Masterman put it: "In point of fact, such a bait was rarely taken. . . . Though they would not take a first-rate article from us, the Germans showed themselves more than willing to push a second-rate article of their own. . . . It appeared that the only quality which the German spymaster demanded was that he should himself have discovered the agent and launched him on his career." Masterman and his crew soon saw that this effort to "throw an agent in the way of the Germans" was a failure and gave it up.

The only exception was the invention of a notional agent supposedly "recruited" as a subagent by a genuine double agent.

B1A's responsibilities didn't end with preparing story lines for the double agents. There was also the need to attend to the care and feeding of these individuals. The Committee found that the running and control of double agents was an infinitely complicated task. Each agent must be provided with an identity card, ration cards and clothes coupons. He must be housed. Each agent needed a case officer to manage and organize him, a radio operator to monitor his transmissions or to do the actual sending, at least two guards to provide around-the-clock surveillance, an officer with a car to collect the agent's information and a housekeeper to look after and feed the whole party. The agent must have an occupation, some means of support, even if it was only notional.

The role of the case officer was especially important. The Committee saw it as essential that every agent should be under the control day by day of an officer who knew every detail of his case and who identified with the individual. Often the case officer was an older man who became a father figure to the young and understandably nervous faux spy, one to whom the double agent could look for companionship, reassurance and understanding. To quote Masterman: "The most profitable cases were those in which the case officer had introduced himself most completely in the skin of the agent."

A rule of the Twenty Committee was to have each agent, to the extent possible, experience what he reported about, to send his spymaster information based on what he himself had seen and heard as if he had actually been living the life the spymaster envisioned him as living. If he was asked about a factory near Bristol, for example, he was driven there to see it for himself.

The Committee tried, in most cases, to keep each agent independent of the others and unaware of their activities. By this means, the members assured themselves that if one double agent was blown for some unforeseen reason, he would not bring down the others or possibly endanger the whole double-cross system. There were exceptions to this rule, especially on the part of those agents who felt more comfortable knowing they had an ally and one to whom they could appeal for help if their money ran short.

Fortunately, money was rarely a problem. German spymasters saw to it that, one way or another, agents they wanted to retain received living expenses. Over the course of the war they managed to dole out to their British operatives sufficient pound notes to make the double-cross system practically self-sustaining.

Masterman summed up the operations of the Twenty Committee with this seven-point creed:

1. To control the enemy system, or as much of it as we could get our hands on.
2. To catch fresh spies when they appeared.
3. To gain knowledge of the personalities and methods of the German Secret Service.
4. To obtain information about the code and cipher work of the German Service.
5. To get evidence of enemy plans and intentions from the questions asked by them.
6. To influence enemy plans by the answers sent to the enemy.
7. To deceive the enemy about our plans and intentions.

To explain how the double-cross system functioned, this account so far has dealt only with the agents in Great Britain. As has been indicated and will be detailed more fully later, however, Britain's system had its counterparts elsewhere in the empire. Wherever Germany and Britain confronted each other, the Germans were up against not just their visible enemy but also a legion of combatants of which they were ignorant.

CHAPTER THREE

ULTRA, THE DOUBLE AGENTS' INDISPENSABLE ALLY

In the secret war that lay behind World War II's shooting conflict, the double agents were not the only powerful unknown enemy the Axis powers faced. Their other invisible but invincible foe consisted of the Allied codebreakers who were piercing the cryptologic shields of Axis communications and reading the supposedly untouchable exchanges between Axis leaders.

Early in the war, a group of British cryptanalysts under Oliver Strachey broke the manual codes used by the Abwehr to communicate with its agents abroad. Reading these coded messages made it possible for the British to monitor what the double agents were asked and what they signaled back to their controllers. The decryptions also disclosed the German spymasters' attitudes toward the agents: which ones were trusted and which ones were under suspicion and requiring remedial efforts. At times the Abwehr messages disclosed fresh attempts to infiltrate new agents into Britain. It was Strachey's decrypts that eventually confirmed that every German agent in the UK was under British control.

The codebreakers' mastery of the Abwehr communications was continued even after the Germans began using machine coding. Actually the Abwehr was quite late in making this switch. All three of the main German military services—the army, navy and air force—had long since placed their reliance on machines rather than hand methods.

The changeover had been prompted by the First World War. The Germans were not alone in seeing that that war had turned into a cryptographer's nightmare. Having to rely on pen-and-paper codes handed down from the past made every nation's communications vulnerable. Readings of Russian communications had given the Germans victory in the Battle of Tannenberg that drove Russia out of the war. A French cryptanalyst's breaking of a German code enabled the French to turn back the Germans in the climactic second Battle of the Marne. British penetration of German naval codes finished off the threats of the German navy's warships and U-boats. And the British breaking of the infamous Zimmermann telegram, in which the German foreign minister Arthur Zimmermann tried to distract the Americans from entering the war by inducing the Mexicans to reclaim their territories in Texas, New Mexico and Arizona, sealed the Germans' defeat by stirring the public outrage that drove the United States into the conflict. German militarists were convinced in the 1920s that the time had come to entrust their radio exchanges only to their carefully selected code machine.

They were confident that the machine they decided upon was an ideal choice. They bought the rights to the machine offered by a German inventor, Arthur Scherbius. Scherbius called his machine the Enigma, allegedly deriving the name from British composer Edward Elgar's *Enigma Variations,* in which he used melodic codes to characterize some of his friends. The Enigma utilized electric-powered rotors to scramble the plaintext letters of a message so thoroughly that no one other than the intended recipient, knowing the original rotor settings, could possibly unscramble them.

Not content with Scherbius's machine, however, the Germans added new scrambling elements that enormously increased the complexities facing the would-be codebreaker. U.S. mathematician Ray Miller has determined that the Germans' souped-up Enigma produced a greater number of variations and permutations than there are atoms in the observable universe. It's no wonder that the Germans never wavered from their certainty that the Enigma was impregnable.

And yet the unthinkable happened. As early as Christmastime in 1932, three brilliant young Polish mathematicians, aided by the sellout of information about the Enigma by a German traitor, began to read

Enigma-enciphered German messages. The Poles continued their successes against the machine all during the 1930s.

Marian Rejewski, the leader of the Polish analysts, made another vital contribution. He realized that the manual methods being employed by him and his colleagues against the Enigma were far too slow to be of value in a fast-moving modern war. He invented a code-*breaking* machine to master the code-*making* machine. His idea came to him, so the story goes, while the three colleagues were enjoying Polish ice cream confections called *bombi*. They called Rejewski's machine the "bombe." When properly set up, the bombe could sort through the variations of a coded message with great speed, rejecting all the possible settings until it came to the correct one. Then it would stop, and the Poles were on their way to reading all the Enigma-enciphered communications until the Germans changed to new settings. In those early years the changeover came only quarterly, but as the decade neared its end and the war drums beat more loudly, the shift occurred daily.

The Poles continued their successes against the Enigma until 1939, when two things happened. One was that the Germans made a change in their Enigma procedures with which the Polish bombes were unable to cope insofar as decoding most of the German traffic. The second was that the Polish analysts could foresee that Hitler was planning to invade Poland and, with the tremendous power of the German Wehrmacht, probably overwhelm the Polish defenses. They called in their French and British allies, to whom they had not previously revealed their triumphs over the Enigma, and disclosed to them their full technology as well as presenting them with clones of the Enigma and plans for the bombes. When the Germans did crush the Polish armies, Rejewski and company fled the country.

At this point the British took over. Two visionary British mathematicians, Alan Turing and Gordon Welchman, saw the flaws in the Polish bombes that left them vulnerable to changes in the German system and developed new bombes that applied different principles. In May 1940, while World War II was still hanging fire in the stalemated "phony war," the British began breaking the Enigma codes of the German Luftwaffe and followed that success by penetrating the codes of the other services.

British cryptologic planners made another smart move. They realized that the type of brainpower needed in breaking code machines was a rare commodity, and instead of allowing these brains to be scattered among the turf-protecting intelligence branches of the military, they congregated them in one place, on an estate called Bletchley Park, northwest of London. They also assigned thousands of bright individuals, women as well as men and civilians as well as uniformed service personnel, in a meritocracy that supported the top brains in mounting an all-out attack on the codes of the Axis. In 1943, some five hundred American servicemen, including this book's author, joined the various phases of the British effort centered in Bletchley Park. The British code-named their program the Ultra Secret, and we U.S. troops assigned to it came to speak of ourselves as the "Ultra Americans."

The Germans were also confident that they had developed a system to thwart and confuse even the interceptors of their radio messages. They turned upside down the practices of commercial radio stations, each of which goes to great lengths to make listeners aware of the frequency on which it transmits—810 kilocycles, say—and the call letters that identify it—WGY, as an example. Instead, each German network of stations would, at a preappointed hour, abruptly disappear from the frequency on which it had been broadcasting and resume its traffic on an entirely different frequency. At the same time, the stations would all change their call letters. What had been CPG on 2,700 kilocycles, for example, would become RMD on 4,400 kilocycles. The stations were given each day the formula they would use to find their new call letters in a fat book of some 40,000 three-letter combinations. Any unguided interceptor trying to deal with these complexities would have been completely lost.

Patient British analysts, however, had also solved this system. By compiling duplicate frequency schedules and call-sign books, and by determining the shift formulas, they were able to inform their intercept stations, including the one the Americans added, where assigned German networks would go on the frequency spectrum and what the shift formula for a given day would be so that the intercept operators would know the new call signs to look for. The result was that the operators never missed a beat in copying down the five-letter code groups in which the German communications were hidden. Those Americans at their intercept station who were trained as cryptographers discovered, to their great disappointment, that they would not be involved in the actual breaking of those masses of encoded messages the operators copied down; their job was to keep the operators informed of coming changes, monitor their output and prepare the messages for teletypists to wire to what we knew only as Station X—in reality, Bletchley Park.

On being demobilized postwar, each American, including myself, had to sign a pledge never to reveal or discuss what we had done in the war. We Ultra Americans and nearly 10,000 British participants kept that promise for thirty years, until British authorities began, in 1974, to allow the story of World War II codebreaking to emerge.

While this conquest of the German codes was going on in England, American cryptanalysts, led by William Friedman in Washington, were breaking the Japanese code machines. First they mastered the machine the Americans code-named Red and subsequently the much more sophisticated machine code-named Purple. As it turned out, the U.S. breaking of Purple had far greater importance in the European phase of the conflict than it did in the Pacific. The machine was used by Japanese diplomats and military attachés serving in Germany and in the neutral countries of Europe. Baron Hiroshi Oshima, the Japanese ambassador in Berlin, spoke German fluently and has been described as "more Nazi than the Nazis." He became a confidant of Hitler and had long talks with the Fuehrer and his subordinates, all of which the baron detailed in long messages back to Tokyo. Also, he and his military attachés were taken on tours of German warfronts, such as the fortifications in northern France, which they duly reported—accounts that were read with much stronger interest in London and Washington than they were in the home islands.

Bletchley Park's success in deciphering the Germans' Enigma-encoded messages was, of course, a closely guarded secret. For a time early in the war, responsibility for the security of Ultra was given to a stubborn young man named Felix Cowgill, head of the MI6 counterintelligence division. He was also the MI6 representative on the Twenty Committee. Cowgill took his security job with such excessive seriousness that he decided some members of the Committee should not be allowed to see any Ultra material whatever and that the Committee as a whole should not be permitted to review information relating to MI6 agents.

As Ewen Montagu wrote of this internecine battle: "Cowgill was so imbued with the idea of security that when he was put in charge . . . of this material, he was quite willing to try entirely to prevent its use as intelligence lest it be compromised." And, Montagu added, "These views inevitably caused friction." In fact, his intransigence soon brought the Twenty Committee's operation to a virtual standstill.

The struggle over Cowgill came to the attention of Stewart Menzies, chief of MI6. He found a solution by easing Cowgill into other work and replacing him on the Twenty Committee with Frank Foley. For twenty of his years with MI6, Foley had been concentrating on Germany. In his new assignment he quickly made himself an asset as an agent who understood the importance of Ultra's decrypts to the double-cross team and who "knew the Germans backwards." He was also recognized, long after the war, as the man who, by devising ingenious escape routes out of Nazi Germany, became, according to the subtitle of the book Michael Smith wrote about Foley, "The Spy Who Saved 10,000 Jews."

To the Twenty Committee, the greatest importance of the Allied codebreaking successes was the aid they gave to Masterman and his cohorts in carrying out deceptions. It would have been next to impossible for the Committee to conduct ever more ambitious deceptions if they had not been able to learn from code breaks that their untruths were being accepted, believed and acted upon by the enemy. With Bletchley Park reading the minds of German commanders, all those collaborating in a major hoax knew whether it was being swallowed.

When Masterman penned his postwar report on the double-cross system, it was still far too soon to discuss the codebreakers' contributions. The most he could say was "secret sources permitted us to observe that the reports of the double-cross agents were transmitted to Berlin, that they were believed."

In turn, the codebreakers benefited from the double agents. Turing's bombes worked on the basis that German military language included stereotyped phraseology that could be presumed to appear in a test message—the term "nothing to report" or the title "commander-in-chief," as examples. The bombes went searching for these "cribs" and stopped when they found the right plaintext beneath the encoded letters. Back when the Abwehr began discarding their manual cipher and using the Enigma, phrases appearing frequently in the earlier messages gave Bletchley cryptanalysts good cribs to be applied in breaking the Enigma code. British analysts read exchanges between the Abwehr and its spies for the rest of the war.

Mention has been made of the codebreakers' long-kept pledge of secrecy about their wartime duties. Britain's Official Secrets Act also applied to the double agents while they remained within British jurisdiction. Official reports and personal memoirs written shortly after the war's end remained classified, precluding publication. While most of the agents disappeared into anonymity, a few wanted to see their stories in print and were nettled by the restrictions. Eddie Chapman and Roman Garby-Czerniawski published partial accounts that excluded the experiences covered by the ban. The wall of secrecy began to crumble in the 1970s when a writer in the know about the double agents published a "novel" that was only a thinly disguised recounting of Garbo's story. J. C. Masterman took Sefton Delmer's telling of *The Counterfeit Spy* as license to bring out his long-suppressed history of the Twenty Committee, even though to escape the ban he had to have his book published in the United States. Masterman was also driven by his desire to restore the intelligence services' reputation after the battering it received following the scandals involving Kim Philby and other Communist sympathizers who used their intelligence jobs during the Cold War to send secret information to the Soviets. Dusko Popov published his memoir—daring the authorities to take action against him. Following these breaks, the restrictions have at last been eased and the sequestered files on most of the double agents—the files on Elvira Chandoir are a notable exception—have been released to public inspection via Britain's National Archives. Out of concern to protect individuals from being traced by disclosures of personal details about them, the names of many who are mentioned in these files are whited out and they are recognized only by their code names.

It has been a pleasure, in the pages that follow, to begin the telling of the full story of the double agents, to present the results of probing as deeply as possible into the official records and of seeking out other sources that allow these men and women to be identified and recognized as the remarkable individuals they were. Here is an all-out effort to present the flesh-and-blood humans behind the masks of their code names. They are a diverse lot, ranging from ex-criminals to wealthy playboys, from a lowly scrubwoman to a diplomat's daughter, and from scared-rabbit "turned" spies to courageous volunteers, but they have one thing in common: they are some of the most deserving unsung heroes of World War II.

The story told here is admittedly a one-sided, pro-Allied account, as though the Axis powers never conceived of using double agents. Of course they did, as in the grim story of the Dutch agent Huub Lauwers, whom the British parachuted into Holland to be a spy for them. Captured, Lauwers allowed himself to be turned, partly because he knew of coded signals that were supposed to alert his British controllers to the fact that he had been compromised. Even though he inserted these signals repeatedly into his messages, his English controllers never seemed to tumble. As a result, his radio exchanges betrayed some fifty agents, who were seized by the Nazis and executed.

So there was an Axis side to the story. The evidence suggests, however, that if all the examples were pulled together, they would still make a very thin book. The really big story—the one that had a substantial effect in the winning of the war—belongs to the cast of characters whose narratives follow.

CHAPTER FOUR

IN THE BEGINNING, SNOW

Arthur George Owens was a slippery character. He was described in an official report as "mean-spirited," an "underfed type," with a "very short, bony face, ill-shaped ears, disproportionately small for size of man" and displaying a "shifty look." The details fit his record as an arrant opportunist, ready to shift his allegiance to whichever side offered him the better deal.

One observer was also put off by Owens's habit of "only wearing his false teeth when eating."

Yet, under the cover name of Snow, this unprepossessing Welshman became the first of Britain's double agents and is recognized as "the cornerstone of the double-cross system." J. C. Masterman has pronounced Owens "the *fons et origo* of all of our activities for the next five years."

Owens made himself a source from which British intelligence learned much of importance about the Abwehr and its methods. He is given credit for helping to put the finger on several agents the Germans tried to infiltrate into England. He also pioneered the use of notional subagents, creating an imaginary network to supplement his own reports. When collected postwar, the messages he and his subagents sent to German spymasters under the Twenty Committee's direction, together with the background information on him, added up to thirty-five volumes.

The beginnings of Owens's career as a double agent, however, were not auspicious. He was an electrical engineer employed by an English firm holding a number of contracts with the Admiralty. He also represented the firm in dealing with customers on the Continent. In his prewar travels he picked up technical information, primarily about German shipping, that he sporadically passed on to the Admiralty's Naval Intelligence Division.

This irregular arrangement was not rewarding enough for Owens. He made it known that he wanted to supplement his income through steady work for the government. His case was passed on to MI6. He quickly became dissatisfied, foreseeing that his compensation from this agency would never amount to more than, to use his term for it, "peanuts." He also worried that MI6, which he saw as a rather slipshod operation, might betray him to the Germans.

During a 1936 trip to Germany, Owens met Luftwaffe major Nikolaus Ritter, of the Abwehr's Hamburg station concerned with aviation intelligence, who affected the code name of Dr. Rantzau. Ritter gave him a lavish wine-and-dine night on the town, at the end of which Ritter appealed to Owens's Welsh nationalist bitterness toward the English as good reason to become a secret agent for Germany. Ritter made it plain there would be ample money in the deal. That was satisfactory enough for Owens. He agreed and was given a Hamburg cover address to which to mail his reports. The Abwehr trained him in Morse code, encipherment of his messages, meteorological observation, aircraft identification and sabotage.

It was not MI6 but Abwehr carelessness that uncovered his double-dealings. The Hamburg cover address should, of course, have been carefully protected. It was not. The British intercepted a letter by Owens disclosing that he had had previous meetings with the German intelligence service and was about to have another. Since this was peacetime, though, the British took no immediate action beyond observing that he continued posting letters to Hamburg.

At the 1936 year's end, MI6 was finally prodded by MI5 into confronting Owens. He confessed but quickly suggested that he play a double role. To the Germans he would continue to be their man, supplying them with information they would consider of value. But he would see to it that his reports to the Abwehr would contain the misinformation his

British controllers wanted him to include. Moreover, he would use his German contacts to uncover as much as he could about the Germans' secret service operations and other matters MI6 would find of interest.

For more than two years, British intelligence went along with this scheme. Then, in January 1939, Owens informed the British authorities that his Abwehr contacts were no longer content with having him write letters; they would send him a transmitter. Later that month Ritter sent him a letter containing instructions for working the set and a ticket from the cloakroom at Victoria Station, where the set would be waiting for him in a suitcase.

However, he was not to begin using it until he heard his favorite German song, "Du Liesst mir im Herzen," played twice in succession on a nightly program Berlin directed toward Britain. Owens and his case officer, Tar Robertson, waited. The signal was not broadcast until September 4, the day after Britain and France had declared war on Germany. By then the British, doubtful about Owens's loyalty, had shut him up at Wandsworth Prison. When transmission from the prison was found to be poor, Owens was taken to another building, where, carefully monitored, he began transmitting to his controller, Major Ritter.

His first message was reassuring. He began with the words *"Ein Glas Bier"*—a joke between him and Ritter. Owens claimed it was the only German phrase he knew, and he had learned it in his night of carousing in Hamburg. It instantly identified him with Ritter. Owens tapped out a message saying he must meet Ritter in Holland at once. He continued with two cryptic additions: "Bring weather code. Radio town and hotel Wales ready."

Owens explained. Ritter had instructed him that, when war began, one of Owens's principal duties would be to transmit daily weather reports. In addition, Ritter wanted him to supply the name and address of a Welsh Nationalist Party member who could help the Germans with sabotage in Wales.

As Masterman noted in his postwar report, "With Snow's first message from Wandsworth Prison the double-cross system was well and truly launched. Very soon he was receiving a variety of orders and requests for information."

Reassured, the British released him from Wandsworth and allowed him to start transmitting from his home the messages prepared for him by the Twenty Committee.

From this beginning, Owens became both the cornerstone of double-agentry in Britain and the linchpin of the Abwehr's spy network there. His importance to both sides was enhanced by two events that, in the war's early days, broke the backs of whatever spy operation each opponent had established on the soil of the other.

Two days after war was declared, Britain followed through on an operation MI5 had been planning for some time. This was to require all enemy aliens in the United Kingdom to report to the police. Investigation of some 62,000 Germans and 12,000 Austrians boiled down to 600 who were classed as "unreliable." This search, although somewhat sloppily conducted, did combine with the list of suspects MI5 had compiled to single out for capture the few alleged spies the Germans had in the UK and, consequently, greatly increased their reliance on Owens.

Britain, on the other hand, had had its continental lineup of spies betrayed by what became known as the Venlo incident. This occurred in November 1939 during the "phony war" when, having declared war, the troops of both Germany and the Anglo-French alliance hung tensely on their battlefronts without fighting. At the Dutch town of Venlo, hard against Holland's border with Germany, two British MI6 officers under diplomatic cover were to meet with Germans supposedly plotting against Hitler. It was a trap. The Germans were under the direction of the head of the Gestapo, Heinrich Himmler. They shot and killed the Dutch officer accompanying the British pair, seized them and dragged them over the border into Germany, to be imprisoned for the rest of the war. Foolishly, one of the British officers had with him a list of British agents on the Continent, who were summarily rounded up.

The desperation felt by both antagonists offered a character as amoral as George Owens a ripe opportunity for exploitation. On the British side, he racked up what was later described as an "enormous salary," one that "would make a cabinet minister's salary look stupid."

He was also well paid by the Germans, who were delighted by the zeal he displayed on their behalf. At this point he increased his value to the

Germans by inventing his subagents. Owens told them he wasn't content to report only the information he himself could uncover; he recruited a team of other Britons with hard feelings toward their countrymen who were willing to forward him reports from strategic vantage points across Britain. What the Abwehr didn't know, of course, was that the information delivered by these subagents was also dictated by the Twenty Committee.

During the phony war period, ferries continued to run between Britain and the Continent, allowing Owens to make repeated trips to meet with Ritter, usually in Antwerp. On his October trip, he was accompanied by Gwilym Williams (called G.W.), a retired police officer who posed as another anti-British Welsh extremist. This time Ritter had them meet with a high Abwehr official who proposed to send arms and explosives to Wales by U-boat for use in any insurrection by the Welsh Nationalist Party. Williams affirmed that he would back such an effort and was ready himself to carry out sabotage operations. He was given explosives detonators hidden in a block of wood.

Owens was introduced to a new technology for increasing the information he supplied. This was microphotography, by which a full-size sheet of data could be reduced to the size of an easily concealed postage stamp. He was also given the name of an agent in Britain who could handle this technology for him.

The agent's code name was Charlie. He turned out to be a Manchester businessman of German-English parentage who, on being naturalized in Britain, had adopted the name Ashborn. During a trip to Germany, he had been blackmailed by the Abwehr: Either cooperate with us or we'll take reprisals against your family here. Confronted in England, and assured that his cooperation would be kept secret, Ashborn proclaimed, and proved, his loyalty to Britain and agreed to work as Owens's photographic aide. A member of the Royal Photographic Society, he brought a high level of skill and technical experience to handling his microphotographic duties.

While Owens was away on that trip, MI5 representatives working on his case intercepted two letters addressed to him at his London home. Each contained a twenty-pound note stamped "S & Co."

Robertson's assistant, investigating the suspicious letters, found that "S

& Co." referred to Selfridges, a large London department store. He also determined that they had been purchased by a woman named Mathilde Kraft, who was of German origin and obviously serving the Abwehr as a paymistress to the likes of Owens. Rather than arrest her, MI5 kept her under surveillance to see if she would lead to other agents.

From Owens's exchanges, the British gleaned further insights into the inner workings of the Abwehr, its procedures and personalities. The questionnaires they dispatched to him provided rich clues to German interests and intentions. A development of special importance was the assistance the Owens case gave the codebreakers at Bletchley Park. Messages prepared by the Twenty Committee for transmission by Owens to his Hamburg spymasters were enciphered in the manual code the Abwehr had provided him. These messages, the British determined, were relayed almost unchanged to Berlin by operators using the Abwehr's Enigma machines. Comparative analysis of intercepts of these messages with the original texts revealed substantial repeats that supplied cribs useful in Bletchley's breaking of the whole system of Enigma-encoded messages.

The phony war extended into May 1940. Major Ritter knew, however, that this stalemate was about to end and that if he was to continue to have face-to-face contacts with Owens, a meeting place other than Antwerp had to be devised. He suggested that Owens secure an English fishing trawler and travel in it into the North Sea. Ritter would arrive at the rendezvous point either by plane or submarine. He also wanted Owens to bring along a new recruit who could be taken back to Germany for training as a sabotage expert. All this the British arranged. The new German spy, Sam McCarthy, code-named Biscuit, was a reformed crook, drug smuggler and con man. He and Owens set off together to board their vessel in the port town of Grimsby.

There was a hitch. British intelligence had failed to inform each of the men that the other was a bona fide double agent. Owens and McCarthy began to suspect that his intended partner in this risky project would reveal to Ritter that his companion was under British control—a betrayal that was likely to have fatal consequences. Aboard the trawler they quarreled violently. When the rendezvous seemed not to be going as McCarthy expected, he induced the crew to lock Owens in the ship's cabin under guard and to return to Grimsby.

This donnybrook happened two days before the meeting with Ritter was actually scheduled. When British authorities had reassured the two agents of their trustworthiness, a hurry-up new effort was made, this time with a disguised Royal Navy crew. In addition, the British Navy ship HMS/M *Salmon* was standing by. Now the whole rendezvous had a new purpose: not just that of meeting with Ritter and turning McCarthy over to him but to capture Ritter and destroy whatever his means of transport turned out to be—something of a British retaliation for the Venlo incident.

It came close to happening. Ritter did try to make the rendezvous. He is reported to have carried out two approaches by seaplane and sought to make contact by firing flares. But the weather over the North Sea was poor and the whole scheme had to be scuttled.

Owens's devious nature did not inspire the confidence of others. His estranged wife, to whom he had been multiply unfaithful, tried to report to British intelligence her suspicions that Owens was a German spy. Walter Dicketts, his favorite drinking buddy in a South London pub, who became a double agent code-named Celery, expressed similar doubts about him.

His British case officer could not shake off similar feelings. Despite all the good work that Owens had done, Tar Robertson held lingering doubts about his reliability. His mistrust was not relieved by the North Sea trawler episode. Before he was released from the ship's cabin, Owens was searched and was found to be carrying the "Important Persons Club" membership list as well as the menu for the club's fortieth anniversary dinner. The importance of these documents was that they disclosed the personnel of Britain's Secret Service Bureau going back to the bureau's earliest beginnings. In German hands, they would have provided a dossier of many of the leaders in British intelligence.

And how did the list come into Owens's possession? He explained that he had been given the papers by a business associate who, short of money, thought Owens could arrange a deal that would be profitable to the businessman—with, no doubt, a cut going to Owens. In fact, the source was not a businessman but MI5 insider William Rolph, who chose to cash in some of his secret knowledge for personal gain. After being questioned by Robertson, Rolph committed suicide.

Although Robertson did not choose to act against Owens at that moment, he did resolve to continue supplementing Owens's notional agents with live ones, ostensibly to help Owens but also to monitor him.

Robertson acted on his suspicions in January 1941 when Owens was to meet Ritter in Lisbon. It was arranged that Walter Dicketts, Celery, would travel separately and join Owens there. Celery was to be introduced to Ritter and to receive training in sabotage. He was to present himself to the Germans as bearing a grudge against the RAF and Britain. During the First World War he had served in Air Intelligence, but when he tried to regain a commission in World War II, he was refused. The Abwehr did not need to know that the turndown was reasonable, considering that during the years between the wars Dicketts had been convicted on charges of bilking people in confidence games.

What happened in Lisbon remains murky. On Owens's return to London, Robertson subjected him to an intense interrogation. Owens admitted that Ritter had commented on Owens's deteriorating condition due to his alcoholism and the pressure of his spy work. Ritter also asserted that he had just recently learned that Owens was under the control of the British. Owens's story was that he admitted to Ritter that this was true: three months previously British authorities had taken over him and his transmitter. For two months, Owens claimed, he had been closely monitored, but during the last month the British had evidently changed their minds about him and he had been allowed to run almost free. At no point, he told Ritter, had his subagents been compromised; the British knew nothing of their existence. Owens had managed, covertly, to maintain contact with them.

These exchanges with Ritter occurred before Celery arrived. Owens reported that he told Ritter that he himself didn't trust Celery and thought he might be double-crossing the Germans. He suggested to Ritter that since Celery was to go to Berlin for training, he should be closely cross-examined.

In his testimony to Robertson, Celery denied knowing any of this. If he had known, he certainly would not have gone along with what Ritter wanted him to do, which was to travel to Germany for three weeks of special training. It was true, he said, that on his arrival in Germany he was grilled at length, but he survived the questioning without damaging admissions. Meanwhile, Owens remained in Lisbon, nursing an illness brought on by his excessive drinking.

Where was the truth in all this? Could it be true that Owens had been so persuasive that he had succeeded in talking himself back into Ritter's good graces? Or had Owens's brains been so addled by alcohol that he had simply imagined this whole improbable series of events?

Or could it be that Ritter was swayed by the German spymasters' reluctance to give up on their spies? Owens was, after all, the bulwark of his spy operation in Britain and had also become his paymaster to other agents. As Owens told his British interrogator, Ritter "had appeared satisfied with the explanation." Also, there was the fact that Ritter sent Celery and him off with £10,000 and more sabotage materials—scarcely the actions of a suspicious spymaster.

Robertson never received a satisfactory answer, but his mind was made up. He closed down Snow along with Celery, Biscuit, Charlie and, for a time, G.W. A series of messages sent via Owens's transmitter informed Ritter that both his health and his nerve had collapsed, that it was impossible for him to carry on and that his gear would be bundled up and hidden away.

To guard against further trickery by Owens, he spent the rest of the war being "detained" in Dartmoor Prison and on the Isle of Man.

CHAPTER FIVE

TRICYCLE, THE ABWEHR'S YUGOSLAV SOCIALITE

People who esteem former FBI director J. Edgar Hoover tend to scorn Dusan "Dusko" Popov. They agree with Hoover in labeling Popov a "moral degenerate" and in claiming that his code name Tricycle reflected not the official explanation that as a British double agent he managed a triumvirate that included a pair of subagents but, instead, that he indulged a penchant for bedding two women at once. The story behind Hoover's disfavor will be told later in these pages.

To his British controllers, however, Popov was a courageous man who achieved great successes in leading German commanders rather than just gullible women down the garden path. Harry Hinsley, a Bletchley Park veteran and postwar chronicler of Ultra, rated him as one of the three "most valuable" double agents in Britain's cause. While Popov was not a man whose looks turned heads, he overcame this lack by the sheer force and appeal of his personality.

There are believers who assert that Popov's combination of cool daring on the job and hot romantic adventures in his off-hours gave his wartime intelligence associate Ian Fleming the model for creating James Bond. Ewen Montagu said of Popov, however, that "he exhibited a basic common sense that James Bond never displayed."

In short, Dusko Popov was another complex man who proved himself capable of winning the confidence and respect of both his German spymasters and his British case officer. In the laudatory foreword that Montagu wrote for Tricycle's autobiography, *Spy/Counterspy*, he speaks of Popov as "one of the bravest and gayest of men, possessing immense charm and personal magnetism."

The beginnings of Popov's role as a double agent trace back to his 1930s days as a student at Germany's Freiburg University. The scion of a wealthy Yugoslav business family with connections to royalty, Popov was educated in England and France as well as in Yugoslavia before matriculating at Freiburg to earn his doctorate in law. At the university two things happened that subsequently shaped his wartime service. One was that he came to despise the Nazi regime—a feeling he was not careful to conceal. The other was that he formed a warm friendship with Johann "Johnny" Jebsen, heir to an even wealthier German ship-owning family fortune. Jebsen, Popov found, was a character of interesting contradictions. His demeanor was that of a highly proper young upper-class German: he affected a monocle, wore impeccable clothes and seemed fully to be one of those aloof and reserved aristocrats who appeared to see merit in the Hitler dictatorship. Beneath this exterior, however, he revealed himself to Popov as a mischievous, irrepressible scamp, a lusty womanizer, a lover of souped-up sports cars, an aficionado of pornographic movies and a fellow Nazi-hater.

Immediately after Popov had received his degree and was planning a celebratory trip to Paris before returning to Belgrade, Jebsen had to rescue him. Popov's quarters at the university were suddenly raided by four Gestapo thugs looking for evidence that he was a Communist sympathizer. He was thrown into prison and threatened with shipment to a concentration camp. It took Jebsen several weeks of frantic searching to uncover what had happened. To avoid being heard on a German phone line, Jebsen drove across the border into Switzerland and called Popov's father. The elder Popov pulled high-level strings to free his son. Dusko had to swear he would leave Germany at once, which he was only too glad to do.

Five months after the war began, and three years after their last meeting, it was Jebsen's turn to ask favors of Popov. He and Dusko met at a Belgrade bar. Popov noticed that Jebsen had changed visibly. His eyes showed an apprehensiveness. While he was still sylishly dressed, his blond hair was unkempt and his mustache looked neglected. "He ordered his whiskies double, neat and frequently."

Jebsen sought Popov's help in a scheme to keep ships blockaded in Trieste harbor, including one from his family's fleet, from eventually ending up in Nazi hands. The plan that Popov carried out for him was to have Yugoslavia, acting as a neutral, to appear to be the buyer while actually serving as an intermediary in delivering the ships to the British. It was a bit of trickery whose success was to make trouble for Jebsen later in the war.

The second favor held a sharp surprise for Popov. That was to find that his seemingly free-spirited friend had become an officer in the German secret service, the Abwehr. Returning to Belgrade to meet with Popov, Jebsen explained: "I want to keep out of uniform. I also want to be free to travel, to keep in touch firsthand with what is happening in the world outside of Germany. I couldn't do that if I was in a military unit destined for cannon fodder. I won't be able to do it either unless I'm well established in the Abwehr. If you want to stay in, you can't pretend or exist on the edges. You have to entrench yourself, and to do that you've got to produce results."

All this was a lead-up to his request. The Abwehr had been asked to make an independent analysis of the French politicians who would be most cooperative with the Germans when France was conquered.

"Don't you mean 'if and when'?" Popov asked.

Jebsen shook his head. The reality was that it was just a matter of when. Germany's enemies underestimated Hitler's aggressiveness and the country's strength. France was going to be conquered. If Popov could once again use his upper-class contacts to determine the most likely collaborator with the Germans, it would be a great boost for Jebsen.

Popov took on the task for his friend. After interviewing many influential acquaintances, he wrote a long report that came down to one name as most likely: ex–prime minister Pierre Laval. The report impressed the Abwehr leaders—especially after France was conquered and Laval did become the highly collaborative head man of Vichy France under the German occupation. The report's success, however, brought Jebsen back to Belgrade for his third favor. He wanted Popov to invite to dinner in his home the top Abwehr official in Belgrade, Major Müntzinger.

At the dinner the jovial major wasted no time in making his wishes known. Popov's report, he said, had been so "clear and reasoned" and his social connections obviously so top-drawer that the Abwehr now wanted him to consider becoming an informant for them in Great Britain. "We have many agents in England," Müntzinger claimed, "quite a number of them excellent. But we would like someone who has entry everywhere. Your connections would open many doors." Müntzinger sought to sweeten the offer by pointing out that Popov's efforts could help to make the inevitable invasion of Britain less bloody and save many German and English lives. He ended by assuring Popov that the Abwehr would "show its appreciation with generosity."

After getting Popov's agreement to consider the proposal, Müntzinger left. "I hope you'll forgive me, Dusko," Jebsen said. "I'm using you. I'm sorry. I can't survive otherwise." Then he added, "One more thing. If you want to destroy a team, the best way is to become part of it."

Popov took the advice. Next morning he hurried to the British embassy in Belgrade and sought out the MI6 representative there. After checking with London, the rep told him, Yes, go ahead, accept the proposition. Let the Germans think you're working for them while actually working for us.

His next meeting with Müntzinger was jubilant. The major presented Popov with invisible ink to be used in answering Abwehr questionnaires and christened him with his Abwehr code name Ivan.

Before Popov could leave for his mission to Britain, though, he had to work his way out of a crisis. It was a test that showed that under his charming exterior there was a core of hardness that could, when necessary, make him ruthless.

The crisis was brought on by Popov's father's chauffeur, Bozidar. When Dusko's BMW broke down, he borrowed his father's car and enlisted Bozidar to drive him on his rounds. His stops included several sessions at the Passport Control Office, which was also the headquarters of British intelligence in Yugoslavia. There came a morning when Jebsen arrived, in a breathless and agitated state, at Popov's door. Major Müntzinger had taken the precaution to check on Popov's loyalty to the Nazis. He had, for a price, enlisted Bozidar to sabotage the BMW so that Popov was dependent on his father's car and chauffeur. Bozidar had compiled a multipage report on Popov's calls in Belgrade, including the repeated stops at the Passport Control Office. Müntzinger was out of town and had foolishly allowed Jebsen to collect the report. Jebsen could recopy the pages and leave out the incriminating passages. But what was to be done about Bozidar? It was too dangerous to try to threaten him or bribe him. What else?

Popov knew the answer. As a lawyer he had defended local toughs. To show their appreciation for his having obtained suspended sentences for them, two young hoodlums promised to do what needed to be done. That night Popov sent Bozidar on a mock errand that brought him near the railroad yards. There the young thugs had arranged an apparent pillaging. When Bozidar's body was found, shot to death, police concluded he had been involved in the crime.

There were no other crises. Popov was free to go to London and begin his career as a double agent.

From Müntzinger Popov received a questionnaire to which, it was hoped, he could supply the answers. The Germans' questions, he wrote in his memoir, "were useful because they showed what they perhaps didn't know. The questionnaire also indicated what areas the Germans were interested in." Their strongest interest was in England's southeast coast, plainly tying in with their plans for the invasion. They wanted to know the locations of divisions, brigades, commands, the names of officers. Specific interests included antitank guns, other weapons and the armaments industry. And there were political questions. Who were Churchill's enemies? Who in Britain thought the war should be ended quickly? Who was in favor of starting to negotiate peace with Germany?

To reach England, he had to go by way of neutral Lisbon. There he met his spymaster, a major who went by the name of Ludovico von Karsthoff, although his real name was Kremer von Auenrode. He was the head of the Abwehr in Lisbon. Popov found the major to be a slim, good-looking man whose movements were those of a big cat. "Amiable as he was," Popov wrote, "you were constantly aware that you must not make a false move in his presence."

Nevertheless, both he and Popov were charmers who got along famously. "I have been instructed," von Karsthoff said, "to handle you with love and care, to help you to the utmost." Even so, this was a game of little trust. The major felt obliged to put his new spy through a rigorous interrogation before letting him go on to Great Britain.

Popov was seen as a desirable catch by both the Abwehr and MI5. Landed in England on December 20, 1940, he soon found himself in conversation with Stewart Menzies, overall head of the British Secret Service, and was subsequently invited by Menzies to join him for weekends at the family's country estate. Popov was given his own business office in Albany House, just off Piccadilly Circus, and assigned the temporary British code name of Scout. He was also introduced to J. C. Masterman, whom he found to be "most impressive" as well as "cool and calculating."

His case officer, he learned, was to be a genial older Englishman who went by the pseudonym of Bill Matthews, although his real name was William Luke. Of him Popov wrote: "Whoever put the two of us together, probably J. C. Masterman, was a fine psychologist. Bill and I got along famously. He was a Scot, of a family of prominent industrialists, and had a sense of humor rarely surpassed by anyone I ever knew. The same went for his courage." When he talked of serious matters with Popov, he "stroked his R.A.F. mustache."

As Masterman expressed it, Popov "created a most favorable impression," adding that "we had in him a new agent of high quality who could plausibly meet persons in any social station, who was well established with the Germans at the instance of an Abwehr official, and who had an excellent business cover for frequent journeys to Lisbon or to other neutral countries."

To make sure he met "all the nibs," as Luke put it—all the right people—Popov was introduced to a woman he in his book calls Gerda Sullivan. Her real name was Friedl Gaertner. She moved in London's highest societal circles and was to be his "social mistress," seeing to it that he made friends with people who could notionally supply the information the Germans were expecting from him.

Gaertner was also, in Popov's estimation, "charming, beautiful, sexy." She and he quickly became a team in more ways than one. Soon it was proposed that she should serve as a subagent to Popov, with the British cover name of Gelatine. Popov was able to justify her willingness to become an anti-British spy by pointing out that her father was Austrian and had been a Nazi party member—facts that Nazi investigation would find to be true. What they were not to learn was that Gaertner, code-named Yvonne by the Germans, did not in the least share her father's political beliefs. She fed Popov a rich diet of informational bits the Germans would find savory. Through her, and with the Twenty Committee's connivance, Popov was able to deliver piquant details about Britain's political leaders and intelligence officials.

A second subagent whom Popov "recruited" was Dickie Metcalfe, a disgruntled ex-officer in the army who had been made bitter by being cashiered after a series of sexual and financial scandals. The Germans were not told that he had reformed himself and was now a responsible intelligence officer. Metcalfe was able to supply Popov with whatever was needed in technical information. He was given the cover name Balloon. In recognition of the triumvirate he now headed up, the British changed Popov's code name from Scout to Tricycle.

The output of this trio soon became too large to be handled by invisible-ink communications and the occasional trips Tricycle made to Lisbon. They resorted increasingly to radio transmissions.

In all, Popov's son Marco reported to *The London Times* in 2004, "my father made fourteen trips to Lisbon during the war to meet face-to-face with his German handlers. He made the trips never knowing what kind of reception he would meet. If his case had been blown since his last visit, he would have been seized and tortured in an effort to make him disclose what he knew, and liquidated."

As a neutral capital, Lisbon was a viper's nest of intrigue, with spies spying on spies. The procedure Popov learned to follow in order to meet with von Karsthoff seemed fictional but was necessary. Popov left his hotel and placed his call to von Karsthoff's office on a public phone. "I'm a friend of the major's cousin from Italy," Popov told the office secretary.

Von Karsthoff himself got on the phone to say, ritually, "A friend of my Italian cousin? You must come to visit. You'll bring much laughter to my house."

"I'll enjoy that very much," Popov answered. "It's rather urgent. Can we make it for Wednesday?"

"Urgent" meant that Popov was requesting the meeting that same day. Mention of the day of the week fixed the hour. Monday meant 6:10 p.m., Tuesday meant 7:10 p.m., and so on.

"I shall come by train," Popov said. This meant he would expect to be picked up at a prearranged spot on the Avenida de Libertade. If he had said "by taxi," he wanted to be picked up on the main Lisbon road one mile outside Estoril.

If von Karsthoff wanted to arrange a meeting, a still more bizarre procedure was followed. Popov would receive a call from a girl, who said she was sorry she behaved so stupidly the other night. Could they meet at a nightclub that evening?

That meant Popov was to go to the Estoril casino. There von Karsthoff's secretary, Elizabeth Sahrbach, would appear. He was to follow her to a roulette table, where she would play three times. The numbers on which she placed her bets indicated the date, hour and minute. Then she would play zero or 36. Zero meant the pickup was to be in Lisbon, 36 in Estoril.

Even with all these bizarre precautions, Popov was instructed to crouch down in the back of the chauffeured car as it approached von Karsthoff's house and remain there until the car was safely inside the garage.

By submitting to all this hugger-mugger, though, Popov did begin to relay to the Germans the blend of straight and false information the British wanted them to receive. In addition, he was able to contribute an inflow of information valuable to the British. The questionnaires passed to him revealed subtle changes in the Germans' outlook toward the war. Early queries disclosed an ebullient assurance that Britain would soon be invaded and conquered. What elements in Britain, Popov was asked, could be expected to come to terms with Hitler and overthrow Churchill? Who among the British Fascist sympathizers was most likely to aid the invaders? What was the state of British morale?

Later questionnaires made it plain that the invasion of Britain had been, if not entirely abandoned, at least put on hold. The questions now left no doubt that the Germans were expecting a long war. Queries about convoys from the United States and the effects of the submarine blockade suggested a new theme: Instead of conquering the British, the Germans hoped they could starve them into submission.

Popov's triumvirate became adept at transmitting misinformation. Ultra decrypts had revealed that the Germans held misconceptions about the battle strength of the British army, estimating that fifteen of the known twenty-seven divisions were fully equipped. In reality, at that early moment, hardly six divisions were ready to take the field. Tricycle fed the Germans details that confirmed their inflated estimate.

A supposedly stolen document that Popov passed on to his spymaster asserted that 30,000 antitank rifles had been distributed to British troops. This was authentic information the Germans could corroborate. The strength that these guns added to Britain's defense, however, was illusory: there was a dire shortage of ammunition for them; hardly one-fifth were usable.

A constant problem for the Abwehr was how to provide the money needed by their agents in Britain. Air drops too often miscarried. Paymasters such as Mathilde Kraft were put out of business. Arthur Owens had been retired. During one of his Lisbon trips, Popov was asked by von Karsthoff to carry back with him a few thousand pounds so as to start Dickie Metcalfe on his career as a spy for Germany. Popov agreed, this once, but pointed out the danger of breaking the British currency regulations that limited the amount of money with which one could enter the country.

Thinking about the problem, Popov hit upon a scheme that the approving British labeled Plan Midas. The cover story needed the notional cooperation of a rich Englishman who was afraid Britain might lose the war and wanted to protect himself from that debacle by building up a reserve of dollars in America.

On his next visit to Lisbon, Popov casually mentioned to von Karsthoff that he had come upon an opportunity to make a bit of extra change. He told of this wealthy Londoner who wanted to shift the equivalent in dollars of, say, £20,000, less losses in the exchange rate and a commission for services rendered, to the United States. Once the dollars had been deposited, the rich man would pay out the pounds in London. Could the major suggest a bank or transfer agent who could arrange the transaction? Von Karsthoff immediately saw that by making the Abwehr the transfer agent, he could pay the Abwehr spies in Britain. All he would need was confirmation that the pounds were paid out not to a bank in the United States but to his nominee in London.

It was done. And who was the nominee to serve as paymaster? None other than Popov's fellow double agent, Wulf Schmidt. In actuality, MI5 collected the money to help support the double-agent system.

Popov carried out the whole scheme successfully, except that his memory played a trick on him. The cooperative rich Englishman was a theatrical agent, Charles Glass. The name Popov gave von Karsthoff was Charles Sand. He realized his mistake when he returned to London.

As Popov tells it: "We rushed to Glass's office, changed his nameplate on his door, mysteriously told him to answer the phone as Mr. Sand, and put a temporary MI5 receptionist on duty at the front door."

It all worked out. Schmidt—code name Tate—became the ostensible paymaster for the German agents in Britain.

One other clever piece of early deception was carried out by Popov and Ewen Montagu. As the navy's representative to the Twenty Committee, Montagu knew that if the Germans did attempt an invasion of Britain, their strength could be diminished by having some of their ships and landing barges blunder into minefields the British had laid along the coast.

Aerial recon had given the Germans a fair idea of the gaps in these minefields by observing English fishing trawlers going out to sea and returning. But what if Popov got his hands on a secret official chart that skewed by a little the actual locations of the minefields? The trawlers could continue to come and go, but a larger fleet following the chart would be deceived into having some of the craft destroyed.

Very well. But how was it possible, plausibly, for Popov to be given such a chart? Montagu had an answer ready. Imagine a barrister who had joined the navy and had access to such documents. Imagine the law man was a Jew who, having heard what the Nazis were doing to the Jews in Europe, wanted to avoid being handed over to the Gestapo if the Germans invaded and he was captured. He was ready to surrender the chart in exchange for a "chit" that would ensure his being delivered to the more civilized Abwehr rather than the barbaric Gestapo.

Popov liked the idea but said that for him to put it over would require a verifiable name and some details the Germans could check. Not to worry, Montagu replied. The Germans could find Lieutenant Commander Montagu in the "Law List" and in the Jewish Year Books that included members of charity committees.

The scheme was carried out. The Germans accepted the chart as genuine. The very welcome stumbling block was that the invasion never came off and Montagu never had to cash in his chit.

Popov's course with von Karsthoff was not always smooth. At one point von Karsthoff informed him that people were "not satisfied with your work. The enormous amounts which you have received so far are absolutely not justified by what we in fact receive here by way of information. . . . You must in future report *many more details* about the formation and disposition of the army, about new weapons, important operations, about possible landings on the Continent."

Characteristically, Popov fought back. "Surely you realize," he replied, "that what I send you has to be judged by its reliability and not merely by its quantity? You would not thank me for sending you pages of rumours which are unconfirmed. There are always stories and rumours. . . . You must make it clear to those people higher up that my letters only contain facts and are much more valuable than if I invented details to make them look better."

Von Karsthoff's criticism, however, was of concern to the Twenty Committee. The decision was that Popov should be seen as trying harder. His next messages included a detailed report about new Royal Navy ships, the building of landing craft, exercises taking place in Scotland and the identification of U.S. forces.

Soon Von Karsthoff was purring again.

Germany's invasion and occupation of Yugoslavia posed a serious problem for Popov. How could he continue to work for the Germans when his country's military had been humbled by their forces? The question came up while Popov was in Lisbon for meetings with von Karsthoff.

When his spymaster sent him an urgent summons for another meeting, Popov knew what was up. He did deplore the Germans' conquest, but the news only strengthened his resolve to continue what he was doing and work against them. Typically, he came up with an inventive answer. Yugoslavia was, as everyone knew, a country made up of discordant elements, primarily the Serbs and the Croats. The war had only increased their antipathy. The Serbs, by and large, sided with the Allies. Many of the Croats supported the Utashe Fascist movement that advocated an independent Croatia under the protection of the Hitler regime. Where was Popov's allegiance? Von Karsthoff plainly wanted him to say he was a Croat, but any such claim would be quickly disproved by even a cursory check. Popov remembered that his hometown was Dubrovnik, whose historical name was Ragusa. He told von Karsthoff that he did not think of himself as either a Serb or a Croat but as a Ragusan. Von Karsthoff, no doubt wanting to avoid the surrender of the chief meal ticket of his easy life in Lisbon, was obviously relieved by Popov's explanation. The show went on.

With adventures such as these, Dusko Popov—Tricycle—was started on one of the most risky yet most productive careers among Britain's double agents.

CHAPTER SIX

TATE, CONVERT FROM NAZISM

The Abwehr trusted Arthur Owens—Snow—to the point of advising him when and where a new agent, who was being sent as his helper, was to be air-dropped onto British soil. So it was that British intelligence learned about the German plans for Agent V-3719, a Swedish mechanic named Gösta Caroli, to land by parachute in a field not far from the Buckinghamshire town of Aylesbury on the night of September 6, 1940.

Before the war, Caroli had lived in Birmingham long enough to become reasonably fluent in English. Then his German-born mother had returned with her son to Germany. When Hitler came to power, the young Caroli joined the Nazi Party. Spotted as a prospect by one of the recruiting scouts of the Abwehr, he was selected for training as a German spy and in Hamburg was given instruction in operating a radio transmitting and receiving set, secret inks, codes and communication techniques. His spymaster was the same as Snow's: Luftwaffe major Nikolaus Ritter. The expectation was that Caroli would establish himself just in time to be of help to Operation Sea Lion, the Germans' invasion of England.

As the result of Owens's alert, Aylesbury's police were warned that "this pigeon is MI5's, so take care there is no spectacular arrest which all can see." Still, the local populace were asked to keep their eyes open for a stranger in the area. Preparing for his flight, Caroli had mistakenly decided to strap his heavy transmitter-receiver to his harness rather than having it parachuted down separately. On landing, he was knocked unconscious. Half coming to in the morning, he cut away his harness but then fell back to sleep in the ditch where he'd come down. He was spotted there by a farm boy, whose employer tipped off the police. Sweeping up Caroli, they delivered him to waiting MI5 officers, who whisked him off to the agency's detention and interrogation center, Camp 020, located south of London in Latchmere House, previously an asylum for the insane.

Despite his tough exterior, Caroli wilted quickly under questioning, especially when he found out how much his interrogators, led by Tar Robertson, knew about him through the decrypts of Abwehr messages by Oliver Strachey's unit at Bletchley Park. Caroli's panicky focus narrowed to how he could avoid being executed. He agreed to cooperate with the British on the understanding he would not be hanged. To clinch the deal, he exacted a promise from his captors that if he informed them of the projected arrival of another spy, a friend of his, his friend would also be spared.

Caroli couldn't know it but he was the first to benefit from a new attitude that B1A had adopted toward captured would-be spies. Five earlier arrivals had been summarily executed. Then Tar Robertson and his MI5 boss, Dick White, almost simultaneously came to the same reaction: Why hang these men when, very probably, they could be "turned" from their Nazi allegiance and become useful double agents? Caroli, given the code name of Summer, presented a good opportunity to test this theory.

Carefully monitored against any trickery, Caroli used his transmitter to signal to Hamburg his safe arrival. Ritter's reply revealed that Agent V-3725 would be the next to be parachuted into Britain and detailed where he would land.

V-3725 was Wulf Schmidt. Caroli and he had lived in the same hotel during their spy training in Hamburg and had become good friends. Although both were rugged young men, their individual characters were nearly opposites.

Caroli was of limited intelligence and was minimally educated. His only advantage over Schmidt was his better command of English. Otherwise, as he had demonstrated, he was relatively easy for his interrogators to break down.

With Schmidt, the British soon found they were up against a much sharper and more sophisticated intelligence. The son of a German father and a Danish mother, he was well educated and widely traveled, including a time in Africa. He had studied for the law at Lübeck University until a reading of Hitler's *Mein Kampf* and the war fever lit up his adventurous spirit and swept him into volunteering to be a Nazi spy. He worked hard at improving his command of English but spoke it only with a marked accent. The Abwehr report on him noted that he was well equipped mentally, energetic and with a good bearing and showed all the signs of a first-rate upbringing. He was described as being well built, of medium height, clean-shaven, quick in movements and with brown hair and blue eyes.

As Agent V-3725, Schmidt boarded a Luftwaffe plane on the night of September 19, 1940, to be parachuted into Britain. He told himself, as he recounted later, "It should be a cakewalk, as they say in England. After all, in a week's time the Third Reich will have installed their own government in London."

Holding fast to his radio set, he came down in the countryside near a village. His parachute got stuck in a tree. Extricating himself from his chute and trying to descend to the ground, he hurt one of his hands and twisted an ankle, which soon became swollen and painful. He spent the night in a hedge. At dawn, he decided to hide the radio equipment and go into the village. He visited several shops, had breakfast, bought a wristwatch, and learned that the village was not far from Cambridge.

Then he made a mistake. He went to the village pump to bathe his foot. His action might have gone unnoticed in a German village, but not in a proper Cambridgeshire hamlet. A passing Home Guard patrol asked to see his papers. The inspection revealed another mistake Schmidt had made. When his German spymaster Ritter had asked him what English-sounding name he wanted on his forged passport, the only name Schmidt could think of was that of Harry Johnson, a man he had once known in the Cameroons. To his British inspectors the name of course seemed at odds with his foreign accent. The patrol detained him and took him to the police in Cambridge.

Representatives of MI5, having been alerted to Schmidt's landing by his erstwhile friend Caroli, were already close by and quickly assumed responsibility for him. He was taken to Camp 020.

There he was confronted by two army officers and Dr. Harold Dearden, a civilian psychiatrist experienced in cross-questioning criminals.

"When I was brought in for interrogation," Schmidt subsequently reported, "I was fascinated by the strange old man in civilian clothes. He was reading a newspaper. He looked at me briefly as I came in and then went on reading. I couldn't take my eyes off him."

Schmidt expected from his interrogation the harsh kind of treatment meted out by the Gestapo. Instead, these men at Camp 020, especially Dearden, confused him by the polite manner of their questioning. This manner of handling 020 prisoners derived not so much from humanitarian motives but because it was more effective. As 020's Major R.W.G. Stephens put it: "Violence is taboo, for not only does it produce answers to please but it lowers the standard of information."

Still, Schmidt was far from being ready to cave in as Caroli had done. As one of his questioners commented, "He was a tough nut to crack. It was hard going questioning him and very wearying."

Transcripts of his exchanges with his interrogators, now available in Britain's National Archives, show how the British hammered away at him, particularly at his original explanation of how, when and where he arrived in England. The story he spun was that he had landed not in September but back in July and not by parachute but by a Danish fishing boat that he had hired to take him to a port on the north coast of Britain. From there he had begun walking south, living on cakes and chocolate, trying to reach the Danish consul in London, a trip that had taken him the rest of July and on through August. Excerpts from the transcripts indicate the way in which Major Stephens, the commandant at 020, tried to prove to him that his tale was unacceptable.

Q: Who cut your hair last?
A: I did not cut it.
Q: You have not had your hair cut for two and a half months?
A: Yes. When I came it was very short.
Q: How much longer are you going on with this nonsense? Do you

know what a man looks like whose hair has been growing for two and half months?

A: It is different. My beard does not grow either.

Q: How often did you shave?

A: Three days or four days.

Q: What did you shave with?

A: I have this knife and these blades.

Q: What laundry did you go to on the way? Which shop washed your clothes?

A: When I came I had two shirts more and socks. This is the last of those I brought.

Q: It looks as if you have been marching all this distance with dirty clothes.

A: I had more clothes and I threw them away.

After a long series of such exchanges, Major Stephens had had enough. "You know the whole of your story is a stack of lies." He added: "It's just a question of whether you intend to help yourself or not. We know a good deal about you, you see. Everything is consistent with your having fallen from a parachute a couple of days ago. Your clothes, in the first place, are clean. Your hair has recently been cut. You probably hurt your hand and foot when you landed. Your health is good, which means you have not been living on buns and chocolates for two months."

Schmidt began to realize that these British did know entirely too much about him. During another series of questions after he had admitted that his cover story was false and that he had, indeed, just arrived by parachute, he commented that he wasn't sure he'd been parachuted into the right place. One of his interrogators said, "Oh, but I'm sure Major Gartenfeld wouldn't make a mistake like that." Schmidt was dumbfounded: these guys even knew the name of his pilot!

Harold Dearden sensed another major confusion in Schmidt's mind. This was September 1940 and in Germany there had been expectation that at any minute the invasion of Britain would begin. Schmidt had expected to see a country devastated by the Luftwaffe's blitz, its buildings smashed, its people humbled and ready to capitulate to the German invaders. These were the thoughts that had prompted his optimism in the plane bearing him over England. Instead, he found Britons going routinely about their business in a largely unscathed countryside. The conversation of his guards in the van taking him to Camp 020 was not that of men in fear of their lives. Cleverly, the MI5 driver transporting him there had intentionally passed by Whitehall, the Houses of Parliament and Westminster Abbey, all of which remained, to his eyes, incredibly undamaged. It bothered Schmidt greatly to realize how Nazi propaganda had painted an almost completely false picture. He wrote, much later, "Gradually I realized that the picture that had been given me of a totally defeated Britain, with the people on the run and resistance to Germany nil, was entirely misleading. . . . It depressed me to think I had been so misled."

Dearden also realized that Schmidt had a sense of humor. At one point in his questioning, Schmidt said, with a sardonic grin, "If we all wait a short while longer, you will all be *my* prisoners."

The oral fencing went on. The British knew they were under a severe time pressure, in that Ritter would be expecting a radio report from him. Could he be turned into a double agent soon enough to avoid arousing the Abwehr's suspicions?

Dearden thought it could be done by playing on Schmidt's disillusionment about not finding Britain in the paralyzed state he'd been led to expect. Dearden also based his hopes on Schmidt's humorous bent.

When told of this attribute of Schmidt, Tar Robertson exclaimed, "My God, how right you are! Do you know, I kept asking myself who Schmidt reminded me of. Now you mention a sense of humor, I know who it is. He is very, very like Harry Tate, the music-hall comedian. So, if we do turn him, I suggest his code name be Tate. What better?"

Could he be turned in time to make Ritter believe that all was well? The British remained patient and polite. Schmidt admitted, long afterward, being impressed that there were no threats of torture if he did not comply. But he was also smart enough to know that at the end of the line, if he did not cooperate, execution was probable. And in Britain in wartime that meant being hanged—in his mind an unspeakable way to go.

Awareness of that grim prospect was only one factor that led to his being turned. A strong element was his growing resentment at being so misled by Nazi propaganda's flagrant lies about the situation in the UK. Also, he was affected by the merciless breaking of his cover story. He knew there was no longer any use in resisting when the British told him that Caroli had also been captured and had talked freely about him and his Abwehr connections. Wulf Schmidt agreed to cooperate.

Schmidt—Tate—was told that he would be required to transmit a message back to Major Ritter. He was warned that he must send it accurately and without any unnecessary pauses and must avoid any mistakes that might tip off his control that he was not a free agent. Otherwise . . . Schmidt said he understood.

He was taken from London back to the country where he had landed, as insurance that his transmission would seem authentic. When his own wireless transmitter was found to be inadequate, he was given a British set.

A troublesome question remained. Schmidt had shown that he was a distinctive individual with a flippant, ironic edge to his sense of humor. He would be expected to communicate in a style all his own. Again he was cooperative. He phrased his first message à la Schmidt, adding a characteristic cheeky request for an urgent transfusion of money.

Despite his apprehensions, Tate efficiently Morse-coded his message to Hamburg. Eventually, a reply came: contact had been established. In a gesture not lost on his monitors, he held up a thumb to indicate that all was well. Then he tapped out, in his own style, the message given him by the Twenty Committee. The sergeant monitoring his transmission signaled it had been done correctly.

Had he, nonetheless, somehow managed to warn the Abwehr that he was held captive? There was nothing for it but to wait. Then Ritter responded and began giving Schmidt instructions on what he was to do.

It was the start of what, for the British involved, was one of the most satisfying double-agent stories of the war. Once his intelligent mind discerned the real differences between the Nazi totalitarian system and the free society he found in Britain, Schmidt underwent what has been described as "an almost religious conversion." He proved that he was not only competent but also trustworthy. Masterman called him "a shining example" of the Twenty Committee's successes in coaxing turned agents to "a better way of thinking."

Tar Robertson took a liking to Schmidt from the start and brought him to his home to live with his family. Masterman regarded him as "one of our most trusted wireless agents" and admired his "terse and virile telegraphese" in sending his messages.

On their side, the Germans trusted him so completely that, as has been told, they chose him to be their paymaster in the wake of Plan Midas.

Interestingly, that role was soon found to present problems for his British controllers. With all that cash available to him, Schmidt was altogether too free to roam the island, sending answers to the increasingly demanding questionnaires sent to him from Hamburg. His movements had to be restricted. He and the Twenty Committee thought up an ingenious solution. He signaled this message to Hamburg: "Was caught in a police raid at Kings Cross Station. Police asked for Identity Cards of all travelers. On being asked whether I had yet registered for military service I answered the truth—that is 'No,' in order not to arouse suspicion by lying. They took the number of my Identity Card, my name, address, etc. I thought it wiser to give my real address to prevent closer investigation about the authenticity of my Identity Card. I was told to register at once, otherwise I would be prosecuted. In order to prevent closer investigation, suspicions, or at the worst arrest and its accompanying investigations, there is nothing else to do but to comply with their orders. I have already made careful plans for answering all likely questions. Now I must only look after myself and get away as easily as possible. I don't think the danger is very great, but it is not a pleasant position to be in."

Only two days later he posted another message: "Do not worry too much. Think will be able to master this situation. I have a good plan."

And two days after that, he reported his happy solution. He had made friends with the owner of a large farm with a modern dairy connected to it. The friend was in need of help, so much so that he was willing to appeal to Schmidt's registry board that Schmidt be exempted from military service in order to work on the farm. Of course, these farm duties greatly limited Schmidt's freedom to travel about, but he could still take on assignments that could be done on his days off.

As another result of having been provided ample funds, the Germans let Tate know that he should begin moving in more influential circles, even if he did have to work on a farm. The Twenty Committee's answer was to give him a fictitious girlfriend named Mary, who worked at Eisenhower's invasion headquarters. In the aura of romance, Mary became indiscreet enough to confide details that made good traffic for the Abwehr. To protect Tate in case the Germans checked up on Mary, the British had a real young woman play the role. The genuine Mary was transferred to Eisenhower's HQ and was also a person who did actually sometimes spend weekends at the farm where Tate resided. In his transmissions, Tate let the Abwehr know of his love interest and on one occasion gave an accurate description of the real Mary, adding, "Don't you think she is quite a tasty dish?"

Gaining the trust and respect of both sides, Wulf Schmidt became the longest-serving double agent in the war—a span extending from his first message sent in October 1940 to a final message from Ritter in Hamburg on May 2, 1945, just a few hours before the city's fall.

During the heyday of his relationship with Major Ritter, the major wrote of him that the information Schmidt sent "was rated especially valuable by the competent authority in Berlin." Ritter thought Schmidt deserved a top Nazi award. He got around the technicality of Schmidt's part-Danish origins by having him naturalized via the wireless. In due course the award was made: Wulf Schmidt—Tate—received the Iron Cross, First Class.

CHAPTER SEVEN

ZIGZAG, THE MOST DARING

From his boyhood on, Eddie Chapman scorned authority and enjoyed making a mockery of bureaucrats. In his adulthood, it was an attitude he retained from the time when he had been a safecracker and a bank robber and had spent time in prison for his misdeeds. After completing his wartime services, he determined that he wanted his story made into a book. He sought out old drinking buddy and journalist Frank Owen. In the foreword of the book that he and Chapman eventually produced, Owen tells of his reintroduction to Chapman.

Chapman called him and told the journalist that if they could meet at one of their favorite pubs, he would repay a ten-pound debt from a years-ago loan. "Where," Owen asked, "did you drop in from?"

Chapman's answer: "Berlin. Would you like a cheque or a tenner?"

In the pub, Chapman pulled out a fat roll of banknotes. Owen reckoned it contained several hundred pounds.

"Come, now, Eddie," he said, "you shouldn't walk around with all that stuff loose. Put it in a bank, boy."

"In a bank?" cried Eddie. "That'd be the place! Why, someone might pinch it!" Then, in a more serious tone: "Honestly, I'm really worried about where I *can* park it."

"How much have you got?"

"About eight thousand quid."

"Where did you get it?"

"Hitler!"

When Owen laughed, Chapman said, "I mean it."

He began to tell Owen the story he wanted made into a book. But this was England, and it was far too soon for breaching the Official Secrets Act. Chapman refused to let that stop him. He got his dictated memoir translated into French, serialized it in a French newspaper and induced a Belgian firm to publish it as a book. For these transgressions he was hauled into court and fined fifty pounds, plus twenty-five pounds in costs. Further, the only way he could publish the English version for the UK market in 1953 was to leave out all the material relating to his service as a double agent. The result, as Owen mentions in a postscript, is that *The Eddie Chapman Story* is "only half of it . . . this is all of Eddie Chapman's story that anyone is allowed to tell."

It's too bad Chapman couldn't have waited. When his full story did become known, Ewen Montagu wrote that Chapman "provided a case which, if it had been recounted as a novel, would have aroused derision."

The half that Chapman does tell begins in Sunderland, a town on the North Sea coast. A product of the Great Depression, he left school on his fourteenth birthday and did odd jobs that bored him. A high point of his early teen years came when he rescued a drowning man and received a certificate for bravery. Even that early, though, he already had an undercover pursuit as a petty thief.

At seventeen, he lied about being underage and joined the Coldstream Guards. He could get away with the lie because he was "six feet, lean and pretty hard." After finishing his training, he was fitted with a red tunic and bearskin topper for duty as a guard at the Tower of London. He enjoyed these ceremonial performances for several years.

In his off-duty hours, though, he continued to demonstrate his complete lack of scruples. As a particularly scurvy example, he indulged in violent affairs with London women and then proceeded to blackmail them by producing compromising photographs taken by an accomplice. He infected a girl with VD and then blackmailed her by threatening to tell her parents that she had given *him* the disease.

His scurrilous escapades finally got him into trouble. He served time in prison and, at the end of his sentence, was discharged from the Guards.

The disapproving stamp on his discharge papers made it tough for him to get legitimate employment. He became a thief again, was caught and served nine more months in prison.

There he met Freddie, just finishing up thirteen years for post-office robbery and safecracking. Released, they formed a partnership, using an explosive still little known to the police. This was gelignite, a mixture of gun cotton dissolved in nitroglycerine and mixed with wood pulp and sodium. So successful were they that they and their associates, who included a getaway car chauffeur, became known as "the gelignite gang." After a foiled safecracking in Glasgow, with Scotland Yard hot on his trail, Chapman flew to the Channel Islands, hoping to go from there to refuge, and new safes to crack, in the south of France. On the isle of Jersey, he was caught and sentenced to a further two years in prison.

He began his term in April 1939. A year more was added when an escape attempt by him was foiled. He was in the Jersey prison, consequently, when the war began and the Germans, in 1940, seized and occupied the island. As his time of release neared, Chapman began to imagine a different future for himself. He spent prison hours learning from grammar books how to read and write both French and German.

His first move after being freed was to go to the Germans' command center on the island and inform an officer there, "I would like to join the German secret service." The officer questioned him and took down notes for a report. It was the first of several interviews, at each of which Chapman told the same story: England had uncaringly assigned him to a poverty-stricken childhood and an inadequate education that left him with no way to survive except through a life of crime. If he left Jersey for England and the British police captured him, he would receive a sentence of at least fifteen years. He was eager for revenge on this inhumane society. If the Germans wanted him to spy for them, he was only too ready.

He backed up his arguments by showing press clippings of his most sensational burglaries.

No one told him directly what the Germans thought of his idea. All he learned was that one day he was ordered to pack his bag. He was driven to the harbor and, under guard, put on a boat to France. The journey ended in another prison cell, this one in the formidable fort of Romainville, near Paris.

In March 1942, his wartime fate was decided when he was called for still another interview. This one was with a German royalist, Baron Stefan von Groening. Chapman liked him "the moment that I saw him"—a tall individual with a pleasant corpulence but also "the benevolent air of a good man." The two of them hit it off from the start. Von Groening became his spymaster, mentor and appreciative father figure. To have in von Groening a man who liked him, admired him and trusted him started Chapman on at least a partial reformation of character.

Von Groening and others in the Abwehr treated Chapman as though considering him a prize catch. German specialists trained him in transmitting by Morse code, the techniques of invisible ink, the art of sabotage and the use of a cipher assigned exclusively to him. When it was decided that he would be dropped into England by parachute, he received a course in parachute jumping. On one of his six practice drops he broke several teeth and was provided dental services that left him with a smile revealing two frontal gold teeth. The peak of all this special care came when he was given the uniform of a German under-officer.

In June 1942, von Groening presented him with a contract. For the sum of 100,000 Reichsmarks he was to land in England and sabotage the airplane factory producing Mosquito fighter-bombers. This was the De Havilland works in Hatfield, north of London. Would he sign the contract?

The answer Chapman says he gave was: "I'll gut the damned place."

After reviewing with him aerial photos of the plant, von Groening equipped Chapman with a wireless set, twenty-four electric detonators, an American Colt .32-caliber pistol, a British entrenching tool, an illuminated wristwatch, a cyanide capsule in case he needed to commit suicide and £1,000. On the night of December 20, 1942, a German plane dropped him northeast of London on the Isle of Ely.

Waiting for word from Fritzchen, von Groening and his Abwehr associates argued about his chances of success. "He's a lunatic and will be caught," one official predicted.

"He's a clever criminal who is used to evading the law," von Groening replied. "His chances of success are improved because of this."

What neither Chapman nor the Abwehr were aware of was that the British were waiting for him. Bletchley Park decrypts of Abwehr Enigma messages had disclosed the Germans' plans for Fritzchen. Following up on the decrypt, the Twenty Committee had researched his case and knew a great deal about his past. As Masterman wrote: "We even knew that he could be identified by certain false teeth, because his departure from France had been postponed as the result of an accident during his parachute training, and the dental repairs had found their place in secret sources"—i.e., Bletchley decrypts. "What we did not know was whether he was really on our side or on that of the Germans."

No need to worry. After his parachute landing and a night of hiding out in a wooded area, Chapman's first action was to call at the nearest police station. He had to overcome the local policemen's doubts about his incredible story, but in the end they agreed to call MI5. The officer who accompanied him to MI5's headquarters asked, as he handed Chapman over, to speak with Tar Robertson. He told Tar: "I don't know what this man may tell you, sir. He came with a German parachute, but I recognized him at once." Chapman, the policeman explained, had been in his Guards platoon all those years before. As Montagu wrote of the incident: "What writer would dare have a spy taken into custody by a country bobby who had him in the same platoon in the Army?"

As with other newly captured spies, Chapman was taken to Camp 020 for interrogation. The camp commander's report on him noted that he was vain and thought of himself as "something of a prince of the underworld," a man "who loved himself, loved adventure and loved his country, probably in that order." The commander added that Chapman "has no scruples and will stop at nothing. . . . Of fear he knows nothing, and while patriotism is not a positive virtue he certainly has a deep-rooted hatred of the Hun. In a word, adventure to Chapman is the breath of life. Given adventure he has the courage to achieve the unbelievable." His hatred of the Hun was not diminished by having his interrogators point out to him that the Nazis had put his life in danger by enclosing the British banknotes they had given him in a German bank wrapper.

His aim all along, Chapman claimed, had been to become a double agent for Britain. He was too shrewd an operator, however, not to exact a price. His demand was that in return for his services he would be pardoned of the prewar charges against him. MI5 granted him this favor, code-named him ZigZag and turned him over to the Twenty Committee to guide him in what he reported to his controllers.

Von Groening, waiting in Paris, heard nothing from him for three days. Then he received Chapman's encoded radio message that he had landed safely and was getting to work. Further reports told how he had gone to Hatfield, had cased the facility and had decided that the best way to put the factory out of business was to destroy its main power plant. From a quarry he knew of in Kent, he radioed his boss, he had acquired the explosives he would need to do the job.

On January 29, 1943, ZigZag's message read, simply, "Will attempt sabotage this evening at six o'clock." Later that night, his second message came: "Mission successfully accomplished." He went on to tell how he had done the job with two improvised explosive devices with timers he had himself constructed using wristwatches, just as he had been taught to do in his sabotage training.

Von Groening was elated. His superiors were skeptical, demanding proof. The Luftwaffe sent planes over Hatfield on reconnaissance flights. Their aerial photos were convincing. They showed great rents in the roof of the power plant and debris from the explosion, including smashed parts of generators and other heavy equipment, scattered over a wide area. The Germans had no doubt that production of Mosquitoes would be crippled for quite a long period.

The recon evidence was backed up by accounts in the British press, with editorials criticizing the security services for failing to detect and prevent this most dastardly of covert operations—good reading for von Groening and his Abwehr team.

How was this seeming catastrophe concocted? The answer is that by this point in the war the British were becoming expert in visual fakery. They had built up a team that included a well-known magician and set designers from the Old Vic theater, individuals adept at producing bogus tanks and artillery out of plywood and papier-mâché, airplanes that were inflated rubber and simulated troops that included balloon soldiers sitting on inflatable latrines. To give the illusion of destroying a power plant was, for them, only an interesting new challenge. This time their fake bombing was given authenticity by a painted canvas showing that the generating plant's roof had been blown off and by bogus parts of generating equipment spread around the landscape. They set off smoke bombs to suggest a devastating blast.

British analysts of the production were more critical than the Germans. National Archives files on the incident show that when surveyed by explosive attack specialists of the Secret Operations Executive and by RAF recon planes the De Havilland "bang" should have been seen as a hoax. The reports reflect concern that had the Germans put any real effort into technical verification of Chapman's claims they would have been revealed as fakes and Chapman himself shown up as being under British control. But the Germans were careless, the British deception team learned from their mistakes and ZigZag went on his merry way.

Life in England as a pseudo-informant for the Nazis did not satisfy his adventurous spirit. He did transmit reports designating the insignia of new American divisions thronging into England. On the night of January 17–18, 1943, he witnessed the German air raid on London and reported sneeringly of its ineffectiveness. "Can't they do better?" he asked.

He repeatedly proposed that the Twenty Committee back him in an attempt to assassinate Hitler, but the Committee just as repeatedly turned him down.

In early February, ZigZag wired von Groening asking that a U-boat come to pick him up. The Abwehr's reply was: Sorry, there were no U-boats to spare. He was instructed to make his way out of the country as best as he could, and to do it quickly, "now that all England is looking for you."

In mid-February Chapman radioed von Groening: "Closing transmission. Too dangerous to work. Am returning via Lisbon."

The Twenty Committee contrived to have him hired as a steward on board the SS *City of Lancaster*. In Lisbon he was to desert the ship and make his way back to von Groening.

While his ship was anchored in Lisbon, Chapman met with German embassy officials to expedite his passage to Paris and Germany. One of them asked if he would help sabotage the ship that had brought him to

Lisbon. He felt constrained to say yes. The official gave him two lumps of coal that were to be inserted into the ship's coal bunker. These simulated lumps were explosives that, when shoveled into the ship's boilers, would detonate and destroy the vessel. Chapman agreed to do the job and returned to the ship. But instead of leaving them in the bunker, he gave them to the ship's captain.

His reunion with von Groening came in Norway, where the baron was now located. It was a victorious occasion. Chapman got credit for destroying not just the power station in Britain. The Germans also believed that he had sunk the *Lancaster* after it had left Lisbon. He was feted as a hero.

For his part in the celebration, Chapman gave a lurid account of how he had blown up the De Havilland works and then had craftily evaded the police and British agents by staying one jump ahead of them, moving from rooming house to rooming house, never remaining in the same area of London for more than a few days. "They thought they had me several times," he told his Abwehr friends. "All they had were empty rooms."

To cap his homecoming, von Groening presented him with the Iron Cross. While other double agents received similar recognition, he was the only Briton to be so rewarded.

Was he ready for a new Abwehr assignment? ZigZag—now Fritzchen again—said yes, but not until he'd had some time to relax and enjoy that reward money the Germans were giving him.

Eddie Chapman, ex-thug, was on his way to being another of the agents highly trusted by the Germans while remaining in the good graces of the British.

In a postwar world that was looking for heroes, he was also on his way to having his story re-created in the film *Triple Cross,* with Christopher Plummer as Eddie Chapman.

CHAPTER EIGHT

CODE NAME BRUTUS

As mentioned earlier, Roman Garby-Czerniawski was another of the double agents who felt compelled to record his wartime experiences in a book. Like Eddie Chapman, he wasn't willing to wait until the British government's ban on double-agent revelations was lifted. His decision was spurred by seeing parts of his story told in other books, most often inaccurately. To comply with the secrets act, his book *The Big Network,* published in 1961, deals only with his earlier wartime experiences in Poland and France. At the book's end, he reports that he "managed to reach England," and that that story would be the theme of his next book, *The Fourth Force.* If he ever did write it, however, there is no record of its being published.

The memoir he did leave is a fascinating one. In it he tells how, despite his imposing height, for ten years he fitted himself into the cockpits of Polish fighter planes and served with the First Regiment of Aviation stationed near Warsaw. He rose to be a captain on the general staff of the Polish Air Force until Poland was overwhelmed by the German attack in 1939. As the Germans approached Warsaw, Garby-Czerniawski was instructed to gather enough reserve officers to fly all the remaining Polish planes to Romania. Fearful of the Germans, the Romanians decided they must intern the Polish fliers. That prospect did not appeal to the Poles, who agreed to split up into groups and make their way to France. Garby-Czerniawski used forged documents to escape from Romania and make his way to Paris.

There he was introduced to intelligence work. He became an intelligence officer in the Polish First Division, which was formed from escapees and sent to the front in Alsace-Lorraine. He was not really interested, he wrote, in becoming a spy.

The image created in his mind by reading spy stories "was a grim one: a life lived in shadows, behind huge spider nets of intrigue, misty with the vapours of alcohol, Turkish cigarettes and the husky voices of décolleté women. . . . A life in which, when you are successful, you receive high pay, but in which failure leads inevitably to an anonymous end against some foreign wall or high on an alien gallows."

His active entrée into that shadowed life became necessary, however, when in 1940 the Wehrmacht crushed the Allied armies in France. That debacle forced Garby-Czerniawski to join his "fourth force," the underground. From the widow of Armand Borni he received her husband's birth certificate, clothing and an old bicycle on which he peddled the three hundred miles to Paris.

It was on another bicycle trip, this time to try to facilitate the escape of a Polish friend in a German prison, that his "big idea" was born.

The Germans were pouring troops into France, both for occupation duties and in preparation for invading Britain. He observed that every German vehicle was distinguished by an organizational insignia. "Here was I," he wrote, "a General Staff Officer, fully trained in intelligence, right in the middle of enemy units! Able to read all these insignia like lines in an open book."

He saw the possibility of forming a secret organization that would collect and analyze these insignia and so determine the makeup of the German forces in France. This, he knew, would be information of high value to the beleaguered British.

Garby-Czerniawski had the intelligence, the energy and the personal associations to begin developing his idea into the Interallié, one of the first substantial resistance groups in occupied France. He has recorded an interesting analysis of the stages of reaction by the French people under the Nazi occupation.

First there was shock; everyone was scared and bewildered. They had to overcome the disbelief that this could happen to their country. Soon they became worried and resigned, adjusting to the reality that the Germans were ruling over them. The next stage was to regard their occupiers with annoyance and impatience. Finally, hatred started to grow, and with it a desire for action. The French, Garby-Czerniawski judged, were at that ultimate stage and were ready for the rallying point his Polish-French anti-Nazi network could provide.

He judged correctly. Even with careful, cautious selectivity the group formed swiftly. Many Frenchmen were eager to undertake the hazardous work of spying on their German occupiers. How many of these French volunteers knew they were working for a Polish-led organization is debatable, but they did gather masses of information to be fed into Garby-Czerniawski's Paris headquarters. Polish radio experts built transmitters with which to send his reports across the Channel to Britain. Couriers learned how to pass into unoccupied France and steal across the Spanish border in order to mail to Britain rolls of film holding more comprehensive reports, maps and diagrams. Garby-Czerniawski himself crossed the demarcation line between occupied and unoccupied France illegally eighteen times and made the crossing with false documents on twelve occasions. He divided occupied France into fourteen sectors, each under an able leader. His organization grew to more than a hundred operatives.

To manage the headquarters office and type his reports, Garby-Czerniawski recruited Mathilde Carré, a bright young Frenchwoman who enjoyed her nickname, La Chatte, the cat. To handle the encoding of his transmissions to England, he sought out Renée Bornet, code-named Violette.

Very quickly Garby-Czerniawski was able to inform the British that his Interallié agents had identified twenty-two German divisions in France. Since the Germans conveniently used a color-coding system to distinguish regiments within a division, Interallié supplied London with an order of battle that extended all the way down to the company level. Added to the informational haul were data on ammunition dumps, aerodromes, naval installations and radar sites.

At that early stage of the war, Garby-Czerniawski's network was Britain's sole regular source of information from France.

Grateful, the British in October 1941 asked Garby-Czerniawski to come to London for a consultation. He left Carré in charge in Paris and hurried to the spot where the RAF landed a small, fast plane to pick him up. During his London stay, the Polish command presented him with the Cross of Virtuti Militari, the highest Polish decoration and the equivalent of the British Victoria Cross. Garby-Czerniawski still had many things he wanted to do in England, but on his sixth day there he received a wireless message from Carré concerning an alarming rift in the Interallié ranks. There was nothing for it but that he return immediately to Paris. And the only way so sudden a change could be handled was to drop him by parachute. He was told to be ready on October 8. In short order he was back at his organization's headquarters and was in control again.

Then, on November 18, 1941, disaster struck. There are conflicting reports on how the betrayal of Interallié came about. The most colorful is that Mathilde Carré became jealous of Garby-Czerniawski's attentions to a younger woman in the group—a jealousy strong enough to impel her to sacrifice the whole network. In his book, Garby-Czerniawski admits to being on warm, kissing terms with both La Chatte and Violette. But his strongest sexual interest seems to have been for his young French mistress, Mademoiselle Deschamps, code-named Moustique, who subsequently reached England and became his wife.

The true story seems to be less romantic. The Abwehr's first break into Interallié came through direction finding that pinpointed the group's radio transmissions. These led to the arrest of and betrayal by the agent Kieffer, code-named Kiki, one of those in charge of the network's Cherbourg intelligence sector. Kiki's betrayal led to the arrests by the Abwehr's Hugo Bleicher of Garby-Czerniawski, Carré and Bornet in Paris. Imprisoned and threatened with torture and death, Carré supplied Bleicher with the names of some sixty of Interallié's agents—and is said to have become Bleicher's mistress as well. Bornet—Violette—also was of help to Bleicher.

That was the end of Interallié. It was also where Garby-Czerniawski's memoir ended. But there was much more of his story to be told.

From Paris, he was taken to the Germans' own high-security prison in France along with his confederates. There they faced execution at the hands of the Gestapo.

At the time, however, the Abwehr was, as an official report put it, "suffering from a serious lack of intelligence agents." Leading the search for recruits was Colonel Joachim Rohleder, who was not above reviewing prison rolls for prospects. His scan of the prisoners at Fresnes prison turned up the name of Garby-Czerniawski. The Pole's history as the leader of a Polish-French resistance group made it seem as though the idea of turning him into a spy for Germany was asking the impossible. However, the record showed that Garby-Czerniawski was a leader with a strong sense of loyalty to his fellow prisoners. Rohleder went to the prison, interviewed Garby-Czerniawski and put to him the proposition: work for the Abwehr as a secret agent in Britain and not only would he himself be freed but also the jailed members of his resistance group would be treated as prisoners of war rather than facing execution.

At first Garby-Czerniawski refused. But at that point in the autumn of 1941 the Germans were overwhelming the Soviet armies. German forces were at the doors of Moscow and were fighting in the streets of Stalingrad. Garby-Czerniawski reconsidered. He informed the Germans he had changed his mind, declaring himself now convinced that since the destiny of Poland lay in German hands, he was ready to put his services at the Germans' disposal.

Although Rohleder and his Abwehr associates were convinced of Garby-Czerniawski's sincerity, they also reminded him that both his mother and his brother were in German hands, as were the Interallié prisoners. They required him to sign an agreement that if he should ever double-cross them, they would be at liberty to execute the hostages held in their power.

How was Garby-Czerniawski, code-named Armand, to reach Britain? Rohleder and his team hatched a scheme and told Bleicher to carry it out. As Bleicher wrote in his own postwar memoir: "I received a strange commission at the beginning of July 1942. I was to fetch Armand out of Fresnes prison allegedly to go to interrogation in Paris, but I was to allow him to make an escape on the way. . . . My duties had hitherto been to catch spies. Now I was to help the chief of a big spy organization to escape. It was a grotesque situation."

Orders, however, were orders. Bleicher let Garby-Czerniawski "escape." The French underground took over and saw to it that he made his way to Madrid. There the Abwehr trained him in spy work and codes and gave him two crystals with which to begin the construction of a radio transmitter. In January 1943, he was also equipped with a questionnaire, plus the usual cyanide capsule, and put on a flight to England.

His arrival in London had already been tipped off by the French resistance. The British found him in what an official report described as "a very nervous condition." When he was interrogated by the security authorities of both Britain and the Polish military in exile, he avoided any reference to his recruitment by the Abwehr. His nervousness and reluctance were understandable, considering the terrible ransom he had left in German hands and his uncertainty as to whether the Abwehr might have penetrated the Polish headquarters in London. At this point, unfortunately, his loyalty to the Allied cause was questioned, causing some of his fellow Polish officers to rise vehemently to his defense. His silence was to cause a serious rift.

Garby-Czerniawski did satisfy the investigating authorities that his escape had been genuine. Otherwise, his only commitment was to tell the chief of the Polish Security Service that he would make an interesting statement in a month's time.

The account he then produced was entitled "Le Grand Jeu," the Great Game. It was a full confession that he had come to Britain with the Abwehr's expectation that he would spy for them. He also produced the two crystals, which he had kept in the heels of his shoes. His principal mission for the Germans, he revealed, was to report on British aircraft production. He had also agreed to use the contacts he would develop among Polish and British leaders to report high-level political information. A more visionary assignment was to form discontent among the Polish armed forces and, if possible, organize a Polish fifth column in Britain.

But that, he insisted, was all on the German side. *His* one aim was to persuade the British to accept him as a double agent doing everything in his power to bring down the Nazi regime.

His confession, in the words of a British analysis, "was a bombshell, particularly for the Polish Services." Many of those officers who had gone out on a limb for him in declaring his innocence felt betrayed and became his bitter opponents. He did not help improve his relations with his Polish colleagues by becoming involved in the inner politics of the Polish military in exile. Polish authorities found that he was playing a leading role in attacking a Polish general whose behavior, Garby-Czerniawski believed, was harmful to the Polish cause. He was tried by court-martial and imprisoned for a week, but then his sentence was indefinitely postponed. An official report on the case concluded, subsequently, that Garby-Czerniawski "was in fact acting in the best interests of his country."

Other top Polish officials smoothed the surface as much as they could manage because they saw that Garby-Czerniawski had the potential to become a highly effective double agent.

His troubles, though, did not end with the Poles. The British, too, were left with doubts. Yes, he had sworn that his whole purpose was to help the Allied cause. But he must have sworn just as convincingly to the Abwehr. Could he be trusted, or might he be attempting some form of triple cross? An official British analysis at the time noted that "the revelation that he had accepted a mission for the Germans made it appear that he was a very much more sinister individual than had been expected." The decision was to keep Garby-Czerniawski under the closest watch, to tap his telephone use and to subject his correspondence to careful inspection.

British authorities had another good reason to be cautious about him. To accept his case meant taking the Polish authorities more into MI5's confidence than in the past, broadening the lists of those in the know and risking a disastrous leak. The British shared Garby-Czerniawski's concern that the Germans might have a mole among the exiled Poles. And it was known that the Poles were in possession of the code the Abwehr had given him and could consequently monitor his radio traffic.

A final troublesome question for MI5 was whether, considering his past work in France for the British, they could be certain the Germans would trust him.

The doubts, though, were soon dispelled. As for his code, he demanded a new one from the Germans, and they complied. Somewhat tentatively, the British decided to try him out as a double agent "for a time at any rate." He would, however, communicate only the routine information the Twenty Committee would supply to him; he would take no part in operational deception.

He was given the code name Brutus and was instructed to report that he had recruited a subagent, code-named Chopin, to act as his wireless operator. The arrangement allowed Brutus to write the messages in his own French style while giving the British control over their transmission.

Handling Brutus turned out to be a tricky proposition—not because of his loyalties but because of his personality. As an official report expressed it, he was "of an intensely dramatic and egotistical nature" and "a vain and conceited man." His successes in France against the Germans, and now in Britain, gave him a sense of self-importance enlarged to the point of regarding himself as "a sort of Joan of Arc of Poland."

Nonetheless, the questions the Abwehr began to send him showed plainly that they trusted him and valued him. He worked his way back into the good graces of the Polish London headquarters and became the liaison officer between the Polish and the Royal air forces. His personal vanity did not get in the way of a trained eye for military observation and a retentive memory, and his liaison position enabled him to pass to the Germans a steady stream of information, cleared for him by the Twenty Committee but expressed in his own vigorous style. His reports were well regarded by the Germans.

By the end of 1943, his case officers were sure enough of Brutus to advocate a change in course. The close watch, phone checks and mail surveillance should be discontinued, they said, "as Brutus appeared not to be engaged in any sinister activity." Most important, they saw him as too valuable an asset to be limited just to an informational role. They recommended that it was time for him to begin sending misinformation as well.

Their recommendations were accepted. Brutus had proved he could be given a major responsibility in the grand deceptions surrounding the Normandy landings.

CHAPTER NINE

TREASURE, FIRST VIOLIN IN THE DECEPTION ORCHESTRA

Nathalie "Lily" Sergueiew, also spelled Sergeyev, had the distinction of being the first woman agent to send messages by radio to the Abwehr. This development came about only well after she had been accepted by the Abwehr in Paris early in the war. Abwehr chief Admiral Wilhelm Canaris did not approve of women as agents and certainly not one to be turned loose with a wireless set. But the Paris office of the Abwehr needed a radio-trained agent in Britain, and Sergueiew was a bright and promising prospect.

The reason she gave for wanting to help the Nazis was that, as a refugee whose family was driven from her native Russia because of their czarist connections, she believed Germany was the best hope for bringing down the Communists. Her record also included the fact that in her youth she, for a time, had expressed admiration for the upsurging Nazi regime.

When she agreed to be a spy for Germany, however, those reasons had been swept away by her loathing of the Nazis and her desire to see them driven out of France—of which, through the naturalization of her parents, she was a citizen.

Her love of France had come early. Her family had fled Saint Petersburg to Paris with her when she was five. She was educated in French schools and first attracted notice as an artist: at nineteen she had a one-woman show of her paintings. At the same time she was succeeding in getting articles published as a journalist. An observer said of her, though, that at that age she was "fat and plain with mouse-colored hair" and had no idea how to dress.

It was as though she overheard this comment and set out immediately to do something about it. She began long hikes—when she was twenty-one she embarked on a walking holiday from Paris to Warsaw and back. In addition to slimming her down, her excursions gave her material for her writings. A collection of them was published with the title *Un voyage à pied.* She also took long bicycle tours. When the war broke out in 1939 she was cycling from Paris to Saigon and had gotten as far as Aleppo in Syria. She immediately canceled the rest of the trip and began training in Beirut as a nurse.

Her self-transformation yielded a young woman who, as described by Ladislav Farago, had a "rough-hewn Slavic face . . . marred by a square chin but mellowed by her gently sloping brow and sensitive eyes. She wore her rich auburn hair down to shoulders that were firm and broad, giving her a somewhat masculine appearance. But Lily was all woman— tender, skittish, vital, high-strung, and set in her ways."

In her diary Sergueiew recorded her reactions when word reached her that France had been defeated. "My brain refused to visualize Paris crowded with Germans: field-gray uniforms strolling along the Champs Elysées or sitting at the café tables; the Swastika flying instead of the French Tricolour. Up to now, I have not hated them, but the thought of Germans parading their mastery about Paris makes me shake with powerful rage and hatred." Her volatile mind began seeking answers to the question: What was the individual, what was she, to do about it? Her preparations as a nurse did not seem enough.

As soon as it became evident that the British would continue to resist the Nazis, she found her answer. She resolved to leave the occupied countries and commit herself to aiding Britain. The idea of a twenty-five-year-old Russian-French woman somehow making a significant contribution to Great Britain's war effort forced her to admit to herself that "in broad daylight, my scheme seemed mad and childlike." She determined, however, to have a go at it.

How? Her memory suggested a course of action. Along the way she had made friends with a German journalist, Felix Dassel, and his family. He had been interested in her wanderings and had written articles about her in the German press. He had, in addition, had her do research for him. Dassel, she had become aware, was not just a journalist; he was also a member of the German Intelligence Service and a recruiting agent for the Abwehr. When she traveled to his home in Berlin and conveyed to him her bitter feelings toward the British for letting the French down so badly, he responded as she hoped he would: he asked if she would consider becoming a German agent in Britain. She accepted at once.

Dassel saw to it that the Abwehr's Paris office took up her case. There she met her spymaster, German major Emil Kliemann, whom she came to think of as "Mustache" because of the heavy upper-lip ornament that went with his bushy black eyebrows. Kliemann was stationed in Berlin but found reasons to visit Paris often because of Yvonne Delidaise, his French mistress. He was an Austrian who did not try particularly hard to mask the fact that he did not like the Germans. He was not a member of the Nazi Party. Still, he was a high and respected official in the Abwehr.

Sergueiew had a series of dinners with Kliemann and Delidaise at expensive restaurants while Kliemann tried to work out where the Abwehr could best use her services. Kliemann's first idea was that she become a spy in Syria, but he gave up that possibility when the British invaded and occupied the country. Then, as weeks went by, he suggested and then rejected Australia. It was the same with Dakar in Africa. Only when Sergueiew disclosed to him that she had a cousin in Cambridge and friends in Bristol, as well as a Polish cousin who was a member of the Polish government in exile in London—contacts that would be potentially useful to her spy work—that he warmed to the idea of her going to the UK. Her code name for the Abwehr would be Solange. The code name she chose for Kliemann was Octave. She received training both as a Morse code radio operator and a secret-ink letter writer.

There remained the problem of obtaining the necessary visa and passport for her passage to London. Weeks of frustration and false starts grew into months before she could start on her way to England. Her first stop was Madrid, where she had to secure a British passport. As justification for her request, she explained that she needed to reach a cousin who lived in Britain. A Mr. Benson from the British consulate called her to come in so they could discuss her passport.

"If what I understand is correct," he said when she met him in his office, "you wish to go to England to rejoin your family."

Sergueiew decided it was time to lay out her cards. "Not exactly. I'm going there to spy." She told Benson her whole story. He went to work to clear the way for her, including permission, in this instance, to overlook British quarantine rules for dogs so that her dog Babs—a male despite his name—could travel with her. After more complications and delays, she finally gained passage on a flight to Gibraltar and from there to England. On November 5, 1943, three years after she originally began trying, she was on British soil. Babs, however, was not with her; Benson was unsuccessful in bending the rules. However, he had promised to keep trying and to see that the dog received good care until he could be flown to her.

With her she carried Kliemann's list of forty-three questions to which she was to find the answers and deliver them to the Abwehr. The questions covered a wide range, including details of the new English Cromwell tank, information on the Camouflet apparatus for safely exploding mines, identification of American forces now in England, location of the staff headquarters of the American Fifth Army and sites of coastal barracks.

Sergueiew saw the start of her enterprise as a test of her courage. "If I succeed," she wrote postwar in her memoir, *Secret Service Rendered,* "from now on I shall be alone, utterly alone. I shall not be able to trust anyone."

Her mood was not improved by finding Britain dank, foggy and bleak. Although she admired the British for their tenacity and power of endurance, she "wouldn't want to be like them. I want to love and hate; to be alive; I found them cold, uncommunicative, undemonstrative, impenetrable."

She was only partly mollified by having British intelligence officials receive her gladly, code-name her Treasure, set her up in her own apartment and assign wise and patient Mary Sherer to be her case officer. As her cover story, she was given notional employment at the British Ministry of Information, where she was assigned to the group producing propaganda films. Tar Robertson came to call on her and told her that because the Germans had complete confidence in her, "we look to you as a trump card in the Intelligence game, worth more than an armoured division."

He added that with her help: "We can go over from the defensive to the offensive and make them think that we have made our preparations to invade an area which in fact we have no intention of going anywhere near. If we succeed in this, the Germans will concentrate their troops in the worst possible places to cope with the landing when it is finally launched."

Mary Sherer guided her in writing her first secret-ink letter to Kliemann, letting him know that she had arrived safely at the home of her friends in Bristol. But there was no time to waste in beginning her flow of information to the Germans. She reported seeing large numbers of troops in the town wearing an insignia that she described. She also overheard two officers discussing an immediate transfer of their units to a town that she identified.

Her time in England was plagued with troubles. Most distressing to her was learning that her dog would not be joining her—he had been accidentally run over and killed at Gibraltar. While she admitted being adept at "artificially roused anger," the news of Babs's death sent her into a heartfelt rage so towering that she threatened to quit her spy work altogether and even to disclose to the Germans what she knew about the double-cross system. They were, of course, threats she did not carry out.

Most serious, in actuality, was that she became ill with an infection brought on by gallstones in her kidneys. British doctors advised an operation. When she refused, she was told that, otherwise, she was likely to have no more than six months to live. Although her illness weakened her and fatigued her to the point of collapse, she reminded herself of her hatred of the Nazis and continued sending her double-layered letters under the direction of Sherer.

To Sergueiew's illness, her loss of Babs and her dislike of Britain and the British was added the disappointment of learning that her cousin in Cambridge, Dr. Elizabeth "Bessie" Hill, wanted nothing to do with her and refused to become involved in whatever underhanded activities she was engaged in. Together, these factors reduced her to indifference, uncaring about her secret work. The British, in her case, broke most of their rules for running double agents. She reported on trips she did not take, described sites and formations she did not observe firsthand. She became little more than a conduit through which her controllers poured the information and misinformation they wanted the Germans to receive.

Fortunately, her old schooltime friend and the friend's husband in Bristol were compassionate and supportive. They took care of her through her illness. Mary Sherer made many trips to Bristol to have Sergueiew pen the messages the Twenty Committee wished her to send to Kliemann.

Through it all, he never wavered in his appreciation of the value and importance of the information his Solange was sending.

By then the winter was receding and the Normandy invasion was fast approaching. Sergueiew had, despite the dire warning of her British physician, begun to regain a degree of her health. Her spirits improved. So did her relationship with Mary Sherer. An official report on Treasure said that she was "exceptionally temperamental and troublesome," but Sherer dealt with her tantrums and kept her on track. For her part, Sergueiew began to see a different side to her case officer. Beneath that all-too-businesslike exterior she realized that there was "a human being and not an automaton," a woman sentimental enough to emerge from a viewing of *Gone With the Wind* with eyes reddened from weeping. Sergueiew grew to like her.

It was time, Treasure's B1A controllers saw, to change her mode of transmission from slow and uncertain letter writing to the speed of radio. To do this, it was necessary for her to secure from Kliemann the special transmitter he had prepared and the instructions and code for using it. This meant a meeting with him in Lisbon.

Her notional work for the Ministry of Information provided a cover story. Her section was planning propaganda films to be used in liberated countries, particularly France, Holland and Belgium. These films would be much more effective, the ministry had decided, if they were done with the counsel of producers who had escaped from their occupied countries. In Lisbon, Sergueiew's mission was to search out these individuals and obtain their cooperation. To guard against slipups in her story, Sherer took her to the ministry, showed her the offices in which she was supposed to work and introduced her to the people with whom she should be familiar. On March 2 she flew to Portugal.

In Lisbon she encountered more delays and frustrations when Kliemann failed to arrive. Even when he did, there were more delays before he could hand over the compact transmitter disguised as an ordinary radio set. In their meetings, though, he assured her she had been doing excellent work. The calendar had moved to March 23 before she was able to return to London. Her film duties allowed her to send the transmitter in an English diplomatic bag.

After a rest with her Bristol couple, she reported herself ready to begin transmitting. Sherer took her to a house in which a room had been set aside for her use. The transmitter was there; so was the young man who would handle the enciphering of her messages. The code she was given took its daily key from a French book, *Montmartre* by Pierre Frondaye.

Her first message, it had been agreed, would be a short one, merely letting Kliemann know that both she and the transmitter had arrived safely and that the Information Ministry authorities had been satisfied with her work.

Her transmissions accelerated. She was soon sending six messages a week and then as many as three a day. B1A continued to break its rule about having double agents first experience what they then reported.

"Well, where have I been this time?" she asked Sherer one Monday morning after having spent the weekend in Bristol.

"You stayed with a colleague from the Ministry on Salisbury Plain."

Treasure wrote in her diary: "I make other imaginary journeys, to places which I did not know existed, and from which I bring back rich harvests of information: the extent of it sometimes frightens me! In this world of fiction, I spend my time in trains, clubs, messes, canteens. And I transmit a hotch-potch of descriptions of badges, vehicles, tanks, planes and airfields, garnished with conversations overheard from which the Germans cannot fail to derive the correct conclusions."

After one vigorous day of transmitting, she was left weak and, she thought, too easily tired. She reminded herself that if that British doctor's diagnosis was correct, she now had only two more months to live. She decided that that was all right. "My aim is actually achieved. I have succeeded! All the plans laid by Beirut, when I lay awake in bed at night, and which in the morning seemed so absolutely fantastic, all have been realized one after the other."

She couldn't know that, even then, B1A was selecting the small orchestra of agents to handle the major D-Day deceptions, and that Lily Sergueiew would be designated as one of "the first violins."

CHAPTER TEN

GARBO, THE GREATEST

Juan Pujol, nom de guerre Garbo, was the Charles Dickens of the double agents. His fecund imagination enabled him to create a large cast of fabulous characters and play out their roles to the vast appreciation of his German audience. For each of his characters, Pujol developed a personal writing style, the words flowing like the output of a steady and copious spring. After the war, his writings for all his broad network of fictional characters were gathered together. Including the background information about him, they added up to fifty volumes on the shelves of Britain's National Archives, truly a Dickensian oeuvre.

Pujol is, simply, the greatest, the most remarkable double agent of the Second World War.

In his achievement he received the aid, guidance and encouragement of another exceptional individual, his case officer, Tomás Harris. Harris's unusual mix of a name is explained by the fact that he was the son of a Spanish mother and an English father. His father, Lionel Harris, was a successful and wealthy art dealer who ran a gallery in London—a pursuit that Tomás prosperously followed. His wartime career as an MI5 case officer resulted from association with the intelligence officers he and his wife entertained in their London home.

Of Pujol, Harris has written: "In 1941 when the Germans were all powerful in Spain, the British Embassy in Madrid was being stoned, France had collapsed and the German invasion of England was imminent,

little were the Germans to know that the small meek young Spaniard who
then approached them and volunteered to go to London to engage in espionage on their behalf would turn out to be an important British agent.
Still less were they to discover that the network which they instructed him
to build up in the United Kingdom was to be composed of twenty-seven
characters who were nothing more than a figment of his imagination."

Together, these two men devised what the historian Mark Seaman has
called "one of the most incredible deception stratagems in history."

Pujol may have been meek on the outside but within him burned
fierce fires of hatred for totalitarian regimes. His was an attitude inherited
from his father. When Juan and his brother were boys in a Barcelona
boarding school, the elder Pujol visited them every Sunday afternoon and,
in their talks, told them of his love for freedom and his loathing for dic-
tators and tyrants—ideas the young Pujol absorbed.

In the shifting tides of the Spanish Civil War, Pujol was forced to serve
for a time with the Republicans, whose numbers were augmented by
Russian Communists. He escaped that despised regimen by fleeing to
Franco's Nationalists. There he found that "Spain, under Fascism, was as
intolerable as it would have been under Communism." He took pride in
reflecting at war's end that he had "managed not to fire a bullet for either
side."

Later, his antagonism toward totalitarianism was fanned by learning
that his brother, who had been in Paris when the Germans marched in,
had disappeared into one of the Gestapo prisons.

Because of the difficult economic conditions in Madrid after the Civil
War, the only job Pujol could find was a dull one as a hotel manager. The
job, however, had an important consequence for him. When it became
necessary for him to travel to Portugal for the hotel, the business nature
of the trip enabled him to obtain a passport—at a time when legal pass-
ports were hard to come by. That passport, even though it allowed him
only passage to Portugal, would play a vital role on his way to becoming
a double agent.

He made the decision to enlist as a spy for Great Britain when, on September 3, 1939, England declared war on Germany. One of the strong
reasons impelling him, he wrote much later in the book on which he and

Nigel West collaborated, was the news he began receiving about Germany's mistreatment of the Jews. "In Spain," he wrote, "few knew of those horrors. But despite censorship, word eventually spread about the horrifying deeds perpetrated by those butchers. . . . My humanist convictions would not allow me to turn a blind eye to the enormous suffering that was being unleashed by this psychopath Hitler and his band of acolytes."

Yet he was so shy that, according to Harris's postwar report, instead of going to Britain's Madrid embassy himself, he sent his wife to offer her husband's services as a spy in either Germany or Italy. Not surprisingly, the offer was turned down. Perhaps, Pujol told himself, the British would become more amenable if he first became a spy for the Germans. This time he himself got up the nerve to approach the German embassy and propose to spy for the Reich either in Lisbon or the United Kingdom. Rebuffed at first, he persisted until he won an audience with an Abwehr official, code-named Federico but whose real name was Friedrich Knappe-Ratey. At the meeting Pujol demonstrated his theatrical abilities, presenting himself as a rabid Nazi enthusiast and fighter for Franco who wanted nothing more than to help the Germans defeat their despicable enemies. "I began to use my gift of gab," he wrote, "and ranted away as befitted a staunch Nazi and Francoist."

Although he impressed Knappe-Ratey with his zeal, the Abwehr required a justification for his going to Britain other than to be a spy for them. The ever-inventive Pujol first concocted a story that he would go to England as the correspondent for a Spanish newspaper. When that didn't fly, he came up with a scheme by which he would go there to investigate dubious financial transactions for a friend at the Bank of Spain.

The Germans were, at last, convinced. They agreed to have him become one of their British agents. They gave him questionnaires indicating German interests in the UK and put him through a crash course in how to write secret messages in invisible ink overlaid by an innocuous letter as camouflage. With a final gift of £3,000 in cash and cover addresses to which to send his messages, the Germans code-named him Arabel, introduced him to his case officer, Karl Eric Kuehlanthal, and sent him off. This was in July 1941.

Pujol used his Spanish passport to return to Lisbon, this time with his wife and son. He confidently expected that with his proofs of being employed by the Abwehr he could gain acceptance from those in the British embassy to serve as a double agent. To his utter dismay, they again turned him down.

He was in a fix. Here he was, supposedly with everything arranged for his passage to Britain but knowing that that whole part of his scheme was a ruse and that the only way he could follow through was to persuade the British to transport him.

Pujol was not to be stopped. He decided that he could win British approval by showing them proofs of the work he did for the Germans. He would pretend to send his reports to the Abwehr from England even though he had never been there.

But how could he send his reports without having the envelopes bear British postmarks? No problem. He explained to the Germans that he had made friends with the pilot of the plane in his flight to Britain. The pilot had proved sympathetic to his tale of being a Spaniard in exile who needed to use an unofficial route to send letters to his family left behind in Lisbon. For a small fee per letter, the pilot had agreed to deliver his mail to a cover address there. To assure his new friend that Pujol was not using this means to convey illegal material, he would leave the envelopes unsealed. Inspection would reveal only innocuous family letters, under which the invisible ink would bear the real messages to the Abwehr. Of course, Pujol himself was the one who posted the letters from Lisbon.

To carry out this seemingly foolhardy scheme, Pujol was able to rely on only an outdated Baedeker guide to the United Kingdom, an old British Railways timetable, a large map of Britain, whatever he could glean from reference books and magazines in the Lisbon library, and visual details derived from watching newsreels at the cinema. His main source was his imagination.

His first regular ink letter was an enthusiastic account of his arrival in Britain. The invisible ink letter between the lines informed the Germans that he had recruited three subagents to cover areas beyond his reach. He had done this by cultivating friendships and finding men sympathetic to the Axis. One of these notional characters was a Portuguese named Carvalho, who was in a position to monitor the English Channel area. The second was British, but of Swiss-German descent, named Gerbers. He was instructed to report on traffic in the busy harbor of Liverpool. The third, a well-to-do Venezuelan identified only as Pedro, who had been educated at the University of Glasgow, was assigned to operate in Scotland.

He managed to keep this risky venture going all through the last five months of 1941 and into 1942. Still more incredibly, his mix of gleaned facts and fancied fiction, despite occasional glaring errors, created an aura of great authenticity and was well received by his controllers.

Then bingo! A message he sent in April 1942 broke through the barrier of British indifference. Interceptors in England picked up a message radioed from Madrid to Berlin in which a German agent in Liverpool reported "the sailing from Liverpool of a convoy of fifteen ships including nine freighters, course Gibraltar and probably going on to Malta, possible intermediate port Lisbon."

British alarm bells began ringing. Berlin was receiving a message from an uncontrolled agent in England! His presence could put the whole double-cross system in jeopardy!

Also puzzling was that the message was obviously a fabrication: no such convoy was scheduled from Liverpool at that time. Subsequent codebreaks by Bletchley Park revealed that Berlin had immediately broadcast an alert to Mediterranean outposts and launched a major effort to intercept the convoy and decimate it. The unknown sender had put the German Navy and Air Force to a great deal of vain searching, useless man-hours and wasted petrol.

British investigators looking into the problem concluded that the agent must be the same man who had approached the British embassies in Madrid and Lisbon. They also determined that now he was not in the UK but somewhere on the Continent. The decision was made that he must be found and brought to Britain. But where was he? At this point an American officer at the U.S. embassy in Lisbon became an intermediary. Pujol, having failed to persuade the British and uncertain that he could continue indefinitely his fakery of the Germans, was contemplating taking flight to Brazil. His visit to the American embassy was one last, desperate effort to salvage his show. There he met with Lieutenant Demorest and told his story. Interested, Demorest promised to consult the British. Happy ending: the British realized their search was over.

Suddenly Pujol became a hot property, so desirable an acquisition that the British security agencies quarreled over which one should take charge of him. MI6 wanted him to spy for them from Lisbon. MI5's wish was to bring him to London and absorb him as another of its double agents.

MI5 won out. He was smuggled out of Lisbon via Gibraltar on April 24, 1942, escorted to London and settled in a safe house in the London suburb of Hendon. Tomás Harris became his case officer. The Twenty Committee was assigned to supply him with information he could write up in any of his various styles. He was given the code name Garbo in recognition of his ability to assume many different roles. As Masterman noted, "He came to us therefore a fully fledged double agent with all the growing pains over—we had only to operate and develop the system which he had already built up."

There was no need now for him to authenticate to the British his acceptance by the Germans. If the British, though, had any questions, he was ready to show copies of thirty-eight letters he had written to his Abwehr controllers during his Lisbon stay, as well as fifteen letters and questionnaires he had received from them.

One can only imagine the pleasure that Garbo felt when he was able to pen his first message on the noninvented, genuine information the Twenty Committee supplied to him. Dated April 12, 1942, it purported to be the result of a conversation with an overly garrulous RAF officer at the British Overseas Club, a friendship Garbo notionally developed. It informed the Germans of the antiaircraft rocket batteries in Hyde Park.

Garbo's subagent Gerbers, who was stationed in Liverpool and had sent the message about the Malta-bound convoy that never existed, was seen as a problem. With the Luftwaffe having closed the Thames as a convoy destination, Liverpool became the main convoy harbor. Gerbers could be expected to report on more convoy arrivals and departures than the British wanted the Germans to know about. Above all, Gerbers would have had to be aware of the preparations in Liverpool for the massive flotilla leaving there to take part in the Allied landings in North Africa. Failure to observe and report this development would, very possibly, not just have blown Gerbers but could have compromised Garbo's whole network. It was essential that he be removed. Garbo handled the problem in his usual imaginative way.

At the beginning of December 1942, his letter to Kuehlanthal recorded his concern about having had no news from Gerbers or even an acknowledgment of the money that had been sent him for the month of November. To see what had happened, Garbo traveled to Gerbers's home in the Liverpool suburb of Bootle. There Gerbers's wife sadly informed him that Gerbers had died. She showed Garbo the obituary of her husband that had appeared in the *Liverpool Daily Post*:

> GERBERS—November 19 at Bootle, after a long illness, aged 52. WILLIAM MAXIMILLIAN. Private funeral. (No flowers, please.)

One wonders whether Garbo shed a tear at having to kill off poor Gerbers, as Dickens did when he had to put away one of his favorite creations, Little Nell Trent. If he did, Garbo recovered quickly enough to forward the clipping to Kuehlanthal and company, who replied with a message of condolence for the unfortunate widow.

Not one to overlook the opportunity to register with his controllers his great compassion for his subagents, Garbo subsequently reported on his efforts to help this loyal wife of an ex-collaborator. First he allowed her to try to replace her husband by sending a couple of messages. She was, however, hopeless as a reporter of espionage. Instead, Garbo saw the advantages of hiring her to look after his household, since he would have complete confidence in her discretion and thus less worry about having his activities discovered. Also, when the volume of wireless traffic became great, she proved herself adept at assisting Garbo with the enciphering of messages.

Gerbers was one of the three notional subagents Garbo had created while still reporting from Lisbon. On his disappearance, Garbo felt obliged to recruit not just one replacement but three.

The first was a good, loyal British government official who worked in the Spanish department of Britain's Ministry of Information. He saw

Garbo as a kindred spirit with whom he could discuss ministry affairs freely. As his friendship with Garbo deepened, this bureaucrat buddy to whom Garbo never gave a name allowed the Spaniard ever greater access to confidential documents. Garbo identified him as Agent J(3)—his way of designating resources who were unwitting of the fact that they were being information suppliers.

Garbo's second new creation, agent number five, was well aware of his role. But he, too, was never named. He was another Venezuelan, the brother of Pedro, but much less prosperous. Garbo hired him as a full-time paid agent. The recognized need now was for subagents who could cover Scotland, which had become the staging area for a largely fictional buildup of Allied forces meant to deceive the Germans into believing that an invasion of Scandinavia was imminent. The threat's objective was to hold German divisions in Scandinavia and away from the coming real invasion of Normandy. Agent five was sent to join his brother for double-agent training in Glasgow and then assigned to cover Scotland's east coast while Pedro continued to report on the west coast Clyde area.

Agent number six was identified only as Dick. He was a South African, a man of independent means and a fine linguist who, in London, had contacts in the Ministry of Information and other government departments. He was willing to work for the Germans because he was violently anti-Communist and was enticed by Garbo's promise to secure him a position in the Nazis' New World Order after the war. One of his early assignments was to help Garbo carry out a complex financial scheme by which the Abwehr made sterling funds available in Britain to provide payments to Garbo and his network.

With this spread of subagents working for him, Pujol was able to markedly increase his flow of information to the Abwehr. The additions only whetted the Germans' appetite for more. By further broadening his network, Kuehlanthal and his colleagues saw, Pujol could cover more of the United Kingdom. Garbo was happy to oblige. His network of twenty-seven subagents operated not only in the UK but also in Canada, the United States and the Middle East.

The demands of his burgeoning network presented Pujol with an increasingly troublesome problem. This was the slow and cumbersome method that had been prescribed for his communications with the Abwehr. Secret-ink letters doubled the work involved in composing a given message. The secret information to be communicated had to be overlaid by an innocuous cover letter dealing with such matters as family issues or health problems or the like. Considering that some of his official reports ran to as many as 8,000 words and averaged between 1,500 and 2,000 words, the invention of accompanying cover texts was a demanding task. Yet it was one that, as Harris observed, "he fulfilled with the greatest ability."

Both Pujol and his British controllers agreed that the time had come for the secret letters to be supplemented by radio. Yet, as will be related later, it took a critical failure in timing to finally convince his spymasters that letter writing was too slow for reporting the war's fast-paced developments and that Garbo should acquire a wireless set and recruit an operator to handle the transmissions. Not until March 7, 1943, did Garbo take to the airwaves. By the end of August he was using radio for nearly all of his messages.

Garbo may have been meek of manner in his first approaches to the Abwehr, but by this time he was receiving the plaudits of both the Germans and the British. The consequence was that in his communications with Madrid he projected a persona of assumed self-importance and a temperament that demanded careful handling. These attributes are reflected rather prominently in the letter he sent Kuehlanthal on February 8, 1943. It said in part:

> A few days ago I completed the second anniversary of my stay here, fulfilling from the start the sacred duty of defending the ideals which inspire me so profoundly against our common enemies, disturbers of justice and social order. I have accomplished a great deal since then, always without thought for the dangers through which I must pass, leaping all obstacles which they put in my way. I believe that I have accomplished my duty to the maximum of my power and ability, in spite of the bad training I had for this work, which, if it were not for the astuteness displayed and the daring of my temperament, it would certainly not have been pos-

sible now for me to be directing a service of such size and responsibility. . . . I know, although at times you smile at my humour, you
appreciate the contents as more valuable than if you read a hundred English newspapers and heard a thousand Anglo-American
transmissions, because through those you would only hear lies, and
my writings only tell you concrete realities. . . . The time has come
to take rather draconian decisions. . . . Why, I ask myself, do not
our high command prepare for an attack against this island? . . .
Why not give them the enormous fright of having their arrogance
brought low? . . . England must be taken by arms, she must be
fallen upon, destroyed and dominated, she must be sabotaged, destroying all her potentialities. . . . I want to take action, and if for
fear of losing the service, you order me and deprive me from moving along the lines I have suggested my co-operation shall still be
the same. With a raised arm I end this letter with a pious remem-
brance for all our dead.

This man, this Spaniard who could spin lines such as these with what
seemed utmost sincerity, came to be regarded by the Germans as their
principal agent in the United Kingdom . . .

. . . even as he was gaining the regard of the Allies for being their foremost hope in pulling off the greatest deception in the history of warfare.

CHAPTER ELEVEN

MUTT, JEFF AND OTHER LESSER AGENTS

The principal players in the drama of the double agents have now made their entrances. In addition, however, several of the large cast of supporting actors must be given their bow. Of the overall total of 120 double agents, Masterman lists 39 men and women for special recognition of their contributions, great or small, in the European theater. As we shall see, these individuals working under the control of the Twenty Committee were not the only show. There were other double agents and alternate versions of the Twenty Committee serving in North Africa, the Middle East and as far away as India.

Mutt and Jeff were two of the double agents on Masterman's list. Code-named after two U.S. newspaper cartoon characters, they were in actuality Helge Moe and Tor Glad. Of them, British journalist John Ezard has written: "To Hitler's Germany the two young Norwegians were intrepid heroes who left a trail of death, destruction and fire across Britain during the Second World War. But to the British intelligence services they were . . . two double agents whose faked sabotage gave them the credibility to mislead Germany over British military strategy in the war."

Their recruitment by the Abwehr reflected the Germans' desperate willingness to enroll agents wherever they could find them. In the Germans' eyes, Moe and Glad were simply two sturdy young Norwegians who had shown at least a mild acceptance of the Nazis by working for the occupying forces in Oslo's German Postal Censorship Office. Both were accomplished linguists. Moe was the son of a Norwegian father and an English mother and could claim to be a British citizen through having been born in London. Glad had studied at a British film company to become a makeup artist. Their command of English recommended them as spies, but the Germans were also in dire need of saboteurs. A German secret services officer, Dr. Muller, proposed that they be given training in both clandestine activities. They accepted.

Moe and Glad were activated by widely differing motives. Moe was an open, honest straight arrow who wanted to do more with his life in this wartime period than continue to be a ladies' hairdresser in his father's salon. His reason for joining the Postal Censorship Office was to use the job to obtain information useful to Norwegian authorities, and in fact he had copied and passed on a list of the names of Norwegians the Nazis suspected of anti-German activities. In agreeing to become a spy-saboteur, he intended from the first to turn against the Germans.

Glad, on the other hand, was a devious character, a clever, self-centered opportunist looking out for his own interests. He saw the work at the censorship office as an additional way to ingratiate himself with the German occupiers. Later, under British interrogation, he amended this to borrow Moe's more idealistic reasoning.

In Glad's interrogation, his harshest critic turned out to be a fellow Norwegian, Captain Martin Linge of the Norwegian army. Linge berated him as "not a good type of Norwegian," a young man who "went round with the worst sort of young Norwegians" and was always "prepared to undertake any sort of job however despicable."

Nevertheless, this was the pair who, on the night of April 7, 1941, was flown by seaplane close to the Scottish coast to be landed in a rubber dinghy. The seas were rough and the plane had to land farther out from the intended site, with the result that Moe and Glad had to row the boat for three miles to reach shore. But they made it, along with a two-way wireless set, ciphers to use in their transmissions, a sum of money, forged travelers' ration books, detonators and instructions for constructing bombs, and a pair of bicycles. As spies, they were to report on troop movements, the locations of airfields and the effects of German bombing on civilian morale. As saboteurs, they were to set fires in food storage facilities, blow up factories, sever power lines and generally try to create panic among the civilian population.

They immediately scuttled all the Abwehr's careful planning by giving themselves up to the British and asserting their true objectives. British intelligence lost no time going to work for them. Since sabotage came first in the Germans' priorities, their MI5 controllers immediately began organizing a demolition project.

At this time of increasing food shortages in Britain, it was decided that the pair's first piece of bogus sabotage should be against a British food storage warehouse. Plan Guy Fawkes was organized for the day in November when the British used fireworks to recall Fawkes's 1605 plan to blow up the Houses of Parliament. This, the first double-cross sabotage of the war, added some real fireworks to the celebration.

For Plan Guy Fawkes, two bombs were constructed that, instead of exploding, burned themselves out to produce intense heat and clouds of smoke. At Wealdstone, east of London, the bombs notionally destroyed a large section of a food storage facility. The planners still had a lot to learn about conducting an operation like this. The two elderly fireguards at the plant had to be roused from deep slumber and lured away from that part of the facility where the bombs had been placed. A local police officer, not knowing of the plan afoot, tried to arrest the onlooking planners. Yet the indignant press reports of the incident, which Moe and Glad were careful to post to their Abwehr masters, did succeed in raising the Germans' estimate of the pair.

The Abwehr had selected electric power plants as special targets for espionage. The British were pleased to oblige. For their second demolition project, Moe and Glad were assigned to blow up an actual power plant at Bury St. Edmunds in Suffolk. It was a "small and unimportant" facility with a section of the building that was no longer used. Further, the site included worn-out equipment waiting to be scrapped. The destruction of the derelict facility and the used-up machinery offered a convincing display to reconnaissance aircraft and generated blaring headlines in the press. As the official report summed it up, "The incident duly took place with complete success."

Moreover, the explosion was seized on by the German press and propaganda broadcasts, which boasted that "over 150 workers were killed, and more than double that number wounded."

By then the two replanted Norwegians were showing themselves to be not just adept saboteurs but good spies as well. Their location in Scotland enabled them to transmit reports keyed to Hitler's fears of an invasion through Norway. Consequently, their observations of the buildup of Allied forces in the north, particularly of the largely notional Fourth Army, were judged of special value by the Abwehr.

Moe settled in to make himself a resourceful and dependable double agent, preferring to drop his Norwegian name and become identified as Jack. Glad, however, had aroused British suspicions from the first. Probes into his past revealed that he had engaged in pro-German activities that he had not admitted during his initial interrogations. This was incriminating enough, but the doubts about him were confirmed when a group of Norwegian refugees landed in Scotland. One of them, Georg Rohde, charged convincingly that Glad had been a prominent pro-Nazi and a supporter of the Norwegian Nazi Vidkun Quisling. That was enough for MI5. Glad was locked away at Camp WX on the Isle of Man. Although the camp was not a penal establishment, it did sequester him for the rest of the war in a place where he could do no harm.

His removal, however, did not end the Mutt and Jeff teamwork. Jeff's role was taken over by an impersonator who used the pair's radio to transmit messages supposedly prepared by Jeff. Jack Moe and the substitute for Tor Glad strengthened their esteem with the Germans to the point where they were able to make a major contribution to the Normandy D-Day deceptions.

A Lady Code-named Bronx

How far would the Abwehr go in order to recruit a prospective agent? If not all the way to Peru, then at least to a Peruvian woman who, as noted earlier, happened to be in France when the Germans occupied the country. She was Elvira Chaudoir, the daughter of a Peruvian diplomat who had served his country in England before being assigned, after the fall of France, to the Peruvian embassy in Vichy. The Abwehr's interest was stirred by knowing she had entrée to influential diplomatic circles in

Britain. On her next visit to her father, Chaudoir was approached by an Abwehr officer with the proposition that she return to England as a spy for the Germans. What the Abwehr didn't know was that Chaudoir was then in France on a secret mission for British intelligence. She acceded to the agent's request with the full intention of immediately betraying the Abwehr.

Back in England she came under the control of the Twenty Committee and was given the code name Bronx. The Abwehr had equipped her to be a secret-ink letter writer. She and the Abwehr agreed to use her bank in Lisbon as the intermediary to forward her letters to her spymasters. The Twenty Committee saw her as a vivacious and beautiful young woman who could provide a perfect conduit for sending the Germans high-level social tattle that included a strategic mixture of valid information and subtle misinformation. The Abwehr valued her letters sufficiently to pay her a regular retainer plus a number of bonuses.

The Lisbon bank connection gave her Abwehr controllers an idea. Already concerned about an Allied invasion of the Continent, and having no firm knowledge of where the attack might fall, the Germans instructed her in a special technique she could use that would be much swifter than communication by letter. If she learned anything about the time and place of the invasion, she was to send a commercial telegram to the bank. A request for £100 would indicate the invasion site as northern France, a £125 request meant the Bay of Biscay coast, £150 the Mediterranean coast, £175 the Adriatic, £250 Norway and so on. Further, words in her telegram would indicate how soon the attack would come: *"toute suite"* meant invasion in one week; "urgent," in two weeks; *"vite,"* in about a month; and *"si possible"* that the date was uncertain.

Prepared thus, Bronx was another who would make a vital contribution to the D-Day deceptions.

The Rebirth of G.W.

British authorities thought the case of the Welsh policeman Gwilym Williams, or G.W., had been blown forever when it was necessary to close down the Snow case. The Germans soon had other ideas. They had absorbed G.W.'s notional admiration of the motto of "Wales for the Welsh" and believed in his affiliation with the extremist Welsh National Party. In consequence they regarded G.W. as an implacable foe of the British whose service they would like to reactivate.

G.W. learned of this by receiving a letter from an official at the Spanish embassy in London seeking to recruit him as a spy whose reports could be channeled through the Spanish to the Germans. The letter was no surprise to Tar Robertson and company, who were aware that the embassy was shot through with officials sympathetic to Nazi Fascism and willing to use their diplomatic status to secure information of value to the Germans. G.W.'s letter was proof of this double-dealing: it was from Miguel Piernaviaje Pozo, using merely Pozo as his code name. The letter suggested a meeting between G.W. and Pozo.

As the later British report expressed it: "Undoubtedly the Germans had kept G.W. on their list of possible agents, had noticed his steady but rather unambitious work for the Welsh National Party and now decided to make greater use of him."

B1A instructed G.W. to go ahead with the meeting. At it, Pozo gave him £4,000 as a down payment on the information he was to supply. He agreed to deliver two reports per week, with emphasis on the doings of the Welsh extremists and on industries engaged in the manufacture of military matériel, most particularly aircraft and parts for them.

The acquaintance expanded fast. Pozo proposed that G.W. buy a car the two of them could use to do sabotage work together.

On February 3, 1941, however, the association was abruptly broken when Pozo, for reasons unknown, left England. On March 31, the British learned, Pozo had been arrested in Madrid and sentenced to prison for six months.

In May, G.W.'s British controllers decided he should make a try at reestablishing himself with the Spaniards in London. He went to the embassy and complained to the porter there that Pozo, on returning to London, was supposed to give G.W. a letter of introduction he could use in his work for embassy officials. The letter had never come. He asked the porter what he should do.

The answer was that he should see another Spanish official, Luis Calvo, press attaché at the embassy. That relationship also quickly blossomed. On

August 8, 1941, G.W. submitted to Tar Robertson a long report on what the Nazi admirers at the embassy wanted him to investigate for "our friends." At that early stage of the war, the Germans were concentrating on starving the English by the shattering of convoys bringing supplies. Consequently, the priority request was for data on food rationing. Calvo wanted copies of all the publications issued by the Ministry of Food and information on the repercussions from the blockade of food, particularly among workers. Other questions concerned developments in food prices and details of where food shipments were coming from.

Calvo's list was also heavy on the need for information on shipbuilding, on authoritative estimates of how well the convoy system was working and on the armaments industries. G.W. was given petrol to enable him to travel in search of information. Because of his supposed pro-Welsh feelings, he presented himself as being willing to do anything he could to discourage the British manufacture of military equipment in factories in Wales. He let the Germans know he would have nothing to do with helping the Luftwaffe bomb those factories, since that would mean killing his countrymen. But he would undertake discriminating sabotage at those factories. Through the Spaniards, the Germans acquiesced.

Just when the G.W. case was progressing splendidly, however, it hit a roadblock. This was not of German or Spanish making; the problem was with another branch of British intelligence, the one investigating sabotage in the UK. Its leaders had been tracking the misdeeds of the unneutral Spanish diplomats and had decided to crack down on Calvo, arrest him and use his case as a warning to others in the Spanish espionage ring. B1A protested vigorously but was overruled; Calvo was seized and jailed. And G.W. was shut down for the second time—this time for the duration.

Masterman wrote that G.W. was a serious loss "for he was by far the best channel we ever had" for the transmission, through the Spanish diplomatic bag, "of documents and information too bulky or detailed for transmission by wireless."

A Not-So-Colorful "Rainbow"

Although the young man named Pierce and code-named Rainbow was English born, he was educated in Germany and worked there until 1938, when he returned to England. His service as a double agent grew out of a friendship with a German, Gunther, whom the Abwehr had sent to England under the cover of representing a German chemical firm but whose real purpose was espionage. Pierce and Gunther lived in the same lodging house. Not knowing of Gunther's secret mission, Pierce began accompanying him on weekend trips into the country, during which Gunther would take photographs, particularly of factories. Gunther's explanation was that his interest was in "commercial intelligence."

Just before the outbreak of the war, Gunther suddenly left for Germany. His suspicions aroused, Pierce received what he felt to be a confirmation of Gunther's true mission when a letter from his former friend suggested that Pierce take over Gunther's agency in England. Interpreting this as a proposal for him to become a spy for Germany, Pierce informed the police. The instructions he received were to arrange a meeting with Gunther in Antwerp to discuss plans. There, surely enough, the Germans' plans for him were made plain: the Abwehr wanted him to be an agent for them in Britain. Agreeing, he was given orders to report on developments for aircraft and air defenses, the effect of air raids and details of transport in the UK.

As his business cover, he was made the English representative of a Belgian firm. His instructions, he was told, would come in the form of microphotographs hidden in the periods after the dates in the firm's letters to him. He was also given invisible ink for his replies, a sum of money and an address in Antwerp through which to pass his letters to Gunther. All this he reported to his British controllers on his return. They awarded him his code name.

In April 1940 he made another trip to Antwerp and was given additional cover addresses to be used in case of emergency. During the period when the Germans were bent on starving the British into capitulation and were seeking the double agents' help in locating food supplies that could be destroyed, Rainbow was assigned the particular job of locating the "large stocks" of food the Germans believed to be stored in Oxford.

While his reporting mainly of industrial and economic information never placed him among the top rank of double agents, Rainbow was sufficiently valued by the Germans that they paid him a salary of £1,000 a year, a tidy sum in those days. Masterman's summation of him was that "Rainbow developed into a more important agent than we had a right to expect."

The Obsession of Hamlet

Of the double agents who helped mislead the Germans, probably the most bizarre was Dr. Koestler, the Austrian Jew and ex–cavalry officer code-named Hamlet. He was wise enough, in the 1930s, to leave Austria before the Nazi takeover and relocate in Belgium. There he founded a business that thrived. Despite his non-Aryan ethnic roots, the Germans tolerated him, out of a desire to use him. After he had established a company in Lisbon to exploit commercial inventions to which he held the patent rights, he approached the Abwehr with the proposal that he supply them with intelligence reports, using his Lisbon business as his cover for espionage. To secure the information, he claimed, he had recruited a network of agents. Actually, all of them were imaginary. The Abwehr agreed.

Hamlet had a fixation. He believed there were elements in both Germany and Britain who wanted to negotiate a peaceful ending to the war. Among those in Germany desiring to break away from the Nazi domination, he was convinced, was a substantial portion of the military. To expedite his scheme, he managed to become an officer in the Abwehr.

In Lisbon, Koestler became acquainted with a man named Thornton and code-named Mullet. Thornton was a British subject born in Belgium of a British father and a Belgian mother. As Mullet, he was planning to make his way to Britain. Deciding that Mullet could be useful to him, Hamlet repeatedly invited him to dinner and long talks in Lisbon. When the time was ripe, Hamlet proposed that Mullet become his business representative in England and, more important, that he explore the opportunities for extending peace feelers to the British. It was Mullet who made British intelligence aware of Hamlet's network and of his offer to have it serve the British.

The situation was a strange one. In Hamlet the British faced this bright but obsessed individual who had suspended himself halfway between the opposing forces in the hope of bringing both sides to the negotiating table. If there was hesitation by B1A about agreeing to work with him, it was swept aside when Hamlet, through Mullet, suggested that the British give him all possible information indicating Britain's great strength, especially the RAF's power to bomb Germany. He felt that German understanding of this overwhelming force would strengthen the resolve of those opposing Hitler.

The Twenty Committee began supplying Mullet with information, which he wrote in invisible ink between the typewritten lines of routine business correspondence.

Mullet was eventually joined by Puppet, whose real name was Fanto. Hamlet assigned him to London as a supporting business rep and double agent. Together, he and Mullet supplied a steady stream of the usual Twenty Committee mix of true and false information—a flow piped directly into the inner circles of the Abwehr.

Hamlet never realized his dream of becoming the central figure in marshaling the forces to overthrow Hitler so that the war could be brought to a swift conclusion. As we shall see, however, Mullet proved of special help to the D-Day deceptions.

There are other double agents—Sniper, Beetle and Watchdog among them—whose stories could be told. But the point has been made: the individuals who came to hate the Nazi regime and were willing to risk their lives to bring it down were an enormously diverse constituency. It is time to begin recounting how this strange and wonderful assemblage of men and women went about the monumental task of helping to achieve their goal.

CHAPTER TWELVE

TRICYCLE'S AMERICAN MISADVENTURE

On his visit to Lisbon in the spring of 1941, Dusko Popov, code-named Ivan or Tricycle according to which side he was representing, received the astonishing news that the Abwehr wanted him to go to the United States. No, this was not an adverse reflection on the job he was doing against the English. On the contrary, the Abwehr badly needed him to go to America and set up the same sort of subagent network he had so successfully established in Britain.

His spymaster, Ludovico von Karsthoff, explained. The Germans had a whole bund full of willing German agents in the United States, but they were all such klutzes at the game that they kept being apprehended by the Federal Bureau of Investigation and subjected to noisy, embarrassing trials that provided fodder for those trying to drive the United States into war with Germany. The Abwehr's chief, Admiral Wilhelm Canaris, had been hauled on the carpet by Hitler. Smarting, Canaris sought someone dependable to go to the United States and do the job right, building outward from a small, discreet, carefully chosen few who would avoid being trapped by the FBI. That someone was Popov. Go to the United States, von Karsthoff told him, and concentrate on the quality, not the quantity, of your chosen agents.

When Popov returned to London to make arrangements for the trip, he found MI5 not at all happy about his new assignment. At that early stage of the war, he had become one of their most reliable and important double agents; to have him shipped off to America did not fit in with their plans for him. But there was nothing for it but to accede to the Abwehr's request. Popov prepared Gelatine and Balloon to carry on without him.

That much about Popov's American venture is agreed on by later narrators. The rest of the story meets a great divide, according to which writer is telling it.

Popov's own version, as reported at length in his postwar memoir, *Spy/Counterspy,* is that in advance of his arrival in Lisbon he made arrangements to meet his Abwehr friend Johnny Jebsen there. The two college classmates climbed to a secluded observation point atop cliffs overlooking the Atlantic near the town of Cascais. There Jebsen related his own recent adventure. He had been asked to join a group inspecting Italian military facilities. "Peculiar," Jebsen said. "The mission was for the Japanese." Jebsen had been chosen to represent the Abwehr because of his family's business connections in the Far East.

At the request of Japan's foreign minister, Yosuke Matsuoka, the Japanese group had toured various Italian bases. Their main interest, though, had been the Italian anchorage at Taranto, on the heel of Italy's boot. The Japanese delegation wanted to learn all they could about the devastating air attack the British had launched against the warships harbored there on the night of November 11, 1940.

The fast new British carrier HMS *Illustrious,* guarded by a protective screen of four cruisers and four destroyers, had slipped stealthily through the Mediterranean Sea to the southwest tip of Italy. Just before 8:30 p.m. her crew began launching the carrier's twenty-one overage Fairey Swordfish torpedo bombers for the fifty-mile flight to Taranto.

The attack had caught the Italians completely off guard. Swooping in at mast height, the Swordfish sent their torpedoes crashing into ship after ship. At the cost of just two planes, the British sank or heavily damaged three battleships, two cruisers and two destroyers. The results were that the Italian navy was cut in half and gave up its Taranto vantage point, retreating to the western side of the boot.

Japanese demands for information about the raid, Jebsen told Popov, were voracious. They wanted to know details that included the effectiveness of the nets that were supposed to protect the anchored ships, the tactics of the bomber crews, even the damage done to the warehouses and petrol installations at Taranto.

It was obvious, Jebsen and Popov agreed, that the Japanese purpose in gathering all this information was to guide their own surprise attack.

But where? What harbor, similar to that at Taranto, did the Japanese have in mind? The two of them could only guess where the blow might fall.

The answer came, Popov believed, when he met with von Karsthoff. Two things happened at that meeting. Popov was given a questionnaire. He was also introduced to the technology of the microdot. Employing this new development, the Germans could reduce a full page of information to be concealed in a drop of plastic the size of a period. The contents could be read only by using a microscope. The device, von Karsthoff advised him, would completely transform the sending and receiving of secret information. The entire new questionnaire, as a case in point, was diminished to a few microdots that Popov would take with him in an envelope. He was also given a typed version of the questionnaire.

Popov's examination of the typed copy showed that the top series of questions was headlined "Naval Information" and included queries on U.S. shipping, convoys, ship names and the like. His eyes riveted on the subsequent headings: "Hawaii," "Aerodromes," "Naval Strong Point Pearl Harbor." The questions sought specifics about naval ammunition dumps and protector nets. If possible, sketches were to be made of aerodromes, including the position of their hangars, workshops and bomb and petrol depots. Fully a third of the questionnaire, Popov saw, was taken up with requests about Hawaii.

"Hawaii is a bit off my beat," Popov reports that he said to von Karsthoff, "unless I can pick up something in Washington."

"No," von Karsthoff answered. "You are to go to Hawaii . . . and as soon as possible."

Popov understood immediately. His mission in the United States to begin building a new spy network was legitimate. But insofar as this added responsibility of gathering information about Hawaii was concerned, he was to be a pawn in the Germans' game of currying favor with their Axis partner. He was to help the Japanese plan a Taranto-style raid on the U.S. Navy's ships and facilities at Pearl Harbor.

What to do with this valuable discovery? Popov sought the British intelligence office in Lisbon. "They got to London," he wrote in his memoir, "and I was instructed to carry my information personally to the United States, since I was leaving in a few days. Apparently, they thought it preferable that I be the bearer of the tidings, since the Americans might want to question me at length to extract the last bit of juice."

According to Ewen Montagu, British intelligence head Stewart Menzies thought Popov's mission was sufficiently important and urgent that he himself called the only U.S. agency then responsible for counterespionage, the FBI. Menzies spoke to the FBI's director, J. Edgar Hoover, to acquaint him with Popov and prepare the way for his meeting with Hoover. According to Montagu, Menzies told Hoover of Popov's playboy lifestyle and explained that the Germans, having given Popov a large sum of money for his expenses in America, would have their suspicions aroused if he didn't continue his extravagant way of life. Menzies also dwelt on how completely the British trusted Popov in his role as Tricycle.

On August 10, Popov boarded the Pan American flight to New York. The large sum of dollars he carried with him came largely from the Germans, supplemented by a gift from a wealthy Yugoslav family. He also had the questionnaire, both in typewritten form and as a series of microdots. When his Pan Am flying boat made an intermediate stop in Bermuda, he was joined by a British intelligence officer who escorted him the rest of the way to New York and got him settled at the Waldorf-Astoria Hotel on Park Avenue.

The account by Popov in his memoir is that he was met in New York by FBI agent Charles Lehman—actually Lanman—who was also his escort when he went to meet the man in charge of the FBI's New York office, Percy "Sam" Foxworth.

Popov was mindful of the clock ticking, the days passing, any one of which could produce the moment for the Japanese raid on Pearl Harbor. "Every twenty-four hours count," he told himself. But the FBI personnel could not be hurried. Foxworth took his time interviewing Popov, reviewing the questionnaire and being introduced to the microdot. As a foretaste of how the FBI underlings catered to every whim of their all-powerful director, Foxworth showed the most interest in the microdot because he was sure that "Mr. Hoover will be very much amused." In fact, the item moved Foxworth to say that he himself would take the microdots to Washington. "And while I'm there I can get instructions about you."

There was nothing Popov could do but wait. Waiting, he bought a new Buick convertible and rented a penthouse apartment. Since his favorite girlfriend of the time, the French movie actress Simone Simon, was shooting in Hollywood and unavailable, he linked up with a young Englishwoman, Terry Richardson, whom he met at a dinner party in New York. His plan was that she would make a lively companion when he made his trip to Hawaii.

A week passed. Then Lanman asked Popov to meet him. Popov hoped to hear about FBI plans for his trip. Instead, Lanman informed him the trip was off. Popov would not be going to Hawaii. To Popov's protests, the only response the agent could make was that "Mr. Hoover will be here in New York in two weeks and will see you then."

Two weeks! No explanation for the delay was forthcoming. But Anthony Summers, a biographer who documents that Hoover was "a closet homosexual" and "a practicing transvestite," has determined that for those two weeks Hoover was away on vacation with his near-constant companion, Clyde Tolson.

Popov decided he could not sit idle for that long. The questionnaire asked that he investigate U.S. military bases, "especially in Florida." Whatever information he could scrape up there could make worthwhile material for the spy network he was supposed to organize. He picked up Richardson, drove her in his new convertible to Miami and lodged them both in a beachside hotel.

On their second day there, while they rested on the beach, so Popov records in his account, they were approached by a formidable figure in a business suit. The man asked Popov to come along with him to the beach bar. There, a second man, "looking like a half-brother," told Popov, "You are registered in this hotel as man and wife with a girl you're not married to."

Hotel detectives, Popov thought, and suggested that he be allowed to get his wallet so things could be "cleared up." They were not, however, house detectives. They showed their FBI badges.

Popov told them he had colleagues of theirs in New York who could, if they would grant him the courtesy of a call, straighten this out.

"We are here on orders from Washington," they informed him, "to warn you that you are breaking the Mann Act." This act, they explained, made it a federal offense to transport a woman across state lines for immoral purposes. Either he was to send the woman home immediately, or he would be taken into custody and face a minimum of a year and a day in prison.

Unfamiliar with U.S. law, Popov couldn't know that prosecution under the Mann Act was virtually a historic relic. He saw no choice but to bundle Richardson on a plane, much to her disgust, send her back to New York and drive north alone.

These, then, were the preliminaries for what Popov described as his audience with Hoover. Called to Foxworth's office, Popov found the FBI director sitting behind Foxworth's desk, "looking like a sledgehammer in search of an anvil." Foxworth, dispossessed, was sitting in an armchair alongside.

"Sit down, Popov," Hoover said with what Popov remembered as "an expression of disgust on his face," as though he found Popov "the equivalent of a fresh dog turd."

"I'm running the cleanest police organization in the world," Popov quotes Hoover as saying. "You come here from nowhere and within six weeks install yourself in a New York penthouse, chase film stars, break a serious law and try to corrupt my officers. I'm telling you right now I won't stand for it." He pounded on the desk with his fist "as though to nail his words into my brain."

Popov defended himself. "I'm not a spy who turned into a playboy. I'm a man who always lived well who happened to become a spy." The Germans, he told Hoover, expected him to live well and would become suspicious if he did not. "But please believe me, if it helped our common cause, I would be willing to live on bread and water in the worst slum you could find."

He then tried to explain the nature of his visit to the United States. "I brought a serious warning," he says he said, "indicating exactly where, when, how and by whom your country is going to be attacked." Popov went on to describe the questionnaire, the microdot development and, most important of all, the plan to organize an enemy double-agent system that would be under FBI control. In the preceding months, he told Hoover, the FBI had successfully broken up the existing German information network in the United States. Obviously, the Nazis had to replace it with a new organization. The Abwehr had assigned him the task. He wasn't to contact any of the former agents. He was there to build his own organization, starting from scratch. Furthermore, he needed information he could send to the Abwehr to establish his credibility before trying to transmit misinformation.

The need was great. "You can't expect a crop," he said, "if you don't put in the seed. You cannot deceive the enemy if you don't—"

Popov was stopped by Hoover's braying laugh. To Foxworth, Hoover said, "That man is trying to teach me my job."

Recognizing the futility of going any further, Popov claims that he said to Hoover, "I don't think anyone could teach you anything." He walked toward the door.

"Good riddance," Hoover yelled after him.

Popov refused to believe, however, that the whole Japanese phase of his mission had been aborted. There were FBI officials, including Foxworth, who saw the value of what had been handed them. And he thought he could count on his British colleagues to try to make the information known in high U.S. government channels.

In fact, according to Montagu, the British did try to persuade Hoover to work with Popov. Sir William Stephenson, respected head of the British Security Coordination outpost of British intelligence in New York City, who had secured Hoover's cooperation on other intelligence issues, sought to soften the FBI chief's attitude toward Popov—with no success.

In the end, the British sent Montagu to the United States to try to help Popov establish an FBI-managed equivalent of the double-cross system. Stephenson assigned Dick Ellis, one of his officials, to be Popov's U.S. case officer.

FBI underlings had, indeed, begun to show a willingness to work with

Popov. They agreed to supply him with information he could transmit to the Germans. This cooperation came after Popov told Foxworth: "The Germans are practically making you a present of their espionage system in the United States and you're rejecting it. My God, man, what more do you want?"

He succeeded in moving Foxworth to say reluctantly that "the aim you propose is worth having a go at." Foxworth thought that rather than have Popov rely on letters written in invisible ink, he should have a transmitter to wire his reports to the Abwehr.

Popov seized upon this possibility. To manage radio transmissions, however, he would have to go to the Abwehr headquarters in Rio de Janeiro to obtain full technical and operating instructions. Before he left, the FBI supplied him with the first batch of material cleared for transmission. Montagu has described it as "pathetically low-level, trumpery reports, wholly out of character with the able working that the Germans had grown to expect from Tricycle." Popov solved the problem by going to *The New York Times* building and selecting from recent issues a fat folder of facts and figures about U.S. production, troop training, marine construction and the like. With about ten times the amount of material the FBI had given him, he flew to Rio.

His visit there with the Abwehr's top agent in Latin America went well. When Popov boarded a ship for his return to the States, he was fully briefed on how to radio his reports to Lisbon. It was while on the ship that he began to hear about a Japanese attack on U.S. shipping. He was sure that "the American fleet had scored a great victory over the Japanese" and was proud he had been able to give the warning to the Americans four months in advance. When the full news about Pearl Harbor became known, he couldn't believe his ears. "How, I asked myself, how? We knew they were coming. We knew how they were going to come. Exactly like at Taranto . . . I couldn't credit what I was hearing."

Of this monumental failure, Masterman wrote: "Obviously it was for the Americans to make their appreciation and to draw their conclusions from the questionnaire rather than for us to do so. Nevertheless, with our full knowledge of the case and of the man, we ought to have stressed its major importance more than we did."

Another huge disappointment was in store for Popov when he returned to New York eager to begin sending factual and notional material
to the Abwehr. Hurrying to Charley Lanman's office, he found Lanman
not pleased to see him. When Popov began to bombard Lanman with the
myriad questions on his mind, Lanman raised his hand to stop the flow.
Sorry, Lanman said, but the use of the radio was to be exclusively an FBI
operation. Popov was not only to have no input to the traffic but was not
even to be shown what was transmitted in his name.

Popov exploded. When it came time for him to leave the United States
and return to Britain, he wanted to know, how could he face his Lisbon
controller without knowing the content of the messages he had supposedly been sending? Couldn't the FBI see that he and his whole system, his
subagents in Britain and those he would recruit in the United States,
would be blown? The answer added up to the realization that, since these
orders had come down from the top, people like Lanman could not concern themselves with what might happen to Popov.

Without knowing it, Popov had been caught in a clash between two
organizations' cultures. British intelligence believed in operating secretly. If they caught a spy, as an example, they tried not to reveal the
fact. The only time they executed a spy was when the uninformed police got to him first and put his capture in the press. The FBI, on the
other hand, living in fear of its glory-seeking chief, sought every possible opportunity to prompt headlines. It became clear to Popov that the
main reason they wanted to run his double-cross system was, as Montagu expressed it, to use Tricycle "as potential flypaper which other
agents would approach, and so get caught—and imprisoned with all
possible publicity." One of the FBI's ploys was to suggest that some of
their material was too lengthy to be transmitted by radio; couldn't the
Abwehr send a courier to pick it up?

Popov consoled himself by getting rid of Richardson and reigniting his
flame for Simone Simon. For a time she flew from Hollywood to spend
weekends with "her darling Dusko." When her shooting was completed,
she rented an apartment near his in Manhattan.

Weeks went by, and then months. Popov fretted. His own country was
under the brutal heel of the Nazis and he was doing nothing about it. Also

he was running short of money, and an obviously disenchanted Abwehr was not to be wooed into sending him more.

Dick Ellis, his case officer, decided it was time Popov ended his American misadventure, try to reestablish himself with von Karsthoff and return to Britain. MI5, agreeing, sent one of Tar Robertson's staff members, Ian Wilson, from London to extricate Popov. Working with Ellis and another MI6 officer, Walter Wren, Wilson prepared a scenario that Popov could use with von Karsthoff in Lisbon.

Tar Robertson put the possibilities to Popov squarely. He could end his double-agent work with British gratitude, or he could go to Lisbon and try to explain away his failure in America. Robertson warned him concerning this latter option, as Montagu recalled, "that his chances were nothing like even money." Montagu's own estimate was: "The odds must be at least two to one that he was blown," with very probable fatal consequences.

Popov resolved to go against the odds and face von Karsthoff in Lisbon. Montagu: "It remains for me the greatest instance of cold-blooded courage that I have ever been in contact with."

With just over a year having elapsed since he flew out of Lisbon, Popov flew back. He remembered to make what turned out to be an astute move: he brought along a gift of silk stockings for Elizabeth, von Karsthoff's secretary and mistress. He met with an outwardly friendly but wary spymaster, who informed him immediately that "some people suspect you have been turned." Following the advice of Wilson and Wren, Popov went on the offensive. He expressed indignation with the Abwehr for shortchanging him on funds, hampering his ability either to accomplish much himself or to secure information. On a gambler's hunch, he went beyond the script and swore he was no longer willing to work for the Germans because of the bad treatment he had received. At one point he found Elizabeth, who had never been a fan of his, defending him (oh, what a few silk stockings would do to a woman, he told himself). The gamble worked. Von Karsthoff backed off from any really difficult questions and began to talk about Popov's future duties. Popov's money troubles were also settled. In triumph he returned to London.

That is essentially the story as told by Popov in his memoir and by his most recent biographer, the very sympathetic Russell Miller. How much of it can be believed?

Most dubious is Popov's claim that the Abwehr ordered him to go to Hawaii in search of answers to his questionnaire. His account is that when he was told that the Hawaiian trip was off, his response was: "If the Germans find out that I never went to Hawaii, it will cause a stink from here to Berlin." Yet never during his yearlong stay did this stink occur. He makes no mention of having von Karsthoff or anyone else in the Abwehr ever inquire about this supposedly highly important assignment.

On close examination, the questionnaire itself seems a strange document. Its Pearl Harbor questions are much more concerned with ammunition dumps, mine deposits, dry docks and airplane hangars than with the U.S. fleet. The idea of a raid on the anchorage there has to be very much read into it. It could well be that the coincidence of his talk with Jebsen and his receipt of the questionnaire so soon afterward did put the possibility of a Pearl Harbor raid in his mind—and in the minds of others such as Masterman and Montagu. But the lack of any subsequent Abwehr interest strongly suggests that the Hawaii questions did not have the importance and urgency Popov attributed to them. As Montagu admitted, well after the war's end, the questionnaire may have amounted to nothing more than "the normal desire of any intelligence service to bring its information up to date."

And why, if British intelligence gave any real weight to Popov's alarm, were they so halfhearted about following up on it? If they had really believed there was hard evidence of a Japanese raid against the United States, would they have not pushed the information up the ladder to the top? Despite Montagu's claim that Stewart Menzies tried to intervene with Hoover on Popov's behalf, there is doubt that the idea ever got to Menzies. If it had, he would certainly have included it in one of his almost-daily briefings of Winston Churchill. Churchill's writings make it plain that for him the news of Pearl Harbor was a complete surprise.

Then there is the FBI side of it. Stung by the denigration of Hoover in Popov's memoir and the gleeful rush of anti-Hoover articles and books it loosed, the FBI released from its files more than 1,400 pages of material about its relations with Popov (it should be noted that at least several hundred pages were *not* released, and many of those the FBI did make public were marred by excisions and blotouts). The files seem to verify that at no time in his first meetings with FBI officials, including ones with the Bureau's assistant director E. J. Connelley, did Popov make any mention of his need to go to Hawaii. The FBI's main purpose in making the files public was to document the claim that there was no meeting, not ever, between Hoover and Popov, and that Hoover knew of Popov only through the reports of underlings. Clarence Kelley, Hoover's successor as FBI director, has asserted in print that "Mr. Popov never personally met Mr. Hoover."

Yet there are highly credible sources who affirm that the meeting did take place. William Stephenson's biographer, for one, says that Stephenson told him, not for publication in the biography for fear of upsetting U.S.-British relations, that Popov had met Hoover and that "Stephenson had no doubt about Popov's credibility and he thought the FBI had totally failed to pick up on what Popov was trying to tell him about Pearl Harbor."

Certainly British intelligence officers shared that opinion. As Tar Robertson said, "The mistake we made was not to take the Pearl Harbor information and send it separately to Roosevelt. No one ever dreamed that Hoover would be such a bloody fool."

For this writer the most preposterous aspect of Popov's account is that the Japanese would give credence to the reports of a Yugoslav spy for Germany who was sent to the United States with orders to travel to Hawaii in order to answer questions that virtually any of Japan's numerous spies in Hawaii could have provided with minimal effort.

It comes down to this: The Abwehr and von Karsthoff did want Popov to go to the United States and set up a more professional spy ring than any the Germans had had previously. But his efforts to also serve his British clients brought him into contention with the FBI, whose only interest in spies, under Hoover, was to generate headlines by capturing them. The result for Popov was an unhappy and frustrating twelve months—certainly not very interesting material for his autobiography. He saw the strange questionnaire and his knowledge of Taranto—whether coming from Jebsen or some other source—providing him the opportunity to raise what was most likely a very sour meeting with Hoover to a fiery confrontation that supplied a dramatic center for his memoir while at the same time enabling him to make a grab for a greater share of historical importance.

To the story must be added one wry footnote. In 1946, Hoover published in *Reader's Digest* an article telling how FBI agents had intercepted a Balkan "playboy son of a millionaire" on his arrival in New York during the war. There was reason to believe, Hoover added, "he was a German agent." In going through his possessions, the FBI had discovered on the front of an envelope this dot that "reflected the light." Under a microscope that magnified the dot's contents two hundred times, Hoover wrote, "we could see that it was an image on a film of a full-sized typewritten letter, a spy letter with a blood-chilling text." And what was that text? Hoover was not about to reveal the text that the FBI had actually seen. He explained that the letter asked the playboy spy to seek out information on how the United States was progressing in nuclear science.

That, certainly, is a lie. Whatever other lies remain wrapped up in this historical worm can are not likely ever to be unscrambled.

CHAPTER THIRTEEN

TRICKERY IN THE MIDDLE EAST

While the Garbos and Tricycles operating in Britain have been the most celebrated of the double agents, attention must also be paid to the dissemblers who served elsewhere in the British Empire. In fact, that mastermind of the double agents in Britain, John Masterman, wrote: "The real home of successful deception was the Middle East. There it really developed early in 1942, and, more fortunately still, double agents were used to assist it."

The Middle East as the home of British deception in World War II owes much to General Archibald Wavell, who at the war's outset was the commander-in-chief, Middle East Command. Wavell was a leader who regarded deception as an essential element in making war against an enemy. When the war began and it became clear that Benito Mussolini's Italy would soon become the partner of Adolf Hitler's Germany, Wavell saw his need for deception as a top priority. He had far too many Middle Eastern countries to guard against enemy conquest and far too few soldiers to carry out the task.

In numbers terms the situation seemed hopeless. In Libya and Italian East Africa, Mussolini faced the British with more than 300,000 troops. Wavell could count only 36,000 men, spread from Egypt and the Sudan to Palestine, Jordan and Iraq. His only recourse, he decided, was to make up the difference through deception. With merely the skeletal beginnings of an intelligence staff to help him, Wavell carried out Operation Compass.

The plan took advantage of the fact that the Italians were then at-tacking Britain's ally Greece. By that time the British had identified pro-Axis sources in Cairo who were eager to pass on the latest rumors. Deliberate leaks of misinformation to those sources indicated that Wavell's desert forces were to be weakened by the withdrawal of troops to go to the aid of Greece. Bogus radio traffic escorted the departing units while administrative paperwork portended a major embarkation. With these indications that an attack was out of the question, Wavell struck. The surprise was complete, and the Italians were routed from Egypt. No clear evidence emerged that the ruses contributed to the British victory, but Wavell's beliefs in the necessity of deception were reconfirmed. In ad-dition to his more pro forma Security Intelligence Middle East (SIME) organization, he created a special unit specifically dedicated to deception. It was named "A" Force in the hope that the enemy, hearing of it, would be misled into thinking it was an airborne security force. To run "A" Force, Wavell secured the transfer of Colonel (later Brigadier) Dudley W. Clarke, the officer much respected for bringing the British Commandos into being.

Clarke's first duty for Wavell was to take over a deception that Wavell himself had devised. This was Plan Camilla, a complex scheme to surprise the Italians in East Africa and drive them out of British Somaliland. To carry out the deception, Clarke employed a bag of tricks he was to use over and over. It included deliberate leaks of false information and fake rumors, misleading air raids, dummy radio messages and spurious ad-ministrative activity. The plan worked. The attack was a surprise and a success.

The first deception that Clarke himself organized was Plan "Abeam," directed against the Italians in North Africa. By that time the British drive against the Italians there had run its course and the two sides faced each other in a desert stalemate. Abeam was born of Clarke's belief in capital-izing on the enemy's known fears. The diary of a captured Italian officer revealed that the Italians were apprehensive of parachutists' landings be-hind their front lines. It was an anxiety, Clarke believed, that he could build into a real "war of nerves." That the British had no parachute troops or glider crews in the Middle East, and none in prospect, was no prob-

lem. He would call upon his visual deception team to create the First Special Air Service Brigade, which would include one parachute battalion
and two glider battalions. The notional brigade was designed along the
lines of the actual Special Air Service battalion existing in the UK. If the
scheme worked, he told himself, the Italians would have to dissipate some
of their frontline strength in order to protect their rear-echelon lines of
communication and airfields against possible airborne attack.

Abeam called for spreading the word that the brigade was just completing its training in Transjordan preparatory to its transfer to Egypt.
From another outfit already in Alexandria, Clarke borrowed two men to
pose as parachutists convalescing from injuries. The men wore uniforms
with their parachutist wings prominently displayed on their shoulders.
They were coached to make themselves very visible in the city and to be
guilty of "guarded indiscretions" in their amiable conversations with the
locals they met on the streets and in restaurants. One of the details they
were to let slip was that they, and all their fellow chutists, had been
trained as demolition experts—just to add to the Italians' jumpy state.

The gliders, Italian air recon would discover, were already arriving.
Clarke's visual deception magicians, which included well-known conjuror
Jasper Maskelyne, were turning out rows of bogus craft lined up on RAF
airfields.

Plan Abeam did succeed in forcing the Italians to withdraw frontline
troops for rearguard protection. It also had an unplanned result. Clarke
saw as his highest overall priority that of creating an inflated order of battle to make up for Britain's actual inadequacy of troop numbers in the
Middle East. He sought to create fictional military forces the enemy
would accept as real. Abeam got Clarke's order of battle deception off to
a good start. The First Special Air Service Brigade, subsequently strengthened by a real parachute unit, entered the enemy's estimation of British
strength and was never deleted.

At this early point in the war, chance also delivered to Clarke the Middle East's first double agent.

His name was Renato Levi. Born in Genoa of Italian-Jewish parents,
he was thirty-eight years old and had lived for periods of time in India,
Switzerland and Australia. Levi had already served as a double agent, hav-

ing been recruited by the Abwehr in 1939 to spy for them in France—an assignment he took on, knowing from the start that he intended to double-cross the Germans. This he did until the war began and the French were defeated. Then he returned to his family. Hans Travoglio, the same part-Italian, part-German Abwehr officer who had enlisted him for his French service, again approached him and introduced him to Kurt Helferich, head of the Abwehr in Italy. Their proposition to Levi was that he go to Cairo, recruit a number of agents, set up a radio transmission operation and then return to Italy to handle the receiving end of the Italy-Cairo exchanges. Levi agreed. The Germans, currying favor with their new Axis partner, submitted the plan to the chief of the Italian army's Secret Service (SIM), Count Scirombo, who approved it.

Levi had various motives. As indicated by his French excursion, his was an adventurous spirit. As a Jew, he feared Germany's Nazis and wanted to join against them. Also, the time he had spent in Australia had been a happy experience, and he hoped that by helping the British, he might, postwar, be granted British citizenship for his service and receive aid in relocating down under.

Assured that Levi had high-level acquaintances in Egypt who could supply him with information of value, the Axis services sent him off with two questionnaires, one German, one Italian. His new controllers equipped him with a code for enciphering his messages, transmission frequencies for his radio operator, a faked passport, a bundle of money and the promise of a radio transmitter. On his roundabout trip he stopped at the British embassy in Belgrade and made his true intentions known to officials there. Thus his arrival in Cairo on February 19, 1941, was anticipated.

Clarke's aides quickly lined him up to be a double agent code-named Cheese. That the promised transmitter did not arrive was no problem. A headquarters noncom, Sergeant R.G.R. Shears—later promoted to lieutenant for his Cheese contributions—agreed to operate a suitable British set, and SIME, taking on the responsibility for the care and running of double agents, assigned as his case officer Captain E. J. Simpson, who had been a novelist in peacetime. Since the Axis expected Levi to return to Italy, the British invented Cheese's Cairo agent, giving him the name of

Paul Nicossof. Levi explained to the Axis: "I believe he is Syrian, but he told me he was born in Egypt." The cover story for the notional Nicossof was that he was willing to work for Cheese and the Germans because he saw Germany as the bulwark against the Communists. Primarily, though, he was in this dangerous game for the money. On May 25, 1941, he began transmitting on a twice-a-week schedule to the receiving station in Bari, Italy. The cipher the Germans had given Levi was slow and cumbersome; SIME supplied a new one that Levi sold to his masters as more suitable. And since Levi had lied when he said he had valuable friends in Egypt, SIME worked up a new list for him.

Levi returned to Rome and solved some radio frequency problems that were interfering with reports from Nicossof. When the logjam was broken and the Germans saw the information that Nicossof was transmitting, they warmly congratulated Levi. But his success also made them want him to return right away to Cairo and begin establishing a new chain of agents throughout the Middle East. For this purpose they would send him back with a thick wad of money to be used to pay Nicossof and other agents Levi could recruit.

He begged off long enough to return to Genoa and tend to some family matters. And then, as far as the British could determine, Renato Levi went over a cliff. They heard nothing of him and could learn nothing of him for more than three years. It wasn't until Eighth Army troops drove up the Italian peninsula in October 1943 that Levi was found imprisoned and was set free.

The story he eventually told was that on virtually the last night before he was to return to Cairo, he was suddenly seized by the troops of the Controspionaggio in Genoa and thrown in jail. He was charged with black market activity, but there is evidence that Count Scirombo was the one behind the arrest. In contrast to Levi's success in Egypt, Scirombo's attempts to establish an Italian spy network there had been a failure. He probably also resented the encroachment of the Germans. To arrest Levi got back not only at a nettlesome competitor but also the whole arrogant German crew.

Did Helferich and company try to rescue Levi? Not with any real fervor. Why rock the boat in their relations with the Italians when

Paul Nicossof was doing just fine by them, thank you. Renato Levi was expendable.

British successes against the Italians in the winter of 1940–41 concluded unhappily. Hitler issued his Directive Number 22, which announced his decision that Germany must come to the aid of Mussolini or face grave problems from the south. On February 12, Erwin Rommel and the first elements of his Afrika Korps arrived in Tripoli, just at the moment Britain's desert forces had been weakened by the transfer of troops and equipment in a vain attempt to help the Greeks in their fight against German invaders.

Rommel gained renown as the "Desert Fox" because of his clever, unconventional generalship. At that early stage of the war, however, he derived a great deal of his foxiness from three distinct advantages in military intelligence. One was his frontline cryptographic team under Captain Alfred Seeböhm that made itself expert in tuning in to British battlefield radio exchanges transmitted in a field code that Seeböhm readily broke. From these decrypts Rommel learned precisely what tactical maneuvers the British were planning.

His second advantage was delivered, unknowingly, by an American. Even though the U.S. was not yet in the war, the British courted American lend-lease aid by granting a military attaché, Colonel Frank Fellers, ready access to their commanders in North Africa. An indefatigable reporter, Fellers interviewed British officers and filed meticulous reports back to Washington, never realizing the code he was using was from a codebook of which a copy had been stolen and turned over to the Germans. Decrypts of Fellers's messages complemented Seeböhm's reports by providing Rommel with top-level insights into British strategic plans.

Rommel's third intelligence superiority came via his own request. He asked for a team of dependable German agents to establish themselves in Cairo and report what they could from behind enemy lines. This was the start of the so-called Kondor mission, organized by the Abwehr's tireless Nickolaus Ritter. A pair of German agents with extensive knowledge of Egypt infiltrated into Cairo with two U.S.-made Hallicrafter radio sets and a thick wad of British pound notes. Heading the mission was John Eppler, a young Abwehr agent born of German parents in Alexandria.

The second was Peter Sandstetter, an oil rig mechanic who had spent much of his life in East Africa. They began seeking reliable sources for their spy reports to Rommel. One who became an avid supplier because of her hatred of the British, according to a SIME report, was Hekmeth Fahmy, one of Egypt's leading belly dancers. Fahmy lived in a houseboat on the Nile, where she regularly entertained a British officer. While she bedded down with the officer, the German spies explored the contents of his briefcase, learning much for their nightly transmissions to Rommel. Another of their sources was Anwar Sadat, then an ardent member of the anti-British nationalist conspiracy.

Combining his own intuition with knowledge from his secret informants, Rommel quickly turned around the situation in North Africa. Moving sooner than Wavell thought possible, Rommel wiped out all the gains the British had made and was soon at the gateways to Egypt. In a swap of generals, Churchill transferred Wavell to the Far East to replace General Claude Auchinleck, who became the new commander-in-chief of Middle East forces.

The Cheese link became very active in helping Auchinleck—and was almost blown as a result. The new commander needed four months of relative quiet on the front against Rommel in order to reorganize and reequip his battered forces. "A" Force put into effect Plan Collect, which consisted of threatening Rommel with a series of offensives, making the Germans think defensively, and then postponing each attack as its date approached.

Nicossof had acquired a new notional subagent, Piet, an anti-British South African. In November, Nicossof relayed a report by Piet that no British attack would come until after Christmas. But then, on November 18, according to plan, Auchinleck struck. What was good for the Auk was bad for Nicossof. While the general achieved complete surprise against the Germans and drove them back toward Tripoli, Helferich's team in Italy let Nicossof know they no longer had confidence in his communiqués and, pointedly, did not respond to them. Everybody in "A" Force felt compelled to give up on what the British continued to identify as "the Cheese channel."

Everybody, that is, except Nicossof's case officer. The wise and patient

Captain Simpson had Nicossof place the blame for false information on Piet and angrily dismiss him as a source. Simpson also kept up the flow of useful information, added meaty bits to it and gradually won back the Germans' approval. Soon Ultra decrypts were verifying that the enemy accepted Nicossof as a genuinely reliable and useful agent.

As time passed, the funding of Nicossof became an increasingly troublesome problem. The Abwehr could not find ways to deliver cash to him and he could not let them fail to do so. The character created for Nicossof was not one who would keep on putting himself in danger without remuneration. His case officer foresaw that if Nicossof kept on working without receiving Abwehr funds, the Germans would suspect that he was on the British payroll. Simpson let the content of Nicossof's messages decline, with Nicossof complaining that he could no longer hire information suppliers and could not, himself, afford to attend the kinds of functions where he could hear, or overhear, high-level indiscretions. The Abwehr was sympathetic and claimed they had made tries to deliver, but no cash came.

Erwin Rommel, unknowingly, gave Simpson reason to revitalize Nicossof. Rommel's defeat of Auchinleck's armies brought him to El Alamein, only about twenty-four hours from Cairo. Nicossof's transmissions radiated a new spirit. Convinced of the imminent arrival of Rommel's troops in Cairo, he imagined them bringing money and honors for the faithful spy who had risked so much to help them along the road. Heedless of his money worries, Nicossof worked feverishly to aid the Germans. Gone were the desultory twice-a-week reports. Now he transmitted daily; he broadcast so diligently that "A" Force had to set up a special committee to prepare the messages. Nicossof persuaded his Greek girlfriend, Marie, code-named Misanthrope, to help him with the encoding and even some of the Morse transmitting. Unlike Nicossof, Marie had a real young woman volunteer ready to impersonate her. Aware that the non-notional Marie carried a pistol in her purse, the irreverent British assigned to the case referred to her covertly as "B.G.M.," the Blonde Gun Moll.

Rommel's drive, however, was spent. He had to halt, just forty miles short of Alexandria, to regroup and reequip his weary troops. Nicossof's spirits also sagged. Now he was so deeply in debt he could no longer borrow more. The Abwehr was also desperate, unable to find a way to deliver funds to him. They claimed that they had tried to carry out a series of rendezvous with Marie, but the efforts went awry and no money was delivered.

Finally, the Germans cooked up a plan to have a go-between dropped by U-boat off the coast of Haifa, in Palestine, and from there make his way to Cairo. British navy operations were warned of the probable arrival of the sub. The plan was to let it deposit the courier and then sink it after it had turned around. But the operators got overeager and sank it on the way in. The courier survived, but no cash got delivered.

SIME, more inventive than the Germans, stepped in. They employed an agent, a financier in Cairo named Cohen and code-named Godsend, who was experienced in handling black market financial transactions. As Nicossof was able to inform the Germans, Godsend would, for a cut of the money, handle a complex three-currency transaction that ended up with Abwehr money in a Cairo bank to be collected by Nicossof.

The Cheese-Nicossof link, now returned to monetary health and to the Abwehr's good graces, became a vital contributor to one of "A" Force's most ambitious deception plans. This was Cascade, the first comprehensive order-of-battle augmentation scheme. It was, again, dictated by the weakness of the Commonwealth forces in North Africa caused by the withdrawal of troops for service on other Middle Eastern fronts. Its objective was to "discourage the enemy from launching any offensive against the Middle East in 1942, except from Libya."

The Middle East command's actual strength in the spring of 1942 was fifteen divisions—ten infantry and five armored. Cascade's goal was to raise the enemy's estimates to twenty-nine divisions—twenty-one infantry, eight armored.

Dudley Clarke relied on his usual tricks, this time only more so. Small administrative units and supply depots "adopted" divisions, referred to them in their communiqués and radio backchat, and displayed their symbols on their vehicles. Detailed histories of the notional divisions were written. Misinformation was adroitly leaked while revealing documents were allowed to fall into enemy hands. And the double agents—now including numerous supplements to the Cheese link—were prepared to answer the inevitable rush of questions from their controllers.

Cascade was continued for two years until it was succeeded by Cascade II. Its greatest coup was to win enemy acceptance of an entire notional army—the Twelfth. In 1943, the plan was broadened to include Dwight Eisenhower's North Africa command and to begin spawning notional U.S. divisions.

By the time of the Allied landings in Sicily, Bletchley Park decrypts were verifying that the Germans believed there were forty-four infantry divisions and fifteen to twenty armored divisions in North Africa and the Middle East. The actual numbers were twenty-three and ten. As will be seen, this near-doubling of Allied divisions meant Allied commanders could notionally launch at the same time several major operations whose manpower demands were well beyond the numbers actually available.

Plainly, the Cheese-Nicossof pairing was the Garbo of the Middle East. As noted, however, just as there were other valuable participants in the double-cross system in Britain, so in the Middle East, and eventually, with Wavell's transfer to command in India, in the Far East, there were additional Janus types working to deceive the enemy. In fact, Levi and his followers deserve a book of their own. The most that can be done here is to give a few examples of these double agents and to sketch in a sampling of the many deception plans they helped to execute.

The Abwehr's officers in Athens seemed to believe that the best way to infiltrate agents into British territories was to give their recruits a bit of spy training and then send them out in groups of three or four. The group that came to be code-named as the Savages was made up of a newly married pair of doctors and their best man. The men were from the island of Cyprus; the woman was Greek. The groom of the married pair apparently meant to serve the Germans. The best man was just as determined to betray them. Landed on the Cyprus coast by one of the small Levantine sailing craft known as caïques, they were captured. Under interrogation, they claimed they were more interested in getting out of occupied Greece than in actually doing spy work for the Abwehr. The British saw a promising double agent in the best man, a young law student whose German code name was Tom. Since "A" Force already had a satisfactory double-cross team in Cyprus—a troupe of Greeks known as the Lemons—the Savages were flown to Cairo. There the doctor pair were sent to a detention camp for the rest of the war, while Tom prepared to begin his transmissions for the British.

What kind of cover story could make this transfer of destinations believable by the Germans? Advised by "A" Force, Tom reported that in Cyprus he had been pressured by the British to become a turned agent for them in Egypt. Not knowing what might happen to him if he refused to go along, he agreed, with the result that the trio was flown to Cairo. Savage I had been able to bring his compact radio set with him. In Cairo, by feigning a health breakdown, he had backed out of the deal with the British. Now, on August 23, 1943, he could begin transmitting to his Abwehr masters in Athens. Savages II and III were notionally employed in a Greek hospital in Cairo and, still loyal to the Germans, were able to supply Savage I with occasional bits of useful information. He himself became adept at tapping indiscreet "unconscious" sources.

Tom's value to "A" Force was as an able Cairo backup and second fiddle to the Cheese-Nicossof channel.

He soon proved himself satisfactory enough that he was given a factual job at General Headquarters in Cairo. The Abwehr was pleased to learn of his job and to observe how cleverly he stepped up the quality of his unconscious disclosures through contacts with headquarters officers. He further broadened his net by his romance with Nikki, a typist who mixed easily with British officers and was willing to help him because she was resentful at having been reprimanded by her superior for talking too freely.

Through their questionnaires the Germans emphasized that they looked to Tom for naval information such as the movement of ships in and out of Alexandria harbor and Port Said. It was a request he could meet because his job required him frequently to visit these port cities. His specialty, however, was to further inflate the Germans' estimate of Allied strength in North Africa and the Middle East. The official records that survive describe his "master stroke" as his report that disclosed practically the complete Middle East order of battle—a coup that resulted from his being able to study an order left open on an officer's desk at headquarters. That was, at least, the story he sent to Athens and that the Abwehr swallowed with warm expressions of appreciation.

Out of the diverse range of double agents active outside Great Britain
during the war, one more example can't be overlooked. This was a Greek
trio trained and dispatched by the Abwehr in Athens. And a strange trio
it was. The leader was George Liossis, a former officer in the Royal Hel-
lenic Air Force who had served with distinction in the battles against the
Italian invaders. His code name was Quicksilver. Second was Rio, a young
tough whose real name was Bonzos. He was willing to serve the Germans
in order to escape prison—he had been found guilty of the murders of the
ravager of his sister and then, obeying a primitive stricture, of the sister as
well. The third was Anna Agiraki, code-named Gala, an adventurous
young secretary added to the troupe at the last minute before their departure on a caïque.

Foretold by Bletchley Park decrypts, the trio's landing on the coast of
Syria quickly led to their capture. Liossis had intended to turn against the
Germans from the first. "A" Force imprisoned the other two but put Liossis up in a house outside Beirut, from which, on October 16, 1942, he
began transmitting to Athens the information prepared for him by a
hastily organized "31 Committee."

The notional opportunities offered by the other two were too rich to
be resisted. Gala was presented as an attractive and promiscuous young
woman who supplied useful information by becoming a popular play-
thing among the British officers in Beirut. Rio, called upon notionally for
service in the Greek navy, added his bit through letters he sent to Quicksilver recording observations on board an actual Greek destroyer in the
Mediterranean.

As for their contribution to beating the Axis, an "A" Force analysis
written late in the war asserts that "this case has been the principal means
of supplementing 'A' Force plans in Syria" and adds that "the deception of
the enemy through this channel has very considerably assisted operations
based in the Middle East."

To read Britain's National Archives files on the multitudinous deception plans conceived and nurtured by SIME and "A" Force is to marvel at
the creativity of Dudley Clarke and his colleagues. The list goes on, file
after file, from the war's earliest days until its end.

Some of the plans were unsuccessful. Plan Anagram, as an example, was designed to disguise the movement of an Australian corps then in Syria. The deception machinery was cranked up to make the Germans believe the corps was going to Crete. The plan was called off when the Australian press published the true story that the corps was being brought back to the Pacific theater.

Other plans were at least moderately successful. Plan Bastion, for one, aimed to dissuade Rommel from continuing his February 1942 advances toward Egypt. Since the British had only a defeated army retreating before him, the plan was to use dummy tank forces and notional troops on his flanks to make him cautious about thrusting his army too far into a trap. Elaborate visual deceptions displayed to Luftwaffe recon planes a powerful massing of troops and armor on Rommel's left flank at Tobruk and on his right in the southern desert. Whether or not the deception contributed could not be proved, but Rommel did show caution, especially about attacking the British fortifications and fake forces at Tobruk. He paused in his drive until late May, a respite the battered British troops sorely needed. Both sides settled into a stalemate at El Alamein.

Another ambitious plan that only partially succeeded was code-named Sentinel. It was attempted when General Bernard Montgomery arrived in Egypt on August 19 to take command of the Eighth Army after Churchill replaced Auchinleck with General Harold Alexander as the Middle East commander-in-chief. Ultra decrypts were making it plain that Rommel was planning, despite severe gasoline shortages resulting from the sinking of a high percentage of his supply ships in the Mediterranean, to end the stalemate at El Alamein and assault the British positions. Montgomery summoned Colonel Clarke and asked him to do everything possible to delay the attack. Clarke's response was Plan Sentinel, whose objective was to make the enemy "feel that the pause gained at El Alamein has been used by us to the best possible value in preparing defenses." In support of the plan, Clarke's visual deception crew almost overnight filled the desert behind the front lines with the greatest assemblage of bogus machinery and false encampments yet seen by enemy warplanes. For manpower, as reported by the Cheese link and other "A" Force agents, these new defenses were manned by two of the notional divisions created as part of Plan Cascade. All of this artful chicanery failed to stop Rommel—he went ahead with his attack on July 31—but it did seem to add to his sense of caution. The attack—his last try at breaking through to Egypt—was half-hearted as well as half out of petrol. It quickly foundered.

By then Rommel's spy network had also run out of gas. All three of his secret intelligence forces had been compromised. Seeböhm's battlefield unit had been overrun in a British raid and he himself killed—a loss the Germans were unable to replace. As for Fellers, their unwitting American ally, Bletchley Park decrypts of German Enigma-encoded messages had uncovered convincing evidence proving his codebook was no longer valid, and that loophole was plugged. And Eppler and Sandstetter, the house-boat spies in Cairo, made mistakes that gave them away. Their most in-criminating error had been to start paying for their bar appearances and prostitute assignations with some of the British pound notes they had brought with them into Egypt. Primarily the Egyptians relied on their own pound notes. The British pounds were acceptable but they did at-tract notice, especially when dispensed with as freely as the German spies were throwing them about. British security forces collected some of the notes and conducted tests of them. The notes, they found, were clever forgeries known to be German. A cordon of British soldiers closed in on the German spies as well as the belly dancer. The Desert Fox lost not only this last information resource but also, not to his knowing, had it turned against him. The British broke the code the spies had been using and con-tinued transmitting to Rommel, except now the information was of British choosing.

The result was that Rommel was left vulnerable to "A" Force decep-tions that were incredibly successful. These were Plan Treatment and Plan Bertram. With Montgomery organizing his offensive, Treatment's aim was strategic: to lull the Germans into thinking no attack could possibly come before the moonless period around November 6. Bertram was on the operational level: to induce Rommel to believe the main assault would come in the south and to mass his main strength there, while in actuality Monty intended only a feint in the south while launching his full drive in the north by the light of the full moon on October 23.

While Rommel was having to rely on hunch and instinct, Mont-gomery had Ultra decrypts to keep him informed on virtually every move

Rommel made. The Cheese link and other secret channels weighed in to detail a scheduled conference that would have drawn General Alexander and other Allied leaders to Tehran at the very time that Montgomery's drive was getting under way. For the visual deceptionists, a masterstroke was the creation of a bogus petrol-supply facility in the south, complete with pipelines, pumping stations, reservoirs and encampments for workers. The complex was camouflaged, but not too carefully. Enemy reconnaissance planes could follow the construction and verify that it was proceeding at a pace that could not possibly reach completion until early November at the earliest. Deceived into believing the attack was not imminent, Rommel, a sick man, had returned to Germany for treatment when the Eighth Army struck. The Germans' second in command, bulbous General Georg Stumme, trying to cope with the complexities, died of a heart attack.

Montgomery had deliberately set the date for his El Alamein drive to begin just two weeks before the Allies were to land in western North Africa. Even though the too-cautious Montgomery allowed too many of the Afrika Korps troops to escape, El Alamein marked the furthest point of German penetration in North Africa. For "A" Force, SIME, Clarke and the Middle East double agents, Montgomery's victory signaled the impressive beginning of the larger roles they would play in the major deceptions yet to come.

CHAPTER FOURTEEN

FOR OPERATION TORCH, STRATEGIC DECEPTIONS

With the Middle East double agents having played a key role in Bernard Montgomery's victory at El Alamein, the next act in the show fell mainly to the tricksters in Britain. Garbo and his colleagues had begun to exploit their credibility with their spymasters by carrying out minor deceptions. Early agents such as Snow and Tate had subtly exaggerated Britain's readiness to withstand an invasion. Coastal defenses were stronger, the number of trained troops higher and the production of aircraft and warships greater than they actually were. By understating the range of British radar, the agents had led German bomber crews to believe they were safely outside the limits when, in fact, they were being tracked for action by RAF pilots and antiaircraft batteries. The morale and fighting spirit of the British people were represented as having only been strengthened by the Blitz.

The double agents had met a special request by Britain's Air Ministry. Concerned about the casualties and destruction resulting from the Luftwaffe's bombing of the cities, the ministry asked the Twenty Committee to advise the Germans that their bombers would have greater effect if they switched to attacking RAF airfields, since these were less well protected than the urban areas. The truth, of course, was the obverse. The ministry also sought, by this change, to increase the attrition rate of German planes. Goering's bombers did make the switch, and more of them came tumbling down.

While these were all gratifying achievements, the double-cross system by the summer of 1942 was ready for a diet of redder meat.

Tar Robertson felt driven, on July 15, 1942, to write an appeal to the military services to make better use of this remarkable instrument—this "powerful weapon"—that was now at their disposal. It was time, he wrote, for the services to go beyond the two hours a week that their representatives spent on monitoring the information the Twenty Committee proposed to transmit. Something more was needed if the German files were to be filled with the information the Allies would like to see there.

Robertson's timing was fortuitous. As historian Michael Howard has put it: "During the last weeks of July the whole aspect of the war had changed." Anglo-American leaders had come to the decision to launch an Allied invasion of North Africa. This meant that the time of defensive operations was past; the Allies were going on the offensive. And as everyone acknowledged, deceptions were more possible and more likely to succeed when the operational plan was forward and aggressive rather than passive.

Archibald Wavell, that great advocate of deception, weighed in. By this time he had been transferred eastward to take charge of the war against the Japanese in India and Burma and had duly established a Far East deception unit. He wired Churchill with a new thought. Isolated deception plans such as those he was initiating in his new command, Wavell wrote, could only be "local and ephemeral" unless they were part of a "general deception plan on a wide scale." He urged a "policy of bold imaginative deception worked between London, Washington and Commanders in the field." The prime minister saw to it that Wavell's memorandum was circulated to all members of the Defense Committee of the Cabinet and to the military involved in planning.

Intelligence authorities responded by organizing still another hierarchical level, one whose whole purpose was to plan and implement deceptions. Both B1A and the Twenty Committee reported to this new entity, given the meaningless title of the London Controlling Section, or the LCS. To take charge of it, the choice was a respected officer in the War Cabinet offices, Colonel John Bevan.

The military services also responded quickly and positively. The army and navy designated full-time staff officers to serve on the Twenty Committee and take responsibility for deception activities. The RAF promised that its representative would be freed to devote more time to the Committee's work. Bevan immediately began attending the weekly sessions of the Twenty Committee.

Much as the Russians were clamoring for a second front in Europe, Operation Torch—the invasion of French North Africa—was the most the Allies could manage in 1942. President Roosevelt and Prime Minister Churchill had decided that the year must not pass without seeing an Allied offensive mounted somewhere in the European theater. Partly the offensive would relieve the pressure on the Russians in their eastern front campaign. And partly it would reconfirm the agreed-upon strategy to give priority to the war against Germany ahead of that against Japan. On July 24 the British and American Combined Chiefs of Staff agreed to recommend that the 1942 attack would fall on the French coast of North Africa, and the two leaders approved.

The seizure of French North Africa was also expected to make the Mediterranean safer for Allied convoys, saving them from having to sail around South Africa to reach the Middle East.

Having made the decision and appointed rising new American general Dwight D. Eisenhower to command the combined forces, the Allied chiefs looked to Colonel Bevan and the newly formed LCS to come up with ways to deceive the Axis leaders into believing the attack would fall somewhere other than the intended targets in Morocco and Algiers. The task of the deception planners was to present the enemy with plausible alternatives.

It was a tall order to carry out. The leaders who made the Torch decision had only a dim idea of what was involved in mounting a successful deception scheme. The time span given the LCS between the making of the decision in late July and the execution of it in October was simply too brief to allow the patient and careful buildup of bits of misinformation that the enemy would string together to arrive at wrong conclusions.

Moreover, the sheer mass of the operation made it all but inconceivable that the true destination could be concealed to the end of the journey. Three large task forces were to converge on North Africa simultaneously: two from the United Kingdom in voyages of more than

2,700 miles and a third from the United States, a distance of some 4,500 miles. The three armadas were to travel through seas where German U-boats were wreaking havoc on Allied shipping, and they would approach coasts that would make them vulnerable to Luftwaffe reconnaissance planes and bombers. Combined, the three fleets totaled 300 warships and 370 merchant vessels carrying 107,000 troops. It was the largest amphibious invasion force thus far in history.

Refusing to be daunted by the magnitude of their task, the LCS, the Twenty Committee and the double agents pitched in with fervor. Bevan and his team had their plans worked out within a week and presented them to the Chiefs of Staff on August 5. The planners knew from Bletchley Park decrypts that the Nazis were aware of a major Allied move in preparation but had no firm conviction as to where the blow would fall. Decrypts also verified that a jittery Hitler was imagining a rationale for every conceivable possibility. The least likely destination, Hitler believed, was French North Africa, because the United States would not do anything that would drive the Vichy government more deeply into German arms.

In the short time they had, Bevan and his deception team concentrated on two main plans. The first, code-named Solo One, was to play to Hitler's anxieties about Scandinavia by making it seem that the massing of ships in Scottish waters for the one convoy of Operation Torch was actually to be directed against Norway. The buildup of Allied troops in Scotland—more of them notional than real—lent plausibility.

The second plan, code-named Overthrow, aimed to scare the Germans into expecting an action against northern France. The plan would capitalize on the growing numbers of Allied troops now training in southern England to make the enemy believe they were preparing for an immediate cross-Channel landing, either a larger Dieppe-type raid or perhaps a real invasion.

Both strategies sought to force the Germans to hold their occupation divisions in place rather than shift reinforcements to the Russian front or to the Mediterranean.

Subsidiary plans included Solo Two, designed to trick the Germans into thinking the troops bound for North Africa were sailing instead to the Middle East by going around South Africa. Other schemes were devised for such purposes as explaining support preparations in Gibraltar and confusing the enemy as to the real destination of the convoys once they had put to sea.

In support of Solo One, Mutt and Jeff used their credibility as dependable observers of developments in Scotland to alert the Germans to the attacks notionally planned against the Norwegian ports of Trondheim and Narvik. Tate reported on a dinner party with officers from both U.S. and Royal Navy ships in Scottish harbors. These officers were sure their vessels, escorted by five destroyers, were due for immediate action and that it must be in another climate, because the personnel had been warned to stock up on cold-weather clothing. A minor agent, Ib Riis, code-named Cobweb, reporting to the Germans by wireless from Iceland, backed up Tate's story by transmitting the true information that two cruisers had sailed north from the island—with their most likely destination being somewhere in Scandinavia. Garbo's far-flung network of sub-agents kept him, and the Germans, informed of the buildup of Canadian, British and Norwegian forces in Scotland.

Deception planners added ingenious details expected to attract the Germans' attention. They ordered 20,000 shoulder patches labeled "Norge" for issue to Norwegian resistance groups, placed large orders for antifreeze and snow chains for vehicles, floated inquiries for the supply of Norwegian currency, and conducted a course in mountain warfare for junior officers. Members of the Norwegian forces in England were summoned to the troop concentration areas in Scotland. And of course the airwaves crackled with bogus traffic linking the largely notional forces assembling for the attack.

Similar teamwork was applied to make the Overthrow threat against northern France as menacing as possible. Centerpiece of the deception was to be an amphibious exercise, Exercise Cavendish, to be conducted in the Channel, temporarily borrowing some of the troops training in southern England for the Normandy landings. It was hoped that one result of this feint would be a major air battle, which would lead to a further substantial preinvasion weakening of the Luftwaffe through the process of attrition.

Touches added by the LCS included a circular letter that went out to all commands asking for the names of officers familiar with the northern French coast, the purchase of quantities of French dictionaries and a search for sea pilots able to navigate the French channel ports. A ban was imposed on travel to the coast areas where Overthrow forces were supposedly assembling, and the departure point of British air service to Portugal was moved from a southwest England airport to one in Northern Ireland.

As a further hopeful tactic, the LCS invented rumors that could, in one way or another, reach German ears and give false impressions of the destination and timing of the notional expeditions. Charles Cruikshank has listed numerous examples of these deliberate rumors. Those in support of Overthrow include:

"I was lunching with a member of the Thames Yacht Club on Friday who told me, after a second glass of port, that all available small craft are to be assembled again along the Kent coast just as they did at Dunkirk."

"My brother, who is a wine merchant in Ashford, is having a devil of a job to supply the demands of the RAF messes in that part of Kent. The number of officers has almost doubled in the past five weeks."

Similarly, created rumors meant to stir up public discussion in the north included these examples:

"My dad is a quartermaster sergeant in the Royal Scots, and when he was home last week I overheard him tell Mum that a lot of arctic clothing had recently arrived at his stores."

"My fiancée is a nurse up in Scotland and when she was last on leave she showed me the new panties with which they had been issued. They are thick wool and would cost £3 a set if you had to buy them. I hope to goodness they're not going to send her to Iceland."

For the double agents, Garbo led the way in support of Overthrow by reporting worrisome movements of troops to southwest embarkation points. In one of his letters he warned that rumors were circulating that "the English cannot invade for lack of tonnage"—rumors put out "with the intention of confusing you and so you do not suspect the improvised plan," which was to overcome the tonnage problem by using "every type of transport." His Abwehr master wrote back: "It is of the greatest importance that you should intensify all your efforts to try to get extensive information and transmit it here quickly by airmail on concentration of troops and matériel, motorized units, aviation and airfields, as well as bases of departure in the south of England and especially the Isle of Wight and regions of Wales." Garbo was asked to send agents to these areas.

While the deception teams did their utmost to make the two plans convincing, the deceptions were given only lukewarm support by the services. With a real campaign to wage, the commanders felt that they could not commit time and resources to bogus operations. True, the RAF did try to stir German worries about a Norway excursion by flying reconnaissance missions over the notional landing sites, and the Royal Navy sent out minesweepers to clear a path for the invasion. True, similar fakery was carried out against French targets. But to do more seemed a probable waste of petrol and possibly of manpower at a time when real needs for both were urgent. Another stumbling block was added when the October date for Torch was delayed into November. October was already viewed as too late in the year for a credible cross-Channel attack to be mounted, and November was out of the question. The coup de grâce for the French deception seemed to come when the main subterfuge of the mock amphibious exercise in the Channel, Exercise Cavendish, was seen by the services as demanding more than they could afford to give it and had to be canceled.

In general, German commanders refused to take Overthrow seriously. But two German leaders did. One was Hitler. On October 5, he ordered the French coast to be put in a state of full alert and coastal defenses strengthened. As Michael Howard has noted, four days later Hitler had one of his "intuitions," which was that Cherbourg was the most likely target, requiring additional attention to the port's defenses.

The other believer was Field Marshal Gerd von Rundstedt, commander-in-chief in the West. Still fresh in his memory was the British raid on Dieppe. He feared that Dieppe was a "dress rehearsal" for "renewed large-scale landing attempts based on the experience gained in that operation." Archives held at the Imperial War Museum in London tell how von Rundstedt's apprehensions continued until almost the end of the year. German observation of the concentration of troops in the south of England and of offshore landing exercises in September "confirms C-in-C West in his opinion that further enemy operations are imminent," including the possibility of "several simultaneous operations at different points." On October 12 von Rundstedt reported "enemy attack possible at any time and in different places." Even weeks later he believed that "operations similar to Dieppe seem likely in November under still favorable weather conditions." Only with the coming of December did the marshal relax his anxiety about a seaborne attack.

In addition to his commands to prepare for a cross-Channel incursion, Hitler acted on his concerns about Solo One. Believing that Norway was "the zone of destiny in this war," he ordered an additional infantry battalion to be sent there and demanded that the Norse coastline, too, be placed on full alert.

In consequence, despite the setbacks, both plans had to be judged as having been successful in achieving their main objectives. No substantial German forces moved either south toward the Mediterranean or east toward Russia.

Deception plans for the convoy departing from the United States dealt mainly with the preparations for combat in a hot climate. If enemy agents were to learn anything about the convoy's destination by overhearing GI chatter, they would have concluded that the ships were bound for the Caribbean and tropical warfare training exercises. That was the cover story the troops themselves were led to believe.

The timing of Operation Torch gave Garbo a prime opportunity to enhance the esteem in which his German spymasters held him. He was allowed, on October 29, to post a letter reporting the sailing of the UK convoy and noting that none of the troops trained in cold-weather mountain warfare had embarked—thus enabling the threat to Norway to be maintained. Just four days later he posted a second letter detailing two urgent findings. The first came from a subagent in western Scotland revealing that additional troop transports had secretly left the Clyde and that the escorting battleships were camouflaged in Mediterranean colors. More important, in a visit to his friend at the Ministry of Information he himself had been able, while his friend was out of the office, to take a quick peek at a top-secret document left lying atop the desk. It was marked "Most Secret" and was entitled "Policy—French North Africa."

Inside he had found a directive that would come into force in the event of Allied action against French Morocco and/or Algeria. Garbo expressed his certainty that the document was connected with the large convoys that had recently been leaving British ports.

It was all fiendishly clever. This was at the early stage when Garbo was still having to deliver his reports by mail. As Garbo and the Twenty Committee knew full well, his letter would reach von Karsthoff and crew only *after* the landings had been made. The Germans' reply:

"Your last reports are all magnificent but we are sorry they arrived late, especially those relating to the Anglo-Yankee disembarkation in North Africa. . . . You must stay in London and continue investigations with your military friends."

So there it was: Garbo had discovered the convoy destinations prior to the landings and had communicated the information immediately by airmail, as the postmark verified. The fact that this urgent message had reached the Germans too late was no fault of Garbo's; he had offered to begin making use of radio transmissions as early as the previous August.

Now his spymasters agreed: Garbo/Arabel should acquire a wireless set and recruit an operator. The Germans also sent him a signal plan and codes to be used in his transmissions—another nice gift to Bletchley Park.

In their passage through the U-boat–infested waters of the Atlantic, the Allied convoys benefited from a strange bit of luck. It so happened that the German U-boat wolf packs had detected a convoy traveling from South Africa to Britain and were so intent on ravaging its ships that the Torch convoys passed by unnoticed. One group's doom was the larger group's salvation.

The task force from the United States, under General George S. Patton, stayed west of Gibraltar and landed at Casablanca in Morocco. The other two pushed past Gibraltar into the Mediterranean. Still having to guess, the Germans decided the convoys' destination was the island of Malta. Making the most of that assumption, the Allied ships made a feint toward Malta and then, on November 8, 1942, turned a hard right to completely surprise the Axis by landing at Oran and Algiers in Algeria.

Hitler is said to have exclaimed, when news of the landings was delivered to him, "We never even dreamed of it."

It seemed as though the war in North Africa would come to a rapid close. Erwin Rommel's Afrika Korps was reeling westward from its defeat at El Alamein by Montgomery's Eighth Army. The expectation was that Rommel's retreating forces would be caught in a vise between Montgomery's army pushing from the east and the masses of new Allied forces moving in from the west. As will be seen, though, Adolf Hitler had other ideas.

The North African campaign united the Anglo-American forces in many vital ways, including the introduction of the Americans to British-style deceptions and use of double agents. Eisenhower made it plain that he wanted the U.S. to become an active partner in both of these black arts. The LCS's Colonel Bevan traveled to Washington to meet with and inform the American officers given these responsibilities. At the meetings, the two sides reached agreement in a formal division of control over deceptions worldwide. The British B1A and "A" Force would control deception in Europe, North Africa, the Middle East and India. Washington's control would extend over the Americas, Australia, the Pacific and China.

Another critical issue was settled by the North African landings: the double agents had proved they could contribute to more than tactical trickery. In the days leading up to the successful landings in Oran, Algiers and Casablanca they had played essential roles in deceptions of strategic importance. Allied leaders were coming more and more to a full realization of the tremendous advantage the double agents were giving them.

CHAPTER FIFTEEN

ANYWHERE BUT SICILY

American caution kept the landings in French North Africa from being as successful as the Allies had hoped. The British wanted the convoys of Operation Torch to sweep past Gibraltar and strike boldly eastward into the Mediterranean with landings at Bizerte and Tunis at the far end of Tunisia. U.S. commanders were wary about so long a reach. What if, they asked, the Germans occupied all of France and pressured Spain into ending its pseudo-neutrality by joining in, or at least acquiescing to, the seizure of Gibraltar? Then this major commitment of Allied troops and equipment would be isolated well inside the Mediterranean with the supply route blocked. The compromise arrived at kept Patton's task force as a safety valve west of the Rock and the Mediterranean landings well short of Tunisia. The expectation was that if the Gibraltar nightmare did not materialize, the Allied forces in Oran and Algiers would drive eastward to join the westward-advancing Eighth Army in crushing Rommel's German and Italian armies between them.

This would have been a sensible script if the Allies had faced only Rommel's battered forces. To the Allies' surprise, however, Hitler decided to make a real fight for North Africa. With stunning speed he pulled troops and equipment off the Russian front and out of France and airlifted a veritable new army into Tunisia. As Rommel noted in his memoir, "What we found really astonishing was to see the amount of material that they were suddenly able to ship into Tunisia, quantities out of all proportion to anything we had received in the past." Hitler also called back from Russia the capable, aggressive General Hans-Jürgen von Arnim, to share leadership with Rommel.

The intended Allied drive eastward had been hampered by poor roads and autumnal rains. Now it also encountered battle-hardened German troops and superior armor. Green American troops were slaughtered at the Kasserine Pass. Allied progress into Tunisia ground to a halt for the winter of 1942–43.

Axis forces, however, were up against those powerful enemies of which they had no knowledge. By this time Bletchley Park cryptologists were reading Luftwaffe traffic routinely, were breaking the Enigma used by the Wehrmacht and had solved a new Enigma key that disclosed Axis shipping schedules. Italy's air force and navy ciphers had also yielded. As a result, Bletchley decrypts informed Allied subs and planes of Axis ships' schedules and courses when they were trying to supply the Axis troops in North Africa.

Allied deceptionists worried that the Germans, in questioning how British submarines were sinking so many of their ships, might suspect breaks into their codes. An alternate explanation was hatched: that the Mediterranean simply teemed with Allied subs. To justify this assumption, the information was leaked to the Germans that eight more new subs were to arrive at Malta from England. Sure enough, German recon planes were able to photograph the subs in Malta waters. What the Germans didn't know was that all eight were full-sized inflated rubber dummies.

It was the same with Allied reconnaissance aircraft: they so blanketed the seas between Italy and North Africa, so it seemed, that an Axis ship could scarcely leave an Italian harbor without its being picked up en route by a hovering observer plane that then led a sub to the kill. The reality was that the plane had been guided there by Bletchley's reading of the Axis mail.

As Ultra cryptanalyst and historian Francis Hinsley expressed it in a 1996 reminiscence: "The Germans and the Italians assumed we had 400 submarines whereas we had 25. And they assumed we had a huge reconnaissance airforce whereas we had three aeroplanes!"

Ships known to be carrying petrol were particular targets. Soon the Axis armies were immobilized by lack of fuel, while many soldiers were existing on two slices of bread per day.

Bletchley Park was also reading the plans of Axis commanders. When Rommel tried to attack the Eighth Army, Montgomery knew precisely where to mass his armor and artillery. The defeat sent Rommel back to Germany a beaten man.

It was a situation made to order for that other unknown Axis nemesis: the deception artists of "A" Force, ably abetted by their double agents. Deception plans were created to convince enemy naval staffs that the future held only increased sinkings for the Axis, making the supply lines ever more tenuous.

"A" Force's final deception plan for North Africa followed the script from an earlier success. Massed dummy tanks were to be seen congregating at one site while the genuine attack forces were secretly gathering, under camouflage netting, at the real target area. This time the question posed to the Axis was whether the assault would be made by Montgomery's Eighth Army driving from the south or by the U.S. First Army attacking from the west. The Cheese channel and others let it be known that the honor would deservedly go to the Eighth. In the night, however, the Eighth's First Armored Division slipped away and was replaced by dummy tanks. The British armor joined the Americans for the victory that sealed the fate of the Axis armies. On May 13, 1943, von Arnim was forced to surrender, along with 215,000 German and Italian troops and all their equipment. The Allies were in control of the whole of North Africa.

"A" Force reaped a rich harvest of new double agents from the conquest. An agent code-named Ram was a sergeant in the French Army who had been recruited in Paris by the Germans and sent to Algiers in early 1942. In fact he was working not for the Abwehr but for French intelligence. Now he willingly came under "A" Force control and continued to flimflam the Germans. Notionally employed in the communications branch of French Army headquarters in Algeria, he specialized in reporting Algiers port activities.

An especially tricky piece of work was that done by an exiled Spanish officer in Algiers, code-named Whiskers. He pretended to be the loyal agent of the pro-German Spanish vice consul there, and in this role, he sent a weekly report to the Abwehr. What neither the vice consul nor the Germans knew was that Whiskers was merely forwarding information prepared for him by new English controllers. His reports were aided a by notional network of agents supplying information from all parts of Algeria.

The acquisition that came to be most highly valued by the Allies was the double agent code-named Gilbert, actually World War I French officer André Latham. His was a strange story. When World War II began, he returned to the army to take command of a battalion that fought well until the French defeat in 1940. He then became involved with Frenchmen so opposed to Soviet Communism they were willing to collaborate with the Germans, even to the extent of fighting against the Russians on the eastern front. Before Latham could make that move, however, the Abwehr recruited him to go to French North Africa as chief of a band of secret agents. Latham's network was to gather both political information of interest to the French Fascist party and military information valuable to the Abwehr. Officially he became an officer on the French Army staff in Tunisia. When Tunis fell, the Abwehr wanted Latham to become a "stay-behind" agent reporting from within the enemy camp. He agreed. The next day, however, he sought out French intelligence and reported he was ready to turn himself in and work for the Allies. On June 10, 1943, his radio operator began transmitting to the Germans in France the mix of true and bogus information prepared by a new variation of the Twenty Committee. He soon became respected by the Germans as a valuable source while continuing to mislead them for fifteen months. Deception historian Thaddeus Holt places him alongside the Cheese channel and Garbo as the most important double agents of World War II.

At the conference of Anglo-American leaders in Casablanca in January 1943, the next step had already been decided. That was the invasion of Sicily, that tricornered island off the boot of Italy. Could the Allied deceivers mislead the Axis into believing the invasion target was *not* Sicily? Winston Churchill, for one, doubted it. "Anybody but a damned fool," he said, "would *know* it was Sicily."

It seemed a most logical conclusion. With only about one hundred sea miles separating the island from Tunisia, Sicily presented the nearest foothold in southern Europe. Capture of it would provide a stepping-stone for whatever larger operation the Allies might want to carry out. Bringing it under Allied control would remove an ever-present danger to Allied shipping in the Mediterranean. The prime minister's assessment seemed inarguable.

"A" Force and the London Controlling Section joined in taking on the mission of proving otherwise. So many Twenty Committee–type units were now supplying agents with information and misinformation for relay to the Abwehr that the new one in Algiers became known as the Forty Committee.

The task these cooperating teams took on was to secure the greatest possible surprise for the Sicily landings. Their scheme, Plan Barclay, had as its main objective that of weakening the enemy garrisons in Sicily by making other attack sites so plausible that the Axis would not only fail to reinforce the island but even diminish the forces that were there in order to reinforce more likely target areas.

Fortunately, the double agents already had a great deal going for them. "A" Force agents guided by Clarke had, slowly but surely, inflated the order of battle of the British forces in the Middle East until the Axis commanders accepted the idea they were facing twice as many divisions as actually existed. This gross overestimation of Allied strength made it feasible to convince Axis leaders that the Allies could mount not just one attack but several simultaneously.

Plan Barclay included three likely scenarios. In the west there would be an invasion of southern France. In the east the target would be Greece as the entrée into the Balkans. In the middle there would be landings not on Italy itself but on the Italian-held islands of Corsica and Sardinia, as support for the French landings.

Clarke's and Bevan's well-oiled deception machinery rumbled into action with its usual mingling of real and simulated measures. In Algiers, French soldiers received special training, ostensibly for landing on French shores. The air forces carried out sorties against Axis installations and conducted reconnaissance flights over possible invasion sites. Small teams of experts made beach landings to gain needed information to guide an invasion force, always leaving behind telltale evidence of their passage. Double agents, French and British, chronicled troop movements and armored concentrations. "A" Force in particular had become adept at making deliberate leakages of interesting information and in starting rumors. Radio deception presented a problem. The actual planning for Sicily could have generated a giveaway volume of traffic at Allied command posts in Tunis and Malta. To avoid this, communications were carried to the extent possible by landlines, while elsewhere reams of bogus messages filled the air.

Plans for the notional Balkan invasion in the east encountered the most serious challenge. The war in North Africa had swept westward, away from that area, leaving miles of empty desert. How could a convincing display of troops and equipment be observed by German recon flights? Answer: dummies and camouflage. The almost entirely notional Twelfth Army that had previously been established in the order of battle accepted by the Axis now had to have its presence substantiated. The creators of dummy spoofery outdid themselves, fashioning bogus quarters for more than 20,000 troops—their tentage, guns, transport vehicles and tanks, with their fake landing craft filling the harbors. Simulated displays of gliders were lined up ready to bear parachute troops to their drop zones. The schemers activated seven separate airfields, chockablock with a dozen squadrons of fighter planes. In actuality, the whole operation consisted of only nine real aircraft. These took to the air, seemingly on routine patrols, when German planes were known to be approaching. In addition to the pilots of these real planes, this whole spread of fakery was peopled by a small cadre of rear-echelon headquarters troops moved out of Cairo plus a South African labor contingent.

It fell to the Twenty Committee to produce what has become the best-known and most admired single deception of the war. This was Operation Mincemeat, the subject postwar of a bestselling book by one of its creators, Ewen Montagu.

Mincemeat was suggested by an actual happening in 1942. A British aircraft, one of many carrying officers around the coast of Spain to North Africa, had crashed into the sea. The body of one of those in the plane washed up on a Spanish shore. The victim was carrying documents that the German-courting Spanish authorities turned over to the Abwehr. On this occasion the documents had not turned out to be of serious import.

But what, B1A's flight lieutenant Charles Cholmondley asked himself, if they *had* been significant? He and Montagu cooked up an imaginative variation of the age-old scheme of a planted body carrying information to mislead the enemy. This time the secured body recovered by the Spaniards *would* be replete with papers of seemingly great value—papers that revealed Allied plans in the Mediterranean.

The two British plotters outdid themselves in covering every detail that would make the story credible to the Abwehr. A primary question was how to make it convincing that the man had drowned, since normal earth-bound corpses don't have seawater in their lungs. The forensic pathologist Sir Bernard Spilsbury assured them this was an unnecessary concern: in air crashes people die for many reasons. The next step was to find a suitable corpse. Their candidate was a homeless derelict named Glyndwr Michael, who had committed suicide by eating rat poison—an ideal choice, they agreed, because there were no relatives to raise questions. The body was placed in cold storage while Cholmondley and Montagu worked out the rest of their dupery.

They gave their intended plant a name and a title. He was William Martin, Captain (Acting Major), Royal Marines, a staff officer at Combined Operations in London. Providing him with an identity card that included a photograph turned out to be a stickler; his dead face refused to be made to look alive. Montagu solved that by finding a man who could have passed as Martin's double.

Next, the man had to be given a military expertise and an individual personality. They made him an expert on landing craft, a valid justification of his flight to North Africa. The contents of his uniform pockets revealed a lot about him. A Lloyd's Bank letter calling on him to pay off a sizable overdraft might indicate he was careless with money, except that it could also be explained by his being in love—he was carrying a bill in his pocket for the engagement ring he'd bought for his Pam. In his wallet was a snapshot of her and two letters well worn from being read and reread.

Also his jacket pocket held the halves of two tickets to the London play to which he'd taken Pam on his last night in England.

Lastly, the connivers had to think up the high-priority documents the major would be carrying. They dreamed up three of them. The first would be a letter of introduction from his superior, Admiral Lord Louis Mountbatten, addressed to Admiral Andrew Cunningham, Mediterranean commander-in-chief. Second were proof sheets of a manual on combined operations sponsored by Mountbatten, to which General Eisenhower had agreed to contribute a foreword—a document deliberately made too large to fit into a pocket, necessitating the major to carry a briefcase. Third was a personal letter from Lieutenant General Sir Archibald Nye to his good friend, General Sir Harold Alexander, Middle East commander-in-chief.

The letters made the claim that the British *wanted* the Germans to think that the landing would be in Sicily—that they were implanting the idea of Sicily as their invasion site in order to keep the enemy from learning the real targets. What *were* the real targets? Knowing that a too-obvious disclosure might arouse suspicion, the schemers inserted in one letter a throwaway line mentioning Greece and casually added the possibility of landings on the beaches of Cape Araxas and Kalamata. The only clue to a second target was in a jocular request in Mountbatten's letter that when Cunningham sent Major Martin back to London, he should carry with him a delicacy rationed in England—a serving of sardines. As Montagu explained, "I thought the rather labored joke about sardines would appeal to the Germans—and help to pinpoint Sardinia as the target of the assault." If the enemy had any question as to why one who was only an acting major had been entrusted with such important mail, the answer came in a note in Mountbatten's letter. The note affirmed how he valued Major Martin and added, "Let me have him back, please, as soon as the assault is over."

Couriers frequently made sure their dossiers were kept secure by chaining them to their clothing. So it was decided for Major Martin. He would be wearing a raincoat, and to it would be chained his briefcase.

How and where would the corpse be delivered? Expert advisers had answers. Packed in dry ice, it would be placed aboard a submarine and, properly uniformed, slipped into the waters off the Spanish port of Huelva. The currents were just right there to carry Major Martin onto the beach. Also, it was known that in Huelva there was a very active German agent who had the supposedly neutral Spaniards cooperating with him. The expectation was that the body would be turned over to the British vice-consul for burial but only after the carefully dried contents of the briefcase had been passed to the agent to be photocopied in Berlin before being returned to the British.

It was done. On the early morning of April 30, 1943, the submarine HMS *Seraph* surfaced, undetected, off Huelva. The *Seraph*'s skipper, Bill Jewel, had let only a few trusted fellow officers in on the secret. They gathered atop the sub, conducted a brief burial service and slipped the major into the sea. To add a finishing touch, a rubber dinghy from a British plane was likewise released.

Did the scheme work? Did it ever. The body was sighted later that same morning by a Spanish fisherman and recovered by local authorities. The postmortem: "asphyxiation by immersion in the sea." The victim's face was found to correspond with the photograph on the identity card. The British vice-consul was informed, and on May 2 Major Martin was buried with full military honors. Pam sent a wreath. The major's name was inserted in Britain's published casualty list, along with the names of two officers who had actually lost their lives in an air crash in the same area. Not until May 13, however, were the major's documents handed over to the British.

As subsequently became clear, the combined effects of the deceptions were all that could be hoped. The German High Command, finding the Mincemeat documents "absolutely convincing," sharply increased the numbers of German divisions in the Balkans and in Greece. Those in Greece included a Panzer division shifted from France to guard against the landings in Araxas and Kalamata. Minefields were laid off the Greek coast and coastal gun batteries installed. The Luftwaffe was ordered to conduct daily recon flights over the whole Greek coast from Corfu to Cape Matapan. A flotilla of torpedo boats was transferred from Sicily to Greece—leaving what was later bitterly recalled by German commanders as a fatal gap in the defenses of Sicily. On the very day of the Allied landings, Rommel arrived in Athens to take charge of the German army in the Balkans.

Similarly, two German divisions were landed on Corsica and Sardinia. To guard against "diversionary attacks during the assault on Sardinia," defenses were improved on the north coast of Sicily—opposite from the actual landing sites.

In his diary, German admiral Karl Doenitz recorded Hitler's convictions: "The Fuehrer does not agree . . . that the most likely invasion point is Sicily. He believes that the discovered Anglo-Saxon order confirms that the attack will be directed mainly against Sardinia and the Peloponnesus"— that is, the southern peninsula of Greece.

An amusing sidelight to Mincemeat was recorded in reminiscence by Noel Currer-Briggs, an analyst in Special Intelligence stationed in Tunisia. He told how he and his crew "were inspected one day by Alexander and Eisenhower. There we were working away at the German wireless traffic coming from the other side of the Mediterranean and we were saying, 'Oh yes. They've moved that division from Sicily to Sardinia and they've moved the other one to the Balkans,' and these two generals were jumping up and down like a couple of schoolboys at a football match. We hadn't a clue why. We thought: 'Silly old boffers.' It wasn't until 1953 when Montagu's book *The Man Who Never Was* came out that we realized we were telling them that the Germans had swallowed the deception hook, line and sinker." Or, as James Gannon preferred to express it: "body, chain and briefcase."

The German certainty that Sicily was not the immediate target held firm even after the Allies seized and made a base of the tiny island of Pantelleria, midway between Tunisia and Sicily. The double agents discounted the island's capture as merely a routine rounding-off of the Tunisian campaign and the removal of an obstacle to reopening the sea route between Gibraltar and Malta.

One final goal of the deception teams was to confuse the Axis commanders as to the timing of the landings. This was done by scheduling several major events the Axis was certain to learn about and then, at the last minute, canceling them. Eisenhower, as one example, ordered that no leave should be granted after June 20 only to countermand the order on

June 15. Similarly, workers at the ports where the invasion fleet was assembling were given a target date for completion of their tasks that was two weeks *after* the real date.

When Allied forces landed in southern Sicily on July 10, the surprise was complete. Only two German divisions, both of them recovering from having been mauled in the African battles, were there to assist the half-hearted Italian Sixth Army in resisting the invaders.

The success of the LCS-"A" Force deception plan extended well beyond its effect in securing surprise for the Sicilian landings. The plan also succeeded to an astonishing degree in meeting the objective of drawing German forces into the Balkans and into the south of France. On March 9 there were eight German divisions in the Balkans—six in Yugoslavia, one in Greece and one in Crete. On Sicilian D-Day, July 10, the total had increased to eighteen divisions. Of these, nine were in Greece and seven in Yugoslavia—a net of ten divisions added to the German Balkan armies. In southern France, the garrison had been increased by two divisions, and as previously noted two more had been sent to occupy Sardinia and Corsica.

To attribute these successes entirely to the deceptionists and double agents would, as military historian Michael Howard has pointed out, be overclaiming. Hitler, he notes in his book on World War II deceptions, was reluctant to commit troops to Sicily in the face of rampant rumors that Italy was about to withdraw from the conflict. The Fuehrer also believed that to send troops to Sicily would be a waste because the coming assault would not be against Sicily but against the Balkans. The German High Command agreed—agreed so strongly that even after Sicily was invaded they persisted in expecting Greece to be the target of a more serious assault. After all, something big must come from all that tremendous concentration of forces in the desert east of Cairo.

With the collaboration of Hitler and the German commanders, the Allied campaign to take Sicily got off to a gratifying start. Partly because of a puerile clash of egos between George Patton and Bernard Montgomery, however, the struggle was longer and more costly than necessary. Further, the opportunity to capture the Axis forces finally entrapped in the island's northeast corner was lost when the Allied generals failed to act on Ultra decrypts warning that evacuation of the men and their armor was under way across the Strait of Messina. Thousands of Axis troops who could have been held in Allied prison camps instead made it to the Italian mainland. There the German forces regrouped, ready to fight again.

Still, the campaign did drive Italy out of the war. On July 25, King Victor Emmanuel III summoned Mussolini to his palace, told him he was dismissed, had him arrested and appointed Field Marshal Pietro Badoglio to succeed him as head of the Italian government.

And the coda to Winston Churchill's original reaction to Sicilian landing alternatives is that the deception teams and their double agents did make fools out of a broad cross-section of German leadership.

CHAPTER SIXTEEN

PRELUDE TO FORTITUDE

Having secured North Africa and Sicily, the Allies faced the question, What next? The issue had been the subject of sharp argument at the Casablanca conference, with Winston Churchill advocating an attack on Italy and U.S. Army Chief of Staff George Marshall opposing it. No agreement was reached. Then the fall of Mussolini and the sudden collapse of the Italian army offered Italy as an opportunity target so inviting that even Marshall changed his mind.

Allied signals intelligence was closely tracking the German response to this fast-changing situation. The German forces in Italy had their hands full in dealing with what the Germans saw as Italy's betrayal that had led to the disemployment of thousands of Italian soldiers. As usual, German leaders could only guess at what the Allies might do. Allied deceptionists, by gaining German acceptance of an ingeniously inflated Allied order of battle, had greatly expanded the Germans' span of possible guesses. Although a drive into Italy was seen as a possibility, the number of divisions the Germans allotted to the Allies would provide the manpower for simultaneous campaigns against other objectives. Corsica and Sardinia were viewed as almost certain targets. The most likely Allied action by far continued to be foreseen as a drive against Greece as an entry into the Balkans.

The German High Command persisted in believing that the Balkans were the Allies' real goal even after Montgomery's Eighth Army made their landing on the toe of Italy's boot on September 3 and the combined

U.S.-British Fifth Army under General Mark Clark landed at Salerno on the west ankle of the boot on September 9.

A new question hung: Would the Germans, having lost the support of the Italian army, withdraw from Italy or would they make a fight for it? The answer came quickly. Hitler rushed in reinforcements both from the eastern front and the west wall.

Patton was out of the picture and in disgrace because of two incidents in which he had slapped GIs hospitalized for psychological troubles whom he considered malingerers.

The Allied campaign badly needed a commander with Patton's boldness. As it was, Montgomery delayed his landings to allow for a three-day bombardment of the nearly unoccupied sites before sending in his troops. The few dazed Italian survivors came down to the beaches to help unload the landing craft.

Clark was just as disastrously cautious in his Salerno landings. He allowed the Germans under the capable field marshal Albert Kesselring to hem in the invaders miles short of their objectives. The result was that instead of spreading out from their beachheads to form a continuous offensive line across Italy, the two Allied armies were pinned down with a 140-mile gap between them. The fighting settled into a virtual stalemate.

Desiring to break out of the deadlock, Churchill advocated a surprise landing farther up the coast at Anzio. The Italian campaign had started just three and a half weeks after the fall of Sicily—too soon to receive much help initially from deception planners or the double agents. By the time of the planning of the Anzio landing, however, the deception machinery was once more functioning. To disguise the Anzio landing, double agents led by Paul Nicossof in Cairo put out the story that Patton's old command, the Seventh Army, would mount pincer attacks against northern Italy, behind the German lines, with one force landing at Pisa on the west coast and the other at Rimini on the east. The usual hocus-pocus was called into play. The notional targets were reconnoitered and bombed. Assault troops were given maps as well as pamphlets explaining what artistic treasures were to be preserved, if possible. On Corsica, from which the attack on Pisa was to kick off, bogus encampments, hospitals and landing craft were made visible to Axis recon planes.

As a result, the Anzio landing on January 31, 1943, was a complete surprise. The invaders met with little opposition on the beaches and pushed inland. But after securing only a thumbnail of territory, the drive was stopped so that Clark and his on-site commander could "organize" their forces. By the time they were ready to resume the attack, Kesselring had moved in superior forces. He gave the Allies a severe beating and hemmed them in close to the shoreline. Churchill complained: "I had hoped that we were hurling a wildcat onto the shore, but all we had got was a stranded whale."

In all of these early operations, Bletchley Park played a significant role. At Salerno, a five-page Bletchley Park decrypt warned of the Germans' all-out attack as described to Hitler by Kesselring and told exactly how he expected to drive to the sea through a gap between the U.S. and British armies so as to mop them up one at a time. At Anzio, the beachhead was saved by what Bletchley Park historian F. H. Hinsley cited as "one of the most valuable decrypts of the whole war." It forewarned Clark of another powerful counterattack planned by Kesselring. The decrypt predicted precisely where the attack would hit. It was shattered not only by land artillery, tanks, tank destroyers and mortars but also by seven hundred Allied aircraft sorties and shelling by two Allied cruisers. The repulse marked the end of Kesselring's aggressive attempts in Italy.

Overall planners of the Italian invasion regarded its main purpose as that of drawing German troops and armor away from the fronts east and west and holding them there. To achieve that goal, though, required the Allies' Italian forces to keep the pressure on the Axis troops. The campaign became a bitter struggle up the peninsula's mountainous center that greatly favored defense over offense. Thousands of Allied soldiers died trying to take the German stronghold atop the massif where the Monte Cassino monastery was located. Only with the help of a bombing that utterly destroyed the monastery were the Allies able to force Kesselring's forces into retreat.

The long and bloody campaign finally climaxed with the capture of Rome by Clark's Fifth Army just two days before D-Day. Even that was a tarnished triumph. To direct his forces toward Rome and the glory of being its conqueror, Clark had to ignore the agreed-on plan that his army's main mission was to strike eastward to block the escape routes for Kesselring's retreating forces. Thousands of German soldiers who should have ended the war in graves or Allied prison camps pressed through to fight again in Normandy.

They could not be transferred there in time for D-Day, however, and that fact alone justified the whole costly campaign.

An unexpected bonus of the control of Italy was "A" Force's acquisition of additional double agents. Such was the low ebb of trust in World War II that Italian intelligence used double agents against their supposed Fascist ally. As the British and American armies drove northward, Italian agents began popping up and volunteering to continue their spying against the Germans, except now it would be for the Allies. Most important of these new recruits was a senior officer in the Italian air force code-named Armour. As Michael Howard has noted, Armour "moved in the highest social and political circles in Italy and was reported to be a personal friend of Marshal Badoglio himself." He was highly regarded by the Abwehr and, now under Allied auspices, continued to supply the Germans with artfully slanted information.

A second addition was Apprentice, a Yugoslav whose hatred for the Communist partisans in his country had gained him the confidence of the German intelligence services. In 1944 the Germans parachuted him behind the Allied lines. He promptly surrendered. As his cover he notionally accepted the task of teaching the Serb language to Allied officers, whose overheard indiscretions gave him material for his reports to the Abwehr. Altogether the new agents opened up a half-dozen additional channels for "A" Force, further broadening the network Dudley Clarke was able to call upon for his deceptions of the Germans.

While all this was happening in what Churchill liked to call "the soft underbelly of Europe," it was also necessary to maintain Allied pressure on the German occupation forces in the north during 1943. Since no real second front was to be opened, the responsibility to keep the Germans on guard until Operation Fortitude—the overall deception for D-Day—would take over fell largely to the deception teams and the double agents.

The Britain-based deception team came up with Plan Cockade, which included three main parts. Plan Tindall called for again cranking up the deception machinery in Scotland to threaten an invasion of Norway and thus hold in place the excessive number of occupation forces that Hitler felt to be necessary. This time the notional target was the port of Stavanger, on the southeast coast of Norway. It was in range of airborne attack from Scotland and had airfields whose seizure could support an invasion force.

Plan Starkey involved another threatened landing on the northern French coast, this time on the Pas de Calais. This seemed an odd choice, considering that the Pas was to figure prominently in the D-Day Fortitude deceptions. Advocates for it argued that "every artifice must be employed to draw his [the enemy's] attention to his most sensitive spot." Roger Hesketh, the chief planner of Fortitude, later wrote: "Whether Starkey was really an asset to deception in 1944 may be doubted."

Whatever its merits, Starkey included a second amphibious feint in the Channel, meant to induce the Germans to believe that landing barges were on the way. The hope also was to stir the Luftwaffe into an air battle in order to pare down the numbers of planes available to the Germans on D-Day.

The third deception, Plan Wadham, was an all-American show. Its purpose was to convince the Germans that U.S. forces would launch a combined seaborne and airborne attack on the western French port of Brest, a haven for U-boats. An American corps already in the UK would cross the Channel to capture Brest, while a second U.S. corps would sail directly from the United States to exploit the capture.

In order to support this complex of plans, "A" Force in Cairo organized its own deception scheme. Plan Zeppelin was devised to pin down German troops in the eastern Mediterranean so they would not be transferred to northern France to oppose the Normandy landings. Middle Eastern forces that included the notional British Twelfth Army would mount threats against Greece, the Dalmatian coast and Crete. The Soviets were to cooperate by a notional attack on the Black Sea and the Greek mainland.

These 1943 plans were far more ambitious than those attempted in 1942. As an example, the Starkey feint toward the French coast was to be made by a naval force that included two battleships, twelve destroyers, twenty-four minesweepers, fifty-nine smaller ships and all the landing craft and merchant shipping that could be spared. Aerial cover would be provided by forty-five British and fifteen American fighter squadrons, while U.S. and RAF bombers would carry out raids on beach defenses.

The services were appalled by the demands. The Admiralty made it clear that it was not going to hazard any of its battleships in such a maneuver. The commander of the U.S. Eighth Air Force could spare only a much smaller number of aircraft and limit them to a fraction of the planned support sorties. As for Bomber Command's air chief marshal Arthur Harris, he ridiculed the deception as "a piece of harmless play-activity" and refused to cooperate at all.

In addition, the plans called for extensive use of dummy gliders, airplanes and landing craft. An example of the unrealistic demands placed on those who would supply the dummy materials was provided by Plan Tindall. The colonel in charge of the preparations was asked to supply overnight camouflage covering for 215 gliders in Scotland. He pointed out that the preparation would require 22,000 man-weeks to do the job, that the material for the task would amount to a rectangle a mile long by half a mile wide and that the metal bracing would consume 5,000 tons of steel. Needless to say, the plans had to be revised drastically downward.

One more problem encountered by the Starkey planners was their overzealous call for a series of fourteen raids on the French coast by small groups of commandos. The aim was to suggest to the Germans that the raiders were seeking information of value to the coming invasion. One raid was supposed to capture a German soldier and bring him back for interrogation. It was not successful, nor were any of the others. The Germans took no notice whatever.

The planned feint toward the Pas de Calais was equally ignored. The convoys had been reduced to two naval and nineteen merchant ships. They approached within ten miles of the coast, in sight of Calais, and awaited the bombardment from coastal guns and attacks by Luftwaffe planes. Neither occurred. Under cover of a smoke screen, the convoys turned for home.

If anything positive was to be achieved by Cockade, it was pretty largely left to the double agents. Once again they responded vigorously.

Bronx and Gelatine used their diplomatic and social contacts to ferret out information about the Allied plans by "overhearing" prominent individuals' indiscreet remarks.

Brutus sent lengthy reports about the preparations he saw for new offensive operations against northwest Europe. In March he was in Scotland to observe troop movements into the area. In April he reported the concentrations being built up along the south coast of England. And in July he was in the southeast and was alarmed by the large numbers of troops obviously moving toward an amphibious assault across the Channel.

Mutt, joined by Jeff's impersonator, once again went into their act of building the threat of a Scotland-based invasion of Norway. They were aided by the local press, which ran accounts of the mostly notional Fourth Army's football matches, and by the BBC in Scotland, whose reporter spent a day with the VII Corps in the field.

By this time Dusko Popov—Tricycle—had returned from his ill-fated American detour and was seeking an opportunity to reestablish himself with the Abwehr. He found it in Cockade. His travels in Britain gave him material for copious reports on offensive concentrations of troops— British divisions in the Midlands, an Anglo-Canadian force on the south coast, the Americans flooding into the west country, the troops being trained in Scotland for an attack on Norway. He described the clever manufacture, in inland factories, of the parts for landing craft that were then sent to coastal warehouses where they could be rapidly assembled when the call came. In July he returned to Lisbon, this time with extensive notes compiled during a notional tour of south coast towns during which he had observed ominous troop movements as well as the preparation of a great number of hospital beds for expected casualties.

As usual, both the British and the Germans relied most heavily on Garbo and his network. In support of Plan Wadham, two of his subagents independently reported U.S. exercises in south Wales as training for a cross-Channel foray into Brittany. In actuality, Garbo was taking advantage of exercises meant not for Wadham but for the D-Day landings.

Plan Tindall received attention both from Garbo's subagent in Scotland and from Garbo himself. The subagent's reports on the preparations for an attack on Scandinavia prompted Garbo to go to Scotland to consult with his aide and to see for himself. From Glasgow he mailed a letter in which he warned of commandos training in mountain warfare, of new camps being built near airfields to accommodate airborne forces and of transport planes arriving, presumably to fly the parachute troops to their drop zones.

Garbo became aware, though, that Plan Starkey took precedence over the other deceptions. On his return to London, he told the Germans, he found himself awaited by his subagent in southern England, who reported urgent preparations for an attack that seemed pointed toward the Pas de Calais. Garbo immediately went to Brighton to see for himself. His trip resulted in a series of messages detailing the concentration of troops and matériel along the south coast. The Twenty Committee got approval for him to tell the Germans that the attack target was Pas de Calais and then to transmit a last-minute alert that the attack would come on the following morning.

What was to be done to keep Garbo from being discredited when the assault never reached beyond mid-Channel? For one with his agile mind, there was no problem. He had one of his imaginary subagents on hand when the troops disembarked, and the agent's report was that they were surprised and disappointed by not being allowed to follow through with the landing. Garbo also seized upon an official announcement in the British press and on the BBC that this had been merely a large-scale training exercise. That was a lie, he thundered indignantly. The convoys were sent on a real invasion attempt meant to focus German attention on northern France while an Allied disembarkation was taking place in Italy. The change in Allied plans, he said, was in response to breaking news of the armistice in Italy, which had made it unnecessary to do more than conduct an exercise in the Channel.

Relaying Garbo's explanations to Berlin, his spymaster Kuehlanthal went beyond merely saying the returning troops were disappointed. "The measure," he told Berlin, "caused disgust among the troops."

Bletchley Park decrypted Berlin's reaction. Abwehr superiors called Garbo's work "first class" and instructed Kuehlanthal to tell him to please continue to keep an eye on troop movements, preparations and possible embarkations.

Despite its shortcomings and failures, Plan Starkey, with the aid of the double agents, once again found believers in von Rundstedt and his staff. They officially reported "the British measures of the previous week to have been a large-scale preliminary rehearsal for a genuine attack to be launched against our west coast. By these measures the enemy has got to know the weaknesses of our artillery coastal defenses and of our air force and air defenses and will be able to turn that experience to his own advantage." The report added that "the transition to a real invasion attack is possible at any time."

Similarly, "A" Force's Plan Zeppelin was successful in helping to maintain German tensions about an offensive against the Balkans. The long buildup of mythical additions to the Middle East order of battle begun by Dudley Clarke never seemed to have been doubted by the Germans. At the beginning of 1943, the British Twelfth Army in the Middle East, consisting notionally of twelve divisions, counted five real divisions and three real, but inflated, brigades. By April, however, the Twelfth's real core totaled only two divisions and three brigades—three divisions had been siphoned off as reinforcements in the Italian campaign. The Germans took no notice when bogus divisions replaced the departed ones. Double agents joined with the visual deception crew and bogus wireless traffic to maintain the illusion of a powerful army ready to spring—an illusion that helped meet "A" Force's goal of holding German forces in southeast Europe well past the date of the D-Day landings.

One other successful deception program deserving mention was Plan Larkhall. Its purpose was to do for the American forces in Britain what plans initiated by Dudley Clarke and his colleagues had been doing for Britain: inflate the order of battle. In May of 1943, when Larkhall was launched, there were only 107,000 American troops in the United Kingdom. By generating rumors and enlisting the aid of double agents, the numbers of American troops arriving in Britain were cannily exaggerated. By August, when the actual number had reached 330,000, the Germans accepted a total of 570,000—a spread between fact and fiction that continued to widen.

How the creation of thousands of mythical Americans was put to use is one of the extraordinary stories yet to be told.

CHAPTER SEVENTEEN

DOUBLE CROSS IN JEOPARDY

In retrospect the double-cross system can be seen as the most fragile of institutions. One discredited or "blown" agent could have set the Abwehr leaders to questioning whether the whole network of their spies in the United Kingdom was suspect. As J. C. Masterman expressed it: "No one can maintain a bluff indefinitely. Sooner or later a blunder or sheer mischance will give it away. If the Germans once gained full knowledge of our procedures in one case, they would inevitably become suspicious of the rest, examine them in every detail, and end by guessing the truth about them all."

Yet it never happened. The German secret services were not peopled by dummkopfs; some of the more intelligent men in the German military were assigned to it. Why did not at least one of them blow the whistle?

There are two plausible answers. One is fear. The Nazi dictatorship was ruled by an eccentric and unstable man who had never hesitated to liquidate a supposed enemy. The whole power structure was shot through with a gnawing distrust of one's neighbors. Many Abwehr spymasters enjoyed comfortable, cushy jobs that depended on continuing to draw from their spies a steady stream of information judged to be of value to the war effort. To admit that a spy had been hoodwinking his controller was not likely to win applause. On the contrary, such honesty was likely to send the official to the Russian front or a concentration camp, if he wasn't summarily shot by the Gestapo.

The other reason was hatred. Behind the majority of those Germans throwing stiff-armed salutes and shouting enthusiastic "Sieg Heils" there was a covert minority who deplored what had happened to their country and wanted to see an end to it. Johnny Jebsen was by no means alone among Abwehr officers in his underground opposition to the Nazis. The Abwehr's chief, Admiral Canaris, was at least sympathetic. He never joined the Nazi Party, was eventually dismissed from his job and, after the failed 1944 bomb plot to assassinate Hitler, was found guilty of being one of the conspirators and was executed.

Of the examples of German officers whose anti-Nazi sentiments stifled their exposure of suspected double agents, the case of Colonel (later General) Erwin Lahousen stands out. His duties brought him into contact with Eddie Chapman. In the diary he kept of his World War II experiences, Lahousen recorded his certainty that Chapman's expressed loathing of the British was only a pose. Other entries in the diary, though, disclose the colonel's growing animus against the Nazis that kept him silent about this probable British spy.

A similar case is that of Georg Sessler, a lieutenant attached to the Abwehr's Hamburg team and another of Canaris's deputies who was anti-Nazi. He became involved in the problems with Arthur Owens, Snow. It will be remembered that for his meetings in Lisbon with Nikolaus Ritter, his controller, Owens was joined by Walter Dicketts, the agent codenamed Celery, whom the Germans wanted to train as a demolitions expert. Sessler took custody of Dicketts for the trip to Berlin, where this new agent was to receive his training and also undergo interrogation. Sessler's contacts with Dicketts convinced him that the man was a British plant. But he kept his misgivings bottled up until after the war when it became his turn to be interrogated—by the Allies.

As for the Abwehr controllers of double agents, postwar analyses found evidence that a number of them did suspect that their agents had been turned but simply ignored their misgivings. A British National Archives file, as an example, relates a postwar interview with a prisoner of war who knew Garby-Czerniawski and repeatedly had the feeling that this agent was "working under control," particularly because Garby-Czerniawski "could have produced very much more valuable information than he did if he had really wished to." The prisoner added that he had voiced his doubts to his superiors and had found that they shared his suspicions, yet nothing was done and Garby-Czerniawski's reports continued to be "considered valuable to the end."

To quote Masterman again: "Information secured after the end of hostilities supports our surmise that some Abwehr officials willfully shut their eyes to suspicions about their agents. They thought it better for selfish reasons to have corrupt or disloyal agents than to have no agents at all."

Then there were the times when an agent was involved in a deception that successfully deluded the Germans. The British case officers could understandably have concluded that when the Germans realized they had been tricked, the agent would be unmasked and his case officer would have to kiss him good-bye. Not so. Invariably the Abwehr spymaster came up with credible explanations of the slipup other than the real one. The most common justification was that the spy had also been deceived by the British. All lapses were excused, and the agent proceeded to his next deception.

Of this tendency for spymasters to reject proof of their agents' betrayal, the prime example is this: the British deliberately tried to blow an agent, to make it unavoidably clear that this one agent was being run under British control—and the attempt did not succeed! The idea was to give the Germans a false idea of the methods used in running such an agent so as to convince them that the other agents were genuine. The scheme failed to work, even though in Masterman's words "the gaffes committed were crass and blatant." The agent's controller waved away all the signs and, at least officially, continued to regard his spy as genuine and reliable.

While these evidences of complicity were reassuring to the British, however, the double-cross officials could not afford to let down their guard. They had to keep reminding themselves there could be one spymaster who, when faced with incontrovertible proof of betrayal, would be brave enough, self-sacrificing enough, to sound the alarm. Even with all the care they could muster, the British were faced with many moments when the whole double-cross system seemed to hang by a thread.

One of the closest calls was precipitated by Gösta Caroli, the double agent code-named Summer. Captured after his parachute landing in Britain, Caroli submitted almost too readily to being turned. Unlike his compatriot Wulf Schmidt—Tate—he apparently never reconciled himself to being a double agent, even though, prewar, he had lived in England and spoke the language well. Unaware of his inner doubts, the London Controlling Section set him up in a guarded house and assigned him a case officer. Trouble developed when his conversations with his case officer revealed that, in his preliminary interviews, he had not told the truth about his previous time in England. No doubt his feelings were hardened when the British closed down his case and put him in prison. While there he made a vain attempt to commit suicide. Deciding to take another chance on Caroli, the LCS once again established him, still under guard, in a house in Hinxton from which he was able to transmit the messages the Twenty Committee prepared for him.

Caroli bided his time until the day came, in January 1941, when he was left with only one guard in the house. Although protesting that "it hurts me more than it hurts you," Caroli attacked his guard, nearly strangled him and took off on a motorbike, with a canoe retrieved from the shed of the house lashed to its side. Apparently he planned to escape across the sea to the Continent. Then his luck ran out. The bike broke down and the manhunt that had been organized caught up with him. Instead of alerting the Germans to his double-agent past, he spent the rest of the war in prison. Wulf Schmidt reported to the Abwehr that Caroli was no longer operative, having been "compelled to suspend security operations for pressing reasons."

If Caroli's escape attempt had succeeded, Masterman later wrote, it "would have wrecked all of our schemes."

In 1943, the system was threatened by another turned agent who regretted having been turned. This was the Norwegian Tor Glad—the Jeff of Mutt and Jeff. He had been found "recalcitrant" and jailed at Dartmoor. But he evidently still dreamed of becoming a hero to the Germans by exposing the whole double-cross system. One way he hoped to do this was by sneaking a letter to a prisoner of war, Erich Karl, who had been a member of the German War Graves Commission before being interned by the British. Now seriously ill, Karl was about to be repatriated and could be expected to bear Glad's information with him. And in fact he was returned to Germany before anyone in the know about Glad's letter managed to stop the transfer. But was Karl too ill to act on the information? Or did he simply decide not to? No one ever found out for sure, but the only thing that came of the incident was a lot of nail biting among those aware of the threat.

Although the British tried mightily to avoid eyebrow-raising coincidences in the messages sent by the various double agents, they did not always succeed. A particularly noticeable trio of potentially incriminating messages was sent on May 24, 1944, by Brutus, Tate and one of Garbo's Welsh subagents. The occasion was an exercise in preparation for the D-Day deceptions. Flights of fighter aircraft based in the Southampton area were sent against targets in northeastern France to demonstrate to the Germans how the Allied planes could shift to airfields closer to the coast in order to reach the Pas de Calais area. If the three double agents had merely observed the aircraft in flight, there would have been no exposure to risk. But all three of the agents also reported the objective of the exercise. As Roger Hesketh has observed, "That this very singular operational intelligence should simultaneously have reached the ears of a Polish staff officer, a Welshman resident in Dover and a German prisoner of war working on a farm in Kent, all of them enemy agents, was indeed straining German incredulity. Had the Germans analyzed and compared the traffic of their agents at the time it was received, their suspicions could hardly have failed to be aroused." But if anyone in the Abwehr did notice, he kept his suspicions to himself.

In June 1943, a huge threat was posed by Mrs. Garbo, Aracelli Pujol. Tomás Harris, Juan Pujol's case officer, characterized her as "a hysterical, spoilt and selfish woman" but also one who was "intelligent and astute." The journey she made in 1942 to join Pujol in London was the first time she had ever been outside the Iberian Peninsula. She was trouble from the first. Life in England did not suit her, she couldn't learn the language and she felt a desperate need to return to Spain to see her mother. Pujol did not help matters by refusing to associate with Spanish people in London. He also insisted on staying clear of the Spanish embassy, on the grounds that he and his work could be endangered if he was known to be in contact with members of the embassy after having told the Germans that he was now out of those circles. He explained to her that it was always possible that someone in the embassy might be in touch with the Germans, and that for him to make himself known there could be most dangerous. For these reasons, he denied her request to return to Spain, even though she threatened to break up the marriage by leaving him.

He did permit a friendship to form with another Spanish couple, the Guerras. The time came, however, when the Guerras invited the Pujols to attend a dinner at the Spanish Club at which all the embassy personnel were to be present. Señora Pujol, of course, was eager to go. When Pujol explained why he could not allow it, she saw an opportunity. To assert that she meant to visit the embassy on her own, she thought, would frighten Pujol's English controllers into paying attention to her request for a visit to Spain. She and Pujol quarreled violently, and Pujol left the house to place a call to Harris warning him of what might happen.

She did call Harris and broadened her threat. If the English didn't act immediately to prepare the papers for her to return to Spain, she said, she *would* go to the embassy and tell what she knew.

Pujol, informed of her call, doubted that she would carry out her threat, but then, considering the worked-up state she was in, he agreed that she very well might. He and Harris planned that after Pujol left the house the following morning, Harris was to call Mrs. Garbo and tell her she would receive her answer by seven o'clock that evening. It was also agreed that the British would keep a watch on the embassy and that if Señora Pujol approached it, she would be apprehended.

When the ever-resourceful Pujol met with the British that afternoon, he had evolved a plan. And what a plan.

He wrote a short note to his wife to tell her he had been jailed and to request that she hand to the bearer his toilet implements and his pajamas. When the note was delivered, she became hysterical and refused to accede to his requests. She did what the planners hoped she would do: she called Harris. The gist of her tearful call was to ask how the Brits could do this to her husband, who had always been loyal and was willing to sacrifice his life for the country.

Harris explained that when Pujol and his controllers had met that afternoon with the chief, the British had decided that Señora Pujol should be given her papers to return to Spain but that Pujol and the children should go with her. Before doing this, Pujol was to write a letter to the Germans giving some excuse for discontinuing his work. Pujol's reaction, she was told, was to become greatly agitated and offensive to the chief. The British, he said, had made a contract with him and he refused to let it be broken. Even if they approved his wife's returning to Spain, they could not force him to do so, and they certainly could not force him to write that letter to the Germans. He would go to prison first. The chief's reply to him was that the British needed the letter to protect their interest against a betrayal by his wife in Spain as she had threatened here in England. She was told that when the word "betrayal" was mentioned by the chief, Pujol completely lost his temper and behaved so violently that his immediate arrest had been necessary.

Señora Pujol's reply was that her husband had behaved just as she would have expected him to do. She said that after the sacrifices he had made, after having his whole life wrapped up in his work, she could well understand that he would rather go to prison than sign that letter.

It sounded as though the scheme had worked. But the señora was not one to give in so easily. That evening she called Pujol's wireless operator and asked him to come to the house. He arrived to find her sitting in the kitchen with all the gas jets turned on. Later that evening she again attempted suicide. The easy verdict was that she was just playacting, but the British took no chances. They arranged for someone to stay the night at her house.

The next morning she requested an interview. At it she said she had been at fault and that if her husband could be pardoned she would never again interfere with his work nor ask to return to Spain. She signed a statement that included these points.

So far so good, but the charade had to be played out to the end. Señora Pujol was told she could see her husband in detention that afternoon. A car would pick her up at four o'clock. At Camp 020, Pujol was brought to her dressed in prison clothing and unshaven. She swore she had not been to the Spanish embassy and never really intended to go there, and that if he was released from prison, she would help him in every way to continue his work with even greater zeal than before. The next day she was told that her husband had made his appearance before the tribunal and it had recommended that he be allowed to resume his work. That evening the Pujols had their grand reunion. The señora was a lady of her word. She did not again cause trouble for her husband—at least insofar as his duties as a double agent were concerned.

In Harris's postwar summary of the Garbo case, as reprinted in the recent publication *Garbo: The Spy Who Saved D-Day,* he includes the whole of the statement Pujol supposedly gave to the tribunal but whose real purpose was to convince his wife not to repeat her performance. In his inimitable overblown style, his statement goes on for too many pages to be included here. As a sample, the passage that nailed down the señora's pledge reads:

> I found, by means of questions, that she did not go to the Spanish Embassy; nor did the watcher placed by you see any sign of her prowling in the neighbourhood. My wife declares that she did not go and never had any intention of going, and is so certain of this, and I presume will still be so in the future, that I am prepared to sign a document making myself responsible for all her future actions which are directly or indirectly related to the services I am voluntarily performing in this country.

*   *   *

The gravest threat to the double-cross system came almost on the eve of D-Day. It involved Popov's friend Johnny Jebsen. Theirs had been a relationship that proved beneficial to both of them. The wealthy Jebsen had aided Popov's family in Yugoslavia during the chaotic times there of partisan strife. His recruitment of Popov to serve the Abwehr was a feather in Jebsen's cap, since Popov was regarded as one of the Abwehr's most outstanding agents. The friendship had deepened when Jebsen confirmed his anti-Nazi sentiments to Popov and agreed to become a double agent code-named Artist. Now, though, the show was coming to a close. Jebsen's financial deals had stirred envy and made enemies, and his open association in Lisbon with known anti-Nazi Germans had aroused the suspicions of Heinrich Himmler's secret intelligence service, the Sicherheitsdienst, or SD.

Knowing he might be in danger if he returned to Germany or German-occupied territory, Jebsen rejected repeated attempts to draw him across into occupied France. The SD was not to be thwarted. Their agent Alois Schreiber went to Lisbon, where he found that Jebsen had invited an Abwehr friend to visit him at his villa in Estoril. The friend was viewed with as much suspicion as Jebsen. Schreiber and a couple of SD underlings purchased two metal trunks big enough for humans and fitted with openings for ventilation. They also bought a knockout potion from a Lisbon pharmacist.

Schreiber called Jebsen and his friend to a meeting in Schreiber's office. There the SD team drugged the pair into unconsciousness, packed them into the trunks and recrossed the border. Jebsen was flown to Berlin to be interrogated in the Gestapo prison there.

Jebsen's arrest, revealed to the British by Ultra decrypts, rang alarm bells in the LCS and the Twenty Committee. The risk involved in running him as Artist had been justified by the excellent inside-the-Abwehr information he delivered. But now the decision to take the risk seemed foolhardy. Here was a double agent living on the Continent, constantly within the Germans' grasp. If he agreed to, or was tortured into, disclosing what he knew, the consequences could be catastrophic. There was hope that Jebsen's arrest was due to his financial dealings rather than evidence of his dealings as a double agent, but who could be sure?

The suspense was heightened by MI5's awareness that the long clash between Canaris and Himmler over which group should operate the German spy system had ended in Himmler's favor. Canaris was ousted and Himmler's deputies took over. The meaning for Jebsen was that as a captive of Himmler, he could no longer look to the Abwehr to intervene in his behalf.

Analysis of the situation convinced the British that their most serious point of vulnerability was Popov. Whether Himmler's organization knew of Popov's ties to Jebsen was not clear, but many in the Abwehr were certainly aware of them. Consequently, although the LCS had expected the Popov link to take a prominent part in the D-Day deceptions, now the decision was made to close down the channel and rule Tricycle out of the artifice altogether.

As it turned out, this drastic step was an unnecessary precaution. Whether or not the Gestapo ever used violent means to force Jebsen to talk is not known. If they did, they failed to break him. He went to his death in the Gestapo prison, and the Germans were no wiser as to when and where the invasion would come.

CHAPTER EIGHTEEN

THE "GRAND STRATEGIC DECEPTION"

The Twenty Committee's kingpin, John Masterman, wrote: "From the beginning of 1944 all our activities were swallowed up in the absorbing interest of the grand strategic deception for the Normandy invasion. The climax which we had hoped for from the beginning was approaching and all other aspects of the work sank into insignificance—at least for the time."

Until then the Allies' deceptions had had the straightforward purpose of holding enemy formations in place rather than allowing them to be transferred as reinforcements on other fronts. This was also a goal for the D-Day deceits. But now the deceptions took on an added dimension, one that derived from the logistics of amphibious operations. In a seaborne assault, success depends on the ability of the attackers to sustain a more rapid rate of reinforcement by sea than the defenders can achieve by land. The challenge in northern France was expected to be especially difficult. There the defenders were well-established and on the alert, and not too far inland were ample mobile reserves ready to move toward the landings on a moment's notice. Allied leaders knew that with all their huge fleet of ships and landing craft, they still could not hope to get enough men, armor and supplies ashore in the opening hours of the invasion to withstand the massive counterattacks the Germans could speedily launch against them. It was up to the deception planners to devise schemes that would hold those reserves away until the beachheads were strong enough not to be dislodged. A special concern was the Germans' veteran, well-mechanized Fifteenth Army, a key element in Army Group B commanded by Erwin Rommel. Stationed in the Pas de Calais, just two hundred miles from the invasion beaches, the Fifteenth had the power and the mobility to fall swiftly upon those first invaders and drive them back into the sea. The Allies also knew from Ultra decrypts that Rommel favored the strategy of attacking the invaders on the beaches, bitterly disagreeing with his superior, Field Marshal von Rundstedt, who believed in waiting until the landings were made before mobilizing his more centralized reserves to crush them. Allied commanders looked to the deceptionists to frustrate Rommel by delaying his attack.

In an interview with a deception planner early in 1944, Dwight Eisenhower expressed his belief that if Allied deceptions could hold the Fifteenth Army away from the Normandy beaches for just two days after the invasion, the Anglo-American forces would gain enough time to secure the beachheads and build up the strength to withstand inevitable German counterattacks.

If one considers only the opening day, Allied shipping did an amazing job. At the end of D-Day the fleet had landed 75,215 British and Canadian troops and 57,510 Americans, while 23,000 Airborne troops had been dropped or landed in gliders. Even so, Allied leaders remained convinced that if on that first day Rommel had been allowed to do as he so vehemently wished to do, the results for the Allies would have been tragic.

That it never happened and Rommel continued to be restrained to the Calais area came as the result of the Allied deception strategy developed over the previous months.

A tremendous reassurance for the Allies was that by the spring of 1944 the intelligence advantage had swung almost entirely their way. In terms of cryptography, British triumphs over the German code machines, combined with American successes against the device used by Japanese diplomats and military attachés reporting from Europe, were enabling the Allies to listen in as German leaders discussed their options and came to their decisions—this at a time when German cryptographers were all but shut out from penetrating Allied codes.

German intelligence was in disarray because the long struggle between

Admiral Canaris's Abwehr and Heinrich Himmler's SD organization for control of German espionage had been resolved in Himmler's favor and the dismissal of Canaris. Alarmed initially by this development, Britain's double-cross organization soon found, to their relief, that the new Nazi chiefs were inexperienced and inept insofar at least as handling the British network. What was originally seen as a loss for the Allies turned out to be a gain, since the bumbling SD proved to be more trusted by German generals than the Abwehr and consequently exerted a more powerful, if more easily misled, influence.

With their cryptanalysts impotent and aerial reconnaissance virtually nonexistent, German commanders faced the coming invasion almost totally dependent for their intelligence on their spy network, never suspecting that their agents in England were telling them only what British controllers wanted them to hear.

The deceptionists of the London Controlling Section in Britain and of "A" Force and SIME in the Middle East had, as we have seen, brought their art to a high point of perfection in everything from visual tricks and dummy armor to simulated radio traffic and the leakage of misleading rumors.

Most important, the slow and patient British effort that had, since the war's earliest days, been adding notional strength to the order of battle had reached a peak, thanks to the Germans' Velcro-like tendency never to remove a formation once it had been pressed onto the Berlin scoreboard. As the result of this steady augmentation, the Germans believed they faced vastly greater Allied strength in manpower than actually existed. The Germans were, accordingly, willing to grant the feasibility of the Allies' launching of several major attacks in unison.

Consider the numbers. In October 1943, when the reality was that Allied strength in the United Kingdom amounted to twelve infantry divisions, four armored and one airborne, for a total of seventeen divisions, Ultra decrypts revealed the Germans' evaluation as forty-three divisions, composed of twenty-six infantry, fourteen armored and three airborne.

In a November speech in Munich, German general Alfred Jodl amplified even those formidable figures. His estimate was that the Allied forces in the UK totaled forty infantry divisions and nine armored, with four independent infantry and eleven armored brigades, two airborne divisions and seven parachute battalions.

A sly note about the Germans' proclivity to cling to an entry in the Allied order of battle once they had acknowledged its existence is cited in Roger Hesketh's book *Fortitude*. He describes how at one point the British invented a largely notional Fourth Army and an entirely fictitious Sixth Army. The Fourth became a valued part of Allied deceptions, but as for the Sixth, he notes: "The Sixth Army we did not need again, but never succeeded in destroying. It remained a part of the German version of the Allied Order of Battle until the end of the war."

The strongest boost of all came from an unlikely source: the seemingly conscientious German officer chiefly responsible for determining the Allied order of battle. He was Colonel Alexis Baron von Roenne, from a distinguished family of the Prussian aristocracy. The trouble the colonel faced as an order of battle analyst was that his reports had to be filtered through Himmler's SD before being passed on to Hitler, and the SD, to "ensure their accuracy," consistently cut Roenne's estimates in half. Roenne feared that these low numbers would persuade Hitler to transfer formations away from the west wall instead of doing what Roenne felt was essential, which was to reinforce the defenders in the west. What to do? A subordinate came forward with a suggestion: *double* the submitted numbers so that when they were halved they would be true and accurate. Roenne rejected the idea but then, in desperation, came back to it. And this time his new totals, submitted in May 1944, went through without being halved—the SD officer who had done the cutting was no longer there. The result was that on the eve of D-Day the Wehrmacht believed it was opposed by eighty-five to ninety Allied divisions and seven airborne divisions instead of thirty-five, including the airborne, which was the reality. It's unclear why Roenne never acted to correct this error, but perhaps by then he had had a change of heart. This much is known: Roenne was found to be one of the conspirators involved in the July 1944 attempt to assassinate Hitler and was executed.

In contrast to the Germans' gross distortions of Allied strength, Allied estimates of the German order of battle turned out to be almost exactly accurate.

One final huge advantage for the Allies was that Ultra decrypts revealed the Nazi leaders' preconceptions as to where the invasion forces would land. Lacking any stone of certainty on which to base their decisions, German commanders could build a good foundation of reason under virtually every possibility from the north of Norway to the Mediterranean. German navy admirals, as an example, felt sure the landings would come near Le Havre, since the Allies would need a large port. Some generals thought the most likely target was the Biscay peninsula; others were convinced the Allies would eschew the dangers of a landing in northern France and invade a less well-protected site such as Bordeaux on the west coast.

In this game of foreseeing the *Schwerpunkt,* the decisive point, no one could surpass Adolf Hitler. As one of his generals reported in a postwar interview: "Hitler was constantly on the jump—at one moment he expected an invasion in Norway, at another moment in Holland, then near the Somme, or Normandy and Brittany, in Portugal, in Spain, in the Adriatic. His eyes were hopping all over the map."

Gradually commanders including Rommel and von Rundstedt narrowed their focus to what they felt sure was the most likely invasion site. That was the Pas de Calais, the jut of land in northern France that shortened the Channel crossing to just twenty miles. The Pas had been, after all, the Germans' chosen jump-off point in those early days when they were planning their own invasion across the Channel and into Britain. They could not imagine the Allies passing up its advantages: the shorter distances that would enhance fighter-plane coverage, the availability of usable harbors and the direct route it offered for a drive toward Berlin and the German heartland.

Hitler was swayed by another key factor. Here were the launch platforms for the V-weapons his scientists were struggling mightily to perfect so that they could be sent crashing into Britain. How could the Allies be so obliging as to strike somewhere else and allow these fearsome weapons to rain down on the British people? How could Allied commanders face the criticism if they made any other choice?

German leaders also felt sure that the Allies, with all that huge preponderance of power, would not be content with only one set of landings.

There would be diversionary attacks—on Norway, perhaps, or on Brittany, or Bordeaux, or the Balkans, or . . .

The time had come for the Allies to cash in on this rich accumulation of assets.

The Allied deception planners under Colonel Bevan had little doubt as to which course to pursue. A primary principle in military deceptions is to base one's plans on the enemy's expectations. Bevan's team hewed to that principle. If the Germans thought the Pas de Calais was most likely, then go along, notionally, with that choice.

In support of Overlord, the code name for the Normandy landings, Allied planners framed three objectives for their deceptions: to mislead the Germans as to the time and place of the attacks as well as the strength of the invading force.

1. Time: the Germans were to be persuaded that Overlord could not possibly come as early as Allied commanders actually scheduled it.
2. Place: the enemy was to be misled into expecting the main attack to be launched from England's southeast ports rather than from farther west.
3. Strength: the invasion armies were to be seen as carrying out only a diversion that left uncommitted in England an even larger force for the main attack.

To meet these goals, deception planners had to replace an earlier plan code-named Bodyguard. Bodyguard had the cachet of deriving from a truism expressed by Winston Churchill: "In war-time, truth is so precious that she should always be attended by a bodyguard of lies." But as D-Day approached, the plan was seen to have its flaws. It had the valid objective of inducing the Germans to believe that the invasion could not come before late summer, but it based this claim on the assertion that the Allies could not possibly have the trained and equipped manpower in place to conduct a cross-Channel invasion any earlier. The Germans knew better than that. They were all too aware of the influx of great numbers of Commonwealth and American troops into the British Isles. In addition, a new plan was needed to address the problem revealed by Bletchley Park decrypts: conscious of the buildup of Allied forces in the west of England, some German leaders were beginning to believe in the probability of a Normandy landing.

Bodyguard gave way to Fortitude, which had two main parts: Fortitude North and Fortitude South.

Fortitude North followed the familiar pattern of a notional diversionary attack on Norway. Its chief purpose remained the same as that of earlier deception plans: to pin down the excess of troops that Hitler insisted on assigning to Scandinavia by threatening a Norwegian landing so that Hitler dared not allow even a battalion to come to the aid of the Normandy defenders. This time the deception was given considerably more teeth. It also received nominal support from the Russians.

Allied services pitched in more cooperatively than before. The purported invasion would require ships. All the shipping that could be rounded up was gathered in Scottish waters, increasing the numbers berthed there from twenty-six at the beginning of April to seventy-one by mid-May. The Royal Navy assigned an aircraft carrier in the North Sea to dispatch planes for aerial reconnaissance. The RAF sent a few real planes to Scottish airfields and supplemented them with dummy aircraft to fill out four medium bomber squadrons together with protective fighter squadrons.

British Special Forces made the kind of raids that could be expected to prepare the way for an invasion. Commandos slipped ashore to sink ships, destroy an oil refinery, mine the German super-battleship *Tirpitz* and attack other facilities. They blew up railways, chemical works and mines. A separate plan sought to force Sweden to put an end to German military traffic across Swedish borders and cease the export to Germany of ball bearings, iron ore, special steel and machine tools.

Fortitude North required manpower. A number of real formations were training in Scotland, mostly for the D-Day operations, but they could be used as centerpieces for a simulated force to invade Norway. The most impressive feat was the creation of an entire fictional army, the British Fourth Army.

In his book *Bodyguard of Lies,* Anthony Cave Brown details how the

Fourth was almost entirely bogus. The Germans were led to believe that the Fourth's commander was a general, Sir Andrew Thorne, whom they knew and respected from his exploits in the Great War and his interwar service as a military attaché in Berlin. Thorne agreed to be the nominal chief, but the real center was Colonel R. M. "Rory" MacLeod, another Great War veteran who was called out of virtual retirement and told, "You will travel to Edinburgh. And there you will represent an army which does not in fact exist. By means of fake signals traffic you will, however, fool the Germans into believing that it does exist and, what is more, that it is about to land in Norway and clear the Germans out of there."

To fake the radio transmissions of a real army, MacLeod was assigned 28 overage officers and, since the deception involved a U.S. outfit, an American liaison officer, plus 334 members of what the British liked to call "other ranks" to create the bogus traffic.

MacLeod made his headquarters in rooms under Edinburgh Castle. Two elderly majors and six junior officers represented an army corps stationed in Stirling, and a similar group established a second corps near Dundee. These small contingents were, by D-Day, to make convincing an army of two corps headquarters, four infantry divisions, one armored division and an armored brigade—a force of more than 250,000 men with its own tactical air command and some 350 armored vehicles.

Calculated leaks to the press and radio helped to confirm the illusion. Local newspapers again published stories about "Fourth Army football matches." This time they added stories about the marriage of "a major of the Fourth Army" to a member of the women's auxiliary of the "VII Corps." Also headlined was a performance by a bagpipe band of the "II Corps" at Edinburgh Castle.

The Germans quickly registered their concern. They used direction-finding equipment to locate the Fourth Army's transmitting station and sent an aircraft to shoot it up. MacLeod's team was startled but no one was hurt. As Cave Brown noted: "The Fourth Army had experienced its first and last combat in the Second World War."

For Fortitude North, not surprisingly, Jack Moe—Mutt—and the impersonator of Jeff took the lead for the double agents. The pair were once again expected to transmit information about troop concentrations for the new Scandinavian operations. A high point for Moe came when he was chosen to report the arrival at Edinburgh Castle of Klementi Budyenny, a Russian military intelligence officer. The Russian's visit was obviously to assist in planning a joint Allied-Russian pincer movement against Scandinavia. Jeff answered a German request to describe the insignia adopted by the Fourth Army and also determined that the formation located near Dundee was the British VII Corps and that at Stirling the British II Corps.

The presence of Polish units training in Scotland—in reality for Normandy, not Norway—gave Garby-Czerniawski/Brutus reason for an extended, though entirely fabricated, Scottish tour. An official report expressed the Germans' reaction to his findings: "An Abwehr source, which has heretofore reported accurately, has been able to provide a clarification of the distribution of forces in Scotland." Among the blanks in the Abwehr's order of battle that he filled in were the locations of the Fourth Army's headquarters in Edinburgh and that of the British II Corps at Stirling. Brutus also confirmed Mutt's disclosure of planned coordination with the Russians by reporting that a Soviet naval and military mission had established itself in Edinburgh.

Popov's subagent and wireless operator code-named Freak—actually another Yugoslav playboy, Marquis Freno de Bono—traveled to Scotland. Among the reports he transmitted to the Abwehr was his account of meeting an indiscreet U.S. officer of the American XV Corps who told de Bono that while his corps was still in Northern Ireland, he himself was stationed in Edinburgh to serve as liaison with the staff of General Andrew Thorne, commander of the Fourth Army, to which his American corps was to be transferred. De Bono's spymaster congratulated him and began boring in with questions about the Fourth, to which the Twenty Committee was happy to think up suitable answers.

As was now customary, the reports about these northern operations that the Germans most valued came from Pujol/Garbo and his imaginary network. On March 7, Garbo received an urgent request for information concerning military preparations in Scotland and northeast England. His response was to allow scarcely a day to pass without some item about Fortitude North being transmitted to Kuehlanthal and company in Madrid, who just as invariably forwarded Garbo's messages to von Rundstedt and the German High Command. As an example, Garbo's subagent in Scotland discovered that the troop transports massing off the east coast were being fitted with special davits with which to lower small assault craft in place of the lifeboats normally carried. The accretion of details such as this slowly pointed to a landing in Scandinavia.

The threat by Garbo and the other double agents, however, hit a snag. It was evident to the British—and so, they thought, to the Germans— that the number of ships that could be concentrated on Scotland's east coast would be inadequate for an operation on the scale of Fortitude North. Thinking the Germans would understand this, they transferred the ships around to the more ample moorings of the Clyde estuary in the west. As Tomás Harris reported: "We overestimated the intelligence of the enemy." All the Germans concluded from the move was that the Norway operations had been abandoned. A whole new effort was required to reactivate the threat.

With Fortitude North doing its job in Scotland, Fortitude South planners took on the more crucial task of deceiving the Germans into believing that no matter what else the Allies might attempt, they were going to land on the Pas de Calais. The decision had been made that the real armies for the invasion of Normandy would be under the command of General Bernard Montgomery. Now the deceptionists had to decide how to use those mythical forces of the Allied order of battle to mount a convincing notional assault against Calais.

As originally drafted, the plan was too small-scale. It foresaw the Calais attack as a "subsidiary operation" with the main purpose of drawing German forces away from the Normandy landings. Assigned to it would be only one assault, one follow-up and four buildup divisions.

The weakness of this plan was seen by the head of Montgomery's intelligence staff, the bumptious but brilliant British officer David Strangeways. He wrote a letter that his superior, Montgomery's chief of staff General Francis de Guingand, agreed to present to a January 1944 meeting of the deception planners. The letter asserted: "I do not agree with the object which has been given for the attack on the Pas de Calais. If we induce the enemy to believe that story, he will not react in the way we want.

I feel we must, from D-Day onwards, endeavour to persuade him that our *main* attack is going to develop later in the Pas de Calais area." The letter added the hope that the Germans would view the Normandy landings as merely a move "to draw reserves from that area."

Strangeways's message, as delivered by de Guingand, became the blueprint for the revised Fortitude South. It turned Fortitude South around. Calais became the big show, with Normandy to be seen by the Germans as no more than a diversion meant to drain away the armies needed to protect against the follow-up main attack.

Where would the Allies find the strength to mount these two demanding campaigns while also contemplating an attack on Norway? Answer: from that inflated order of battle the Allies had offered and the Germans had swallowed whole. Fortitude South called for two substantial army groups to man the 1944 cross-Channel operations. The Twenty-first Army Group, commanded by Montgomery, would claim most of the Allies' real strength for the Normandy landings. The second group would be another grand mix of real and notional units. Consisting mostly of American forces, it was given the name of the First U.S. Army Group (FUSAG). FUSAG would be held back in southeast England, awaiting the moment when the Germans withdrew forces from Calais to reinforce their troops in Normandy. Then, the Germans were led to believe, FUSAG would strike.

To be FUSAG's commander, Eisenhower released George Patton from his punitive limbo. Patton was unhappy about being in charge of a largely fictitious operation, but he accepted the post as better than nothing and strutted about southeast England, leading his bulldog mascot and brandishing his pearl-handled pistols. But he was a good choice. The Germans respected and feared him—Hitler called him "their best general"—and it made sense to them that the Allies had chosen him to lead their most important campaign.

To inform the Russians about the invasion and secure their agreement and cooperation, Colonel Bevan and his American counterpart Major William H. Baumer traveled to Moscow on January 22, 1944. After weeks of vodka-soaked negotiating conferences and countless off-duty evenings watching the Bolshoi Ballet, Bevan and Baumer were astonished when, in the wee hours of May 5, the Russians suddenly called them to the Kremlin and gave them the news that the original plan had the top Soviet leaders' complete approval.

Allied visual deception teams went to work to fill southeast ports with dummy landing craft. Their largest feat was to create a fake oil dock at Dover. Made of scrap materials, it occupied nearly three square miles of the Dover shoreline and, like the similar facility faked in North Africa, included every detail from bogus pipelines and storage tanks to powerhouses and antiaircraft gun ports. To guard against having a valid spy discover this fakery and to improve overall security, a ten-mile-deep restricted zone was imposed along the entire Channel coast from Land's End in the west to Dover in the east and one hundred miles up the North Sea coast. Visitors to the zone were barred, and passage of residents in or out was closely controlled.

Still, the whole deception program was breathtakingly fragile and vulnerable. Imagine what would have happened if just one real German agent had crept ashore on the coast and had discovered the fakery of the oil dock or the pretense of the landing craft. The entire premise of the Calais invasion would have been discounted, leaving what? Normandy would have been pinpointed as the only plausible alternative.

To further guard against any such giveaway, the use of coded telegrams was limited to the Allied military, and neutral diplomats were forbidden to send out diplomatic bags that had previously been immune from search. All airmail between the UK and the Continent was suspended, while delays of regular mail were so long as to make any information in them useless.

German commanders had a good reason to dismiss Normandy beaches as the landing sites: they lacked a major port. An Ultra decrypt disclosed a May 8 report by von Rundstedt in which he expressed the certainty that it would be essential for the Allies to seize Le Havre, Cherbourg or a similar port to ensure the inflow of needed supplies. Certainly past Allied practice justified his belief: in all of their previous landings, in North Africa, Sicily and Italy, the Allies had assured themselves of a usable harbor. Again the Germans were outsmarted. For eight months preceding the landings, a British workforce was busy constructing artificial harbors code-named Mulberries, huge structures that were hauled into place by tugboats and, floating up and down with the tides, provided the capacity to handle 12,000 tons of equipment and supplies per day. Similarly, work was proceeding on Pluto, the acronym for "pipeline under the ocean," to carry petrol from southern England to the invasion armies on the Continent.

This time the LCS had no difficulty persuading the services to support the deceptions. The Allied air forces were careful to ensure that nothing was given away by their pattern of bombardment. German airfields in the Pas de Calais area were more heavily bombed than those in Normandy. Rail junctions supplying Calais were attacked. Attacks on bridges pointed to the Calais sector. Bombings of coastal defenses and radar installations there were twice as heavy as in Normandy. To overcome the thicker concentration of fighter planes and bombers on airfields in the west, on May 29 squadrons of RAF planes used southeast airfields for massive attacks against the Pas de Calais.

The Royal Navy simulated operations against radar stations and made feint landings north of the Seine estuary and against the Pas de Calais itself. Even Montgomery's Twenty-first Army Group overcame its earlier reluctance to join in sham maneuvers and simulated airborne landings in divisional strength as well as smaller airborne operations.

For wireless deception, the United States contributed the 3103 Signals Service Battalion, which arrived in Britain in the early spring of 1944 fully equipped and trained. To simulate the radio traffic that a force the size of FUSAG would generate, the battalion was able to represent three army corps and nine divisions as well as the headquarters of an army group and an army. Its wireless trucks moved through the country as though accompanying the formations to which they were notionally assigned.

That all these measures came together to totally deceive the Germans was made evident by their urgent strengthening of the Calais defenses. New concrete bulwarks were poured, fresh batteries of artillery were hurried into position and additional minefields were laid off the coast. The Pas de Calais was made into as impregnable a fortress as the Germans could manage.

Meanwhile, the Middle East's "A" Force had accepted responsibility for deception plans covering the whole Mediterranean area. The plans' intent was to keep German divisions assigned to this area from being transferred to northern France, not just until D-Day but well after.

"A" Force planned deceptions for both ends of the Mediterranean, east and west. The deceptionists knew the enemy would find it credible for the Allies to mount two campaigns because the Germans in this region, as in northern France, accepted the falsely enlarged order of battle that "A" Force had foisted on them.

In the east, the goal of the deception was to pin down German formations in Greece and the Balkan Peninsula by once again threatening a drive out of Egypt and Syria. This time the attack would be coordinated with a threatened push by the Russians toward northern Greece. In this deception, too, the services cooperated fully. The RAF in northern Syria augmented their actual strength by displaying dummy aircraft and made recon flights over notional targets. The Royal Navy conducted elaborate exercises in the area's harbors. The largely notional Ninth Army drew together a few real units and added bogus formations, complete with dummy armor, to stage displays of force near the Turkish frontier, where German observers presumably watched.

In the west, "A" Force was called on to carry out Operation Vendetta, whose purpose was to threaten landings in the south of France in order to tie down German occupying divisions there past D-Day and into July. The deception team faced a problem: the Allies had scheduled a real invasion of southern France in August. Knowing that the real landings were to be made on the eastern beaches of the Riviera, the planners targeted their notional thrust to fall on the far western border with Spain.

Ultra decrypts had disclosed German anxieties about the large forces remaining in North Africa. A good share of these were bogus. Banking on the German willingness to accept mixes of false formations with real ones, "A" Force created the U.S. Seventh Army of twelve divisions, nine of which were nonexistent. A varied round of simulated preparations built to an actual amphibious exercise between June 9 and 11 that included 13,000 men, 2,000 vehicles and 60 naval vessels and troop transports. The British aircraft carriers HMS *Victorious* and HMS *Indomitable*, which were passing through on their way to the Far East, paused long enough to take part. Fighter aircraft attacked coastal targets while heavy bombers raided further inland. An especially imaginative touch was that the Spanish government was asked for Red Cross facilities to enable casualties from the operation to be evacuated.

These were the principal deceptions hatched by the LCS and "A" Force. The planners again looked to the double agents to take the lead in making them successful. The agents had done their best for Fortitude North. For Fortitude South they went all out.

In Britain the decision was made to limit participation in Fortitude to only a few of the most well established and trusted agents, with help from others as needed.

Originally, Popov—Tricycle—was on the list. As previously noted, however, his close ties with Johnny Jebsen motivated B1A to close down his case following Jebsen's arrest. Before the ax fell, however, he made one significant contribution to Fortitude. Carrying a Yugoslav diplomatic bag that held a number of "looted" documents, he traveled once more to Lisbon and meetings with von Karsthoff. One of the documents was an inflated order of battle slanted toward indicating a large increase in forces moved into the southeast of England. Although Karsthoff sneered at the report as "warmed-over gossip," Popov persuaded him to send it on to Berlin. To Popov's great relief, German intelligence headquarters reacted to it as supplying "particularly valuable information" that "confirms our operational picture"—i.e., that the Allied main attack would be directed at the Pas de Calais.

Wulf Schmidt—Tate—whose activities had been deliberately limited by having him notionally assigned to do farm work in the south of England in order to avoid being drafted, was now given a stronger role. His employer had another farmer friend who lived in Kent and occasionally needed Tate's help. In April 1944 the Germans urged him to exert every effort to find out about Allied invasion preparations. Tate responded by taking the risk, on his next trip to the southeast, of carrying his transmitter with him. Recognized by the Abwehr as one who made friends readily, Tate soon struck up an acquaintance with a gabby railway clerk who was very forthcoming on relating railway arrangements for moving the

FUSAG forces from their concentration areas to southeast embarkation points. Tate's reports were so highly appreciated that one Abwehr official was of the opinion that they could "even decide the outcome of the war."

With Tricycle sidelined, Garby-Czerniawski—Brutus—had to shoulder a heavier burden. On May 19 he was able to report to his controllers that he had been shifted to a new position. He was now to serve as a liaison officer between the Polish High Command and Patton's headquarters for FUSAG. He was an acute observer. Within a week, he began the transmission of a series of nightly messages which disclosed to the Germans by D-Day the entire chain of command, all that great union of real and notional units, that made up Patton's FUSAG. To add to the information he gleaned in his new assignment, Brutus made tours of Kent and East Anglia.

A deft piece of deception was supplied by Hamlet's subagent Thornton/ Mullet. Prewar, Thornton had been a respected official in a Belgian insurance firm. In his wartime role as a double agent, he notionally had joined one of England's largest insurance companies. In peacetime, as he pointed out in reports to his German spymasters, this firm had carried out a great deal of insurance work for companies and factories in the Low Countries and in northern France. From his current employment he was able to transmit to the Germans a flow of updated industrial and economic information regarding those areas. Of particular interest, he noted, were the British government's requests for information that dealt with the Pas de Calais. Thornton had, as he was pleased to report, been placed in charge of the collection and arrangement of the data. He made sure the Germans understood that this expressed interest on the part of high British authorities was probably of greater significance than the information itself.

At this point, deception plans were afoot to hold German forces in Scandinavia via Fortitude North, in the Pas de Calais by Fortitude South, in the south of France by "A" Force's Plan Vendetta, and in Italy and the Balkans by Plan Zeppelin. There still remained the problem of keeping German forces on France's west coast from becoming reinforcements for Normandy. These forces included the strong and mobile German Eleventh Panzer Division stationed at Bordeaux. The task of holding these formations in place fell to Elvira Chaudoir, Bronx. She had gained the Germans' respect, and a regular influx of cash, for her secret-ink letters full of items from her friends in diplomatic circles. Now the Twenty Committee decided it was time for her to activate the special code based on her instructions to her bank in Lisbon. On May 15 she sent her telegram: *"Envoyez vite cinquante livres. J'ai besoin pour mon dentiste."* Decoded, the message meant that "a landing will be made on the Bay of Biscay area in about one month." In a letter, she explained that she had picked up this valuable information when she had been in a nightclub with a British officer who let himself become indiscreet when he drank too much.

Tate backed up the story. On May 23, he transmitted a message that told why he hadn't seen Mary, his girlfriend stationed at Eisenhower's headquarters, for quite a while. She had been sent on a special mission to Washington to help with preparations for a U.S. expeditionary force to sail for Europe. The force consisted of six divisions, and its objective, in Mary's opinion, was a landing on France's west coast.

Juan Pujol—Garbo—delivered the clincher. That U.S. assault division that had landed at Liverpool and was waiting for repair of its landing craft was, Garbo discovered, one prong of a two-pronged American attack. The assault division was to cross the Channel to attack the Brest area of western France while that large expeditionary force mentioned by Mary would land on the west coast to back up the attack.

To give himself an out, Garbo expressed skepticism about the report. But whether or not the Germans believed this visionary tale, this much is true: they did not move the Eleventh Panzer Division or any of the other outfits away from the Bordeaux area.

With the approach of D-Day, Lily Sergueiew—Treasure—stepped up her reports to Kliemann, her spymaster. Accustomed to spending weekends with her friends in the western city of Bristol, which bustled with Allied preparations for Normandy, Treasure reported the opposite, that the scene there was quiet, with hardly any troop movements.

Treasure found it expedient to turn herself into a romantic figure. First she became involved with a staff officer of the notional American Fourteenth Army in Bristol. To her great pleasure, the Fourteenth Army headquarters moved to Essex, much closer to London, allowing her to see her friend more often. The headquarters also had the advantage of being close to the North Sea and the approaches to the Pas de Calais. She was kept busy reporting the movements of the formations now arriving to fill the ranks of FUSAG.

Alas, Treasure announced to Kliemann that she "had broken off her friendship with her friend at Fourteenth Army." In only a short time, though, she found another American suitor. This was an officer in the U.S. Judge Advocate General's branch. In addition to giving her good reason to continue developing news about FUSAG, her new friend helped prepare monthly military crime reports, division by division. His reports gave her another way to verify the divisions being added to FUSAG's growing order of battle.

With D-Day approaching, Garbo augmented his network by recruiting six new subagents from British members of the "Brothers in the Aryan World Order" and placing them at strategic points around the UK. He also had to introduce a new system for sending his information to Kuehlanthal. The ban on airmail precluded secret-ink letters sent directly by his subagents. The only recourse was for them to send their reports to him for wireless transmission to Madrid. Gerbers's widow took on more of the encoding and transmission. Also, Garbo called in from Scotland his most reliable agent, Marquis de Bono, who became both an added helper and a deputy to take over if anything should happen to Garbo.

So much poured in notionally on Garbo by his network of subagents that he was transmitting five to six messages daily, running up a total of well over five hundred messages exchanged between London and Madrid in the period from January 1 to D-Day. The press of traffic ruled out Garbo's usual florid style. He had to begin reporting almost as tersely as Tate.

It was satisfying work. Bletchley decrypts confirmed that Garbo's transmissions were so highly valued that they were immediately retransmitted to Berlin.

The Germans were, unknowingly, very obliging in the requests they sent to Garbo. Just at the point when the Twenty Committee, Harris and Pujol were concentrating on putting together a new order of battle for transmission, the Abwehr specifically asked for the information. Garbo was pleased to report on the real Twenty-first Army Group under Montgomery and the largely fictional First U.S. Army Group under Patton. His reports supplied accurate information regarding the identity and role of formations that were to take part in the initial phase of Fortitude South. The expectation was that when the battle began and the Germans found proof of his accurate unit identifications, they would be that much more inclined to believe his subsequent messages.

Garbo made a move that greatly increased his access to secret information. Earlier he had gained the Abwehr's approval to take a job at the Spanish Department of the Ministry of Information. Although he gave up that work in January 1944, he maintained contact with the official there who, he led the Germans to believe, was the department's head. In May, this official induced Garbo to come back to work in his spare time. His task was to help prepare propaganda about the Second Front for use in Spain and Latin American countries. Before he could take the job he had to sign Britain's Official Secrets Act. Olé! Garbo was on the inside, able to send secret information—and misinformation—the Abwehr would otherwise consider beyond his reach.

If reassurance was needed that the Fortitude South deceptions were succeeding, it came when Allied codebreakers deciphered a report by Baron Hiroshi Oshima, the Japanese ambassador in Berlin, who used his Purple code machine to send his messages to Tokyo—and unknowingly to London and Washington. His May 28 message detailed the conversation he had just had with Hitler. The Fuehrer told him that "about 80 divisions had already been assembled in England" and that "these British and American troops had completed their preparations for landing operations." Asked in what form the Second Front would materialize, Hitler said that "at the moment what he himself thought was most probable was that after having carried out diversionary operations in Norway, Denmark and the southern part of the west coast of France and the French Mediterranean coast, they would establish a bridgehead in Normandy or Brittany, and after seeing how things went would then embark upon the establishment of a real Second Front in the Channel." In other words, the German chancellor had swallowed whole the deceptionists' order of battle and, in trying to guess where the attack would come, his eyes were still "hopping all over the map."

In his transmissions, Garbo also succeeded in advancing the program for confusing the Germans about the timing of Overlord. Another of his subagents reported that an American assault division had landed at Liverpool and was awaiting redeployment. The division could not be effective, however, until some of its assault boats could be repaired, and that wouldn't be completed until after June 8. The Soviets helped by leaking misinformation that their summer offensive in support of the invasion would be delayed until July.

The Allied effort to deceive the Nazis into believing the invasion could not come as soon as early June was completely successful. On June 5, the very eve of D-Day, von Rundstedt issued a report that in his considered opinion the invasion was not imminent. A Bletchley Park decrypt revealed that German commanders in the West were predicting that the time from June 12 onwards must be considered the new danger period.

Garbo was given the approval for a measure that would solidify his reputation with the Germans. This was to transmit to them, on the morning of the landings, an advance warning that the invasion ships were on their way toward France. Eisenhower agreed that this alert could be sent, but not until three a.m. Still, this was three and a half hours before the landing barges were scheduled to touch down on the Normandy beaches. The alarm would come soon enough to bolster Garbo's credibility but not in time for the Germans to do much about it. There was a problem, however. The Abwehr's radio operation in Madrid was now closing down from midnight to seven a.m. How could they be made to remain on duty to receive Garbo's message? Again he displayed his ingenuity. One of his subagents had the task of keeping watch on the troops and ships congregating on the west coast of Scotland. As the crucial hour approached, this agent was foolish enough to break off his surveillance in Scotland and come to London for a personal report to Garbo. Angered by the agent's leaving his post at this critical time, Garbo sent him back immediately to check on whether the fleet that was gathered in the Clyde estuary had departed. Further, he gave the agent a code word he could use in a telephone call to let Garbo know when the troops had started to embark, which would presumably be on the eve of D-Day. The cleverness of this scheme was that Garbo used it to convince the Abwehr's Madrid office to maintain their radio monitoring around the clock in order to receive, at any hour, his vital message that the invasion was about to commence.

D-Day was set for June 5. The weather was so foul it was moved back a day. To their belief that any such timing was much too soon, German leaders added the certainty that the Allies would not attempt so huge an operation in bad weather. The Allies had to be able, the Germans thought, to anticipate at least four days of good weather before launching their attack. They were so sure the invasion could not come then that Rommel went back to Germany to confer with Hitler, and the troops in northwest France were permitted to stand down from their alert status.

When the morning of June 5 came, the Allied chiefs knew one thing about the weather that the Germans, whose weather ships in the North Atlantic had been located by Bletchley Park and sunk by the Royal Navy, did not know. That was a temporary letup in the stormy weather. "A barely tolerable period of fair conditions," the Allies forecasters reported, "far below the minimal requirements, will prevail for just a little more than twenty-four hours."

That was good enough for Eisenhower. He made the decision: the invasion of Normandy was on.

Promptly at three a.m. on June 6 Garbo sent his message of warning. To his dismay and despite the assurances he had received from the Madrid office of the Abwehr, no radio operator was on duty. Garbo's message did not finally get read until eight a.m. In his wrath, Garbo fired off a message that built to this blast: "I am very disgusted as, in this struggle for life and death, I cannot accept excuses or negligence. I cannot masticate the idea of endangering the service without any benefit. Were it not for my ideals I would abandon the work as having proved myself a failure."

The Abwehr was contrite. Kuehlanthal wired back at once: "I wish to stress in the clearest terms that your work over the last few weeks has made it possible for our command to be completely forewarned and prepared."

Soothed, Garbo went back to work and got his notional network to report on the post-D-Day situation. The long analysis he sent to Madrid added up to the point that no FUSAG forces had taken part in the Normandy landings. They were still there awaiting the moment for the real assault to begin.

Both Churchill and Eisenhower aided the deception by including in their D-Day speeches references to the Normandy landings as, in Churchill's phraseology, "the first of a series of landings in force upon the European continent."

German reaction to the landings was slowed by Hitler's fiat that nothing could be done without his approval. On D-Day morning he was in a drugged sleep, and no one dared awaken him. Chafing, Rommel had to keep his Fifteenth Army sitting tight on the Pas de Calais.

With the first day's attacks falling well short of their goals, the Allies' foothold in Normandy was very tenuous. There is no telling what would have happened if Rommel had had his way and loosed his Fifteenth Army from the Pas de Calais.

He had, in fact, received Hitler's guarded agreement to begin sending to Normandy all the troops of the Fifteenth Army that were immediately available. The reinforcements that Rommel rounded up included five infantry and two Panzer divisions, which, if they had been unleashed against the bogged-down Allies, could have overwhelmed them. At this point Garbo delivered what Harris labeled "the most important report of his career." On D-Day plus three he wired, "It is perfectly clear that the present attack is a large-scale attack but diversionary in character to draw the maximum of our reserves so as to be able to strike a blow somewhere else with assured success. The constant aerial bombardment which the area of the Pas de Calais has suffered and the strange disposition of these forces give reason to suggest attack in that region of France which at the same time offers the shortest route for the final objective of their delusions—Berlin."

The effect was dramatic. Garbo's message went straight to Hitler, who ordered Rommel not only to stand pat on the Pas de Calais but also to call back the forces he had sent toward Normandy.

Churchill, General Marshall and the Allied chiefs in London were congregated in London's Operations Room when a secretary brought in the Ultra decrypt that revealed Hitler's order. Ron Wingate, one of the generals at the meeting, later recalled, "We knew then that we'd won. There might be very heavy battles, but we'd won."

German general Bodo Zimmermann, in a postwar interview, agreed. For Germany, he wrote, the war was lost at that point.

It was left to Dwight Eisenhower to sum up most ably the results of the grand strategic deception:

> Lack of infantry was the most important cause of the enemy's defeat in Normandy, and his failure to remedy this weakness was due primarily to the success of the Allied threats leveled against the Pas de Calais. This threat, which had already proved of so much value in misleading the enemy as to the true objectives of our invasion preparations, was maintained after 6th June, and it served most effectively to pin down the German Fifteenth Army east of the Seine while we built up our strength in the lodgment area to the west. I cannot over-emphasize the decisive value of this most successful threat, which paid enormous dividends, both at the time of the assault and during the operations of the two succeeding months. The German Fifteenth Army, which, if committed to battle in June or July, might possibly have defeated us by sheer weight of numbers, remained inoperative throughout the critical period of the campaign, and only when the breakthrough had been achieved were its infantry divisions brought west across the Seine—too late to have any effect upon the course of victory.

All in all, it seems fair to say that the publishers of a new book on Juan Pujol were not overclaiming when they entitled it *Garbo: The Spy Who Saved D-Day*.

CHAPTER NINETEEN

DECEPTIONS BEYOND D-DAY

Many of those in the know about the double agents felt sure that with their D-Day deceptions at a glorious end, they had done their bit and should retire from the game as gracefully as they could. Who among the Germans would give them credence after such a flagrant display of misinformation? Moreover, hadn't the war's center of gravity shifted to the Continent and to stay-behind turned agents there rather than those such as Garbo, Brutus and Tate, who had been left in the backwaters of England?

Colonel Bevan, Tar Robertson, B1A, the LCS and the Twenty Committee rejected these pessimistic thoughts and soldiered on. They were buoyed by the Abwehr's reactions. Kuehlanthal, von Karsthoff and their ilk quickly let it be known that the surprise of the Normandy landings did not diminish their estimations of their agents nor their need for the agents' continuing efforts.

It was good that this positive decision carried the day, since events soon made it plain that there was still a great deal of work for the agents to do.

Foremost was the necessity to keep Fortitude South alive and well. Eisenhower had been given his two days free of attack by forces on the Pas de Calais and had seen two reserve divisions that had headed for Normandy change their course, instead, to prepare for the invasion by FUSAG. But the situation in Normandy remained uncertain, what with

Montgomery's troops still held short of Caen and the Americans under Omar Bradley bogged down in the hedgerows of the bocage country around Saint-Lô. Normandy became such a meat grinder that some of the real units of FUSAG had to be called in as reinforcements—a change that quickly became known to the Germans through battlefield identifications. The time also arrived for Patton to leave off his spurious role as commander of FUSAG and take on his real assignment as leader of the U.S. Third Army when it was transferred to Normandy.

A new plan, Fortitude South II, came into play. Its aim was to make credible the continued buildup of FUSAG by the arrival of new U.S. divisions, both actual and notional, to take the places of the divisions that had left for Normandy. The threat of an imminent crossing to the Pas de Calais was also maintained by the formation of three new armadas of ships gathered along the southeast coast, most of which seemed real only to Luftwaffe recon planes having to fly too high up to detect the fakery.

Patton's change to his lesser command as a subordinate to Bradley was explained. Once again he in his remarks to the press had been indiscreet, and this time Ike lowered the boom by "demoting" him.

The Germans learned of these developments through deliberate leakages in the communications from their agents in Britain.

Within a week after D-Day, the double agents faced the new challenge of Hitler's secret V-weapons—V for *Vergeltungswaffe,* or Vengeance weapons. On June 13, the first of these, the V-1s, began to fall on London. Since the war's beginnings, Adolf Hitler had been looking to German science to provide him with weapons superior to any the Allies might develop. The Allies knew of the progress on these weapons through Bletchley Park decrypts and other sources. German scientists were hard at work on a variety of awesome options, including nuclear bombs, jet aircraft, snorkels for U-boats and guided missles such as the V-1 and V-2.

Until that June 1944 date, however, the Allies had been able to delay the launching of these weapons. They were aided by the intensifying hatred that many Europeans were feeling toward Hitler and the oppressive Nazi regime—a hatred strong enough to impel them on life-risking missions against the Germans.

German atomic bomb development had been thwarted when the Allies realized that a weak point in the Germans' plans existed in a facility in Norway producing the heavy water needed in processing the plutonium for the bombs. A team of courageous Norwegians trained in Britain successfully reentered their country and destroyed the heavy water plant's stainless steel cells in which the heavy water was concentrated. After the Germans put the plant back in operation and produced a new quantity of heavy water, they decided to move the whole facility to Germany, along with the store of water. Knowing that Germany lacked the huge amounts of electricity needed to operate such a plant, the Allies did not worry much about the machinery's transfer. But they did not want that heavy water to reach German nuclear scientists. Again, daring Norwegians saw to it that a boat carrying the water's containers across a deep Norwegian lake was sunk—and Hitler's hopes of atomic bombs to add to his V-list were sunk with it.

Jet plane development was similarly hampered. Bletchley Park decrypts and Nazi-hating informants combined to locate the planes' development and production sites, which were heavily bombed by Allied aircraft. While a few jet fighters began to make their appearance, Hitler never got to fulfill his fantasy of squadrons of German jets sweeping Allied airpower from the skies.

The arrival of the V-1s over London was also far later than Hitler had planned. Anti-Nazi sentiment was once more a key factor in the delay. Development of the rockets demanded that Germany press into service skilled workers from occupied countries. Brave men and women in these ranks were eager to inform the Allies about their work, even if it meant bringing Allied bombs down on their own heads.

This was precisely what happened at Peenemünde, the island off the Baltic coast where development of the advanced aerial weapons was under way. On the night of August 16, 1943, British bombers pulverized the facility. German rocket scientists had to start over in a new underground center in Bavaria and a test site in Poland.

French resistance forces also reported the locations of V-1 launch sites in northern France so that a high percentage of these could be knocked out by Allied bombers.

With the arrival of the V-1s over London skies, the double agents accepted a new responsibility. Actually, Garbo had started probing Kuehlanthal about the V-weapons as early as October 1943. A press report had quoted a Swedish journalist who had written an article about what Garbo termed in his message to Madrid "an enormous rocket gun," which, installed on the northern French coast, could bombard London and other cities within a 125-mile radius. If the article was true, Garbo wrote, he wanted to send his wife and children out of London and into the country.

The answer from Madrid was that "there is no cause to alarm yourself."

By mid-December, though, the story had changed. With the Germans again confident that the launching of the V-1s would soon start, Kuehlanthal wired Garbo that "circumstances dictate that you should carry out your proposition with regard to setting up your home outside the capital."

Kuehlanthal was overly optimistic about the V-1's debut. Design problems and other delays pushed back the date into June. Even so, Garbo had taken the precaution, as he reported, to move his family to the country, give up his house and find himself lodging in a London pension.

Dusko Popov received a warning in May that he should vacate London as soon as possible to escape Hitler's secret weapons targeted on the city. Garbo, however, received no such advance warning and sent a sarcastic message of complaint to Madrid after the first attack. Kuehlanthal protested that he himself had not been forewarned.

Then came the special challenge the new weapons presented to the double agents: the Germans' need to know where the V-1s came down and at what time. The need was dictated by the nature of the weapon. The V-1 was a small pilotless aircraft propelled by rocket fuel. Aimed at London by its launchpad, the explosives-laden plane would fly until its inner "air log" had clicked off the requisite number of miles. Then its fuel supply would shut down and the plane would go into its deadly dive. This whole process was inexact enough that the weapons' demolition points could vary by miles. The Abwehr looked to the agents' reports to help the launch officials correct the V-1's range so that more of them landed in the crowded center of London. Garbo, for one, was asked to find a certain map of the city on which he could pinpoint the explosion sites and transmit them to his controller, who held a copy of the same map.

The double-cross system was faced with a terrible dilemma. How could they not have the double agents do as their spymasters asked? Yet how could they join in measures whose results would be the killing of greater numbers of Londoners?

For Garbo a solution was quickly found. He disappeared! He failed to show up for a scheduled meeting with his deputy subagent. A check with Mrs. Garbo found that he had not been at home. She immediately became hysterical and threatened to make inquiries to the police, a possibility that the deputy saw as highly dangerous. He wired the alarm to Kuehlanthal and asked for advice.

Garbo reappeared, very shaken. His story, all of which was of course fictional, was that he had dutifully gone to investigate the damage caused by a bomb. His questions at the site, delivered in English with a marked foreign accent, had aroused the suspicions of a plainclothes policeman there. Garbo had ended up in jail. How had he finally gained his release? His influential friend at the Spanish Department of the Ministry of Information had vouched for him.

Needless to say, Kuehlanthal relieved Garbo of any further bomb-reporting duties. He was not alone. Brutus's spymaster wired him: "Stop immediately all observation on destruction caused by flying bombs and only communicate to us information on locations of troops, etc."

As for the other double agents, they were rescued by another exercise in British ingenuity. This came in the form of Dr. R. V. Jones, the director of Scientific Intelligence at the Air Ministry and Churchill's personal scientific adviser. Jones's scheme was to have the agents not increase the deaths from the V-1s but to lessen them. The agents would report only the weapons that overshot central London. But they would attribute to these bombs the timing of others that had fallen short. The result was that the bomb directors back in France reduced the range of the missiles so that many of them began to fall in the more open country south and east of London.

In his book *Reflections on Intelligence,* Dr. Jones includes the mocking comment that German scientists had in their own hands the answer to solving their tracking problems: all they had to do was install radio beacons in the warheads of their V-1s and thus themselves electronically monitor the paths of the weapons.

The doctor's solution of how the British could minimize the carnage done by the V-1s did not sit well with the home secretary, Herbert Morrison. Did the agents think they were God? Morrison wanted to know. Would they take unto themselves the power of sparing the lives of one lot of Britons while consigning others to their deaths? In the end Morrison was overruled, with the result that many more Britons survived the V-1s than would otherwise have been the case.

While Garbo was recuperating from the shock of his prison experience, he received a message that gave his spymaster "great happiness and satisfaction." Kuehlanthal announced that the Fuehrer had conferred on Pujol the Iron Cross as a reward for his "distinguished and meritorious service." The award was extraordinary, Kuehlanthal pointed out, because the decoration was, without exception, granted to first-line combatants. For Garbo to receive the Cross meant that the Germans considered him a battlefield soldier. In his response, Garbo returned to his florid style: "I cannot at this moment, when emotion overcomes me, express in words my thanks for the decoration conceded by our Fuehrer, to whom humbly and with every respect, I express my gratitude for the high distinction which he has bestowed on me, for which I feel myself unworthy, since I have never done more than that which I have considered to be the fulfillment of my duty." His words flowed on to bestow the credit also on his comrades in the network. Then he concluded: "My desire is to fight with greater ardour to be worthy of this medal which has only been conceded to those heroes, my companions in honour, who fight on the battlefront."

By late summer, Allied countermeasures against the V-1s had become so successful that only a trickle of them were getting through the protective screen the Allies had erected. On the south coast, crews massed their antiartillery guns and made use of U.S.-designed proximity fuses to bring down the V-1s before they reached land. Of the ones that got through, some were shot down over open countryside by RAF Spitfires while others were hung up on wire nets raised by barrage balloons over barren heath country. The danger diminished to the point where even Hitler conceded: "The V-1 unfortunately cannot decide the war."

He placed his new hopes on the V-2s. These were real rockets, the precursors of intercontinental ballistic missiles, that were fired from northern France to crash down without warning on England. The V-2s began to arrive in September, and their psychological impact on frayed British nerves was worse than the actual damage they inflicted. They descended so swiftly and penetrated so deeply that, while anything directly in their path was vaporized, their blast areas were much less than those of the V-1s.

To counteract the V-2s, the double agents resorted to a variation on Dr. Jones's prescription for the V-1s. The German launch crews knew, as an example, that they had fired a V-2 at twelve thirty p.m. and that it had probably landed about four minutes later. What they did not know was *where* it came down. The agents reported the real point of impact of rockets that hit central London but tied these to shots that fell miles short—a stratagem that convinced the Germans the shorter-range settings were correct. By the time the Allies finally overran the last of the V-2s' launch sites in February 1945, the missiles that were fired fell well short of London.

During the last months of the war, double agent Wulf Schmidt— Tate—took on a special task for the Naval Ministry. A new development had made German U-boats more menacing than before. This was the snorkel, the air intake and exhaust tube that allowed the U-boats to remain submerged rather than come to the surface to recharge batteries and supply fresh air to the subs' interiors. Snorkels enabled new U-boats to lurk beneath the surface for up to ten days. Operating close inshore to the British Isles, the U-boats were once more endangering the shipping that was Britain's lifeline.

The only effective countermeasure the ministry could devise was to lay deep minefields that would snare the U-boats but over which surface craft could safely pass. Deception was needed because of a shortage both of mines and minelayers in home waters.

Tate, it was remembered, had earlier become acquainted with a "minelaying friend" who had served on a minelayer and supplied Tate with information the Germans had considered of value. The friendship was now revived. Yes, the friend was still busy on his mine-laying boat. When not at sea, he met with Tate and gave him advance information about creating extensive new minefields that in fact did not exist. He also attributed to minefields the sinking of U-boats whose cause was not known to the Germans. U-boat command sent out warnings to their skippers at sea.

Corroboration of Tate's reports came as the result of a stroke of good fortune. A U-boat captain reported that his craft had been so damaged by a mine that it had to be scuttled. He did not specify the boat's precise position, but it was close enough to one of Tate's notional minefields that the Germans concluded the U-boat had blundered into it. Convinced that all of his reports must be true, the Germans closed 3,600 miles of Britain's western approaches to the U-boats. As Masterman summed up the deception, Tate "ensured the safety of many of our vessels which would otherwise have run considerable risk, and it is possible that his information moved U-boats from areas where they were safe to areas where they emphatically were not."

On the Continent, meanwhile, the Allies were discovering and capturing agents left behind in the Germans' retreat. The left-behind agents were supposed to report to their spymasters whatever they could determine of Allied troop movements and intentions. Faced with cooperation or death, at this late point when German defeat seemed inescapable, they invariably chose to be turned and serve the Allies. One of the best of these was code-named George, who was caught transmitting from Cherbourg. His mission for the Germans was to report whether the Allies could make use of the city's battered harbor. Very well, his new masters would let him continue with his reports, assuring the Abwehr that the Allies were finding it impossible to reconstruct the harbor. In actuality, Cherbourg was repaired sufficiently for it to take the place of one of the Mulberries that had been destroyed in a storm.

Even though the Germans' feared Fifteenth Army remained idle in the Pas de Calais, awaiting an invasion that was never to come, the Allies continued to be stalled in Normandy. Montgomery was unable to break through at Caen, and Bradley was checked at Saint-Lô. The situation became more alarming when Ultra decrypts began telling the Allies that Hitler, in his desperation, had finally decided that Rommel could leave just enough of the Fifteenth Army's armored strength in Calais to withstand an invasion but direct most of it to a new drive against Montgomery's forces. Allied leaders saw that it was essential to break the two deadlocks before Rommel could get his forces reorganized, moved and ready to strike. Montgomery and Bradley planned their own two-pronged offensive to break through the weaker formations opposing them. Montgomery's attack was code-named Goodwood, Bradley's was Cobra. Goodwood was to begin July 17 with an unprecedentedly massive aerial and artillery bombardment followed by a charge by 250,000 men and 1,500 tanks. Cobra would follow, days after, with an all-out drive at Saint-Lô.

The march of events seemed to favor the Allies. On the same day that Goodwood was launched, Rommel was badly injured when RAF planes swept out of the skies, shot up his command car and caused it to crash. In addition, the Allies were receiving a rising volume of reports indicating that at least a broad segment of the Wehrmacht leadership might be distracted from their battle decisions: they were joined in a conspiracy to assassinate Hitler and take over control of Germany.

Montgomery had another advantage. The left-behind agents had misled German commander-in-chief General Gunther von Kluge, who had replaced von Rundstedt, into believing that the British and Canadian phase of the attack would come from another direction three or four days later than was actually planned. Kluge was taken completely by surprise.

Yet Goodwood foundered. Montgomery's troops dented the German line but could not break it. They did, however, kill enough Germans and destroy so much German armor that Cobra stood a better chance.

Delayed by bad weather, Cobra did not kick off until July 25. At first, it also faltered, but then on the 26th the Americans broke through. At the foot of the Cherbourg peninsula they opened a corridor through which Patton sent his Third Army, after directing their traffic himself, to circle around to the south of Kluge's army.

Having survived the July 20 attempt to assassinate him and starting the investigations that ended with the conspirators being shot or hanged, Hitler in his distrust of his generals had taken command himself. He fancied he saw an opportunity. At the seaside town of Avranches on the western end of the Cherbourg peninsula, the Allied corridor was very thin.

Hitler believed that by directing Kluge's troops to take Avranches he could cut the American forces in two and annihilate them one at a time. He ordered Kluge to attack.

Kluge was aghast. Hitler's strategy would require him to thrust his men and armor much too far westward, with the danger that the Allies could close in on either flank and catch him in a trap. He would have been further dismayed if he had been aware that two unknown foes were also arrayed against him. Double agent George was asked by his spymaster to report on the state of the bridges that Kluge's army would have to cross to reach Avranches, thus disclosing the exact route the Germans would follow. Bletchley Park's cryptanalysts joined in by issuing a last-minute warning that revealed the timing of the attack. Learning of the threat, Patton ordered enough of his army to turn back and reinforce the game U.S. Thirtieth Infantry Division, which was taking the brunt of the German assault. At the town of Mortain, twenty miles east of Avranches, Kluge's attack was checked.

Bletchley Park decrypts also guided Bradley's forces in springing the trap that Kluge had feared. Turned back at Mortain, the Germans had to seek escape by running a gauntlet pressed in on either side by the Allies and wracked from above by hordes of bombers and fighter aircraft. By the time remnants of the German army escaped through a narrow gap at Falaise, an estimated 10,000 Germans had been killed and another 50,000 captured, along with masses of their armor and equipment.

The success carried jubilation among the Allies and raised hopes that the war would be ended by Christmas. It was not to be. The triumphs of 1944 also bred complacency. Montgomery, thirsting to lead the charge to Berlin, diverted too weak a force to shut off the passage that allowed some 70,000 German soldiers, including many from the Fifteenth Army, to escape from Normandy along the northern coast and regroup in Holland. The Belgian port of Antwerp was captured and should have opened a direct entry for supplies, especially gasoline, from England. But the Germans were not dislodged from the approaches to the harbor, making it useless. The result was that Allied armor, especially the tanks of Patton's marauding Third Army, were hampered by shortages of petrol, which had to be trucked from faraway ports.

Montgomery's desire to be the captor of Berlin drove him to another disastrous action. This was his decision to carry out airborne landings in eastern Holland in order to seize and hold the bridge at Arnhem that led across the Rhine into Germany. British paratroopers were to capture the bridge while American airborne divisions held the road and its bridges along which an armored British corps was to reach Arnhem after breaking out of its beachhead more than fifty miles away. Many voices were raised against this scheme, including those of Bletchley Park codebreakers, whose decrypts had ascertained that not only was the regrouped Fifteenth Army near the landing sites but that two other Panzer divisions were in the Arnhem sector to be reequipped with new tanks. These powerful forces were joined by battalions armed with heavy antitank guns. Another Bletchley Park decrypt disclosed that Field Marshal Walther Model had established a headquarters only four miles from Arnhem, putting him in the position of mobilizing and directing the countermeasures against the attackers.

Nothing would dissuade Montgomery. He ignored all the warnings and ordered the landings. The result was a slaughter. Of the original force of 10,000 soldiers, only about 2,000 escaped, many of them having to swim the broad expanse of the Rhine. The others were killed or taken prisoner.

The Germans formed a new line along the Rhine and held Germany's frontier against all Allied attacks through the fall and into the winter.

A big difference for the Allies was that in their drive across western Europe, they no longer had a grand, overarching deception plan as they had had for the Normandy invasion. As Anthony Cave Brown has noted, the war had become for the Allies a grim spectacle of frontal assault against dug-in defenses, of bludgeoning force rather than skillful artifice, of attacks that lacked surprise. All of these together caused the struggle to "deteriorate into dull carnage," with Allied casualties greatly exceeding those of the deception-aided Normandy battles.

In mid-December came the harshest blow of all. After being tricked repeatedly, Hitler planned a trick of his own. He could not hide from the dominant Allied air forces that he was gathering troops for a counterattack, but he could mislead his enemy from knowing where it would strike. Allied commanders were sure that the most he could achieve with his diminished forces was a "spoiling action," probably against the Allied formations assembling for their own attack against the northern German city of Aachen. Instead, Hitler planned to drive through the Ardennes forests, which the Allies so lightly regarded as a possibility that it was defended only by a thin line of green, newly arrived, half-trained American troops and a few battle-weary units sent there for rehabilitation. To make sure his plan remained secret, Hitler maintained communications not by radio but mostly by landlines and motorcycle couriers. The consequence was that not even Bletchley Park was able to give adequate warning of what was to come.

Hitler's dream was to smash through the weak American lines, turn north into Belgium, drive to Antwerp, cut off the British divisions in the north and force them into another Dunkirk, so demoralizing the British people that they would insist on Britain's dropping out of the war.

This was the Battle of the Bulge—a dark cloud that had something of a silver lining. It was a brutal shock to the Allies and the death knell for altogether too many young soldiers. But it achieved none of Hitler's goals and used up his waning resources of men and materials. Its defeat marked the start of the crumbling of the German war machine, allowing the Allies to slash into the heartland from the west while the Russians closed in from the east.

Winston Churchill summed it up: "This was the final German offensive of the war. It cost us no little anxiety and postponed our own advance, but we benefited in the end. The Germans could not replace their losses, and our subsequent battles on the Rhine, though severe, were undoubtedly eased."

Victory in Europe Day, or V-E Day, came on May 8, 1945. By then Hitler had committed suicide in his Berlin bunker, the Americans and Russians had joined hands on the Elbe, the Soviets had taken Berlin, the Allies had discovered the Nazi concentration camps and exposed to the world's horror and pity the emaciated bodies of the Holocaust victims stacked like cordwood, and the Allied leaders had turned their attention to the defeat of Japan.

A number of the double agents were asked to stay on the alert in case

German diehards tried to organize some post-conflict trickery. But none surfaced. For the most part the agents let themselves fade into an obscurity that held during the thirty years in which Britain's Official Secrets Act remained fully in force. Although the ban has largely been lifted, there are undoubtedly still-unreleased files in the National Archives at Kew that may one day add interesting new chapters to the story whose telling this book has been privileged to present.

CHAPTER TWENTY

THE FINAL RECKONING

As the war in Europe drew toward its close, Dusko Popov burned with desire to find out what had happened to his friend Johnny Jebsen. Popov refused to accept the probability that Jebsen was dead. Driven by the belief that he himself was mainly responsible for Jebsen's fate, whatever it was, Popov began a series of extraordinary efforts to find out. From his brother Ivo, who had also known Jebsen, Popov got clues that led him to Paris, only recently liberated. There he tracked down people who knew of Jebsen's arrest but could tell him little more than that Jebsen had been accused of high treason and sent to the concentration camp at Oranienburg, just north of Berlin.

With the end of the war in Europe, the concentration camps, including Oranienburg, were of course liberated. Still, there was no word from or about Jebsen. Popov ran down clue after clue. One of his stops was with a man who had at one point been in a cell next to that of Jebsen. He recalled Jebsen being brought to his cell after a vicious beating that had bloodied his shirt. As his guards shut him in, Jebsen called out, "I trust I shall be provided with a clean shirt." Yes, Popov thought, that certainly fitted in with his own memories of the impeccable Johnny.

Finally convinced that Jebsen had been killed, Popov resolved to track down whoever was responsible and take vengeance on him. One name that kept coming up was that of Walter Salzer, reputed to be the minor official who carried out the dirty work for his boss in the SD, the German secret intelligence service. Popov dressed himself in the uniform of the rank the grateful British had awarded, that of lieutenant colonel, and returned to Paris determined to find Salzer. He rented a jeep and drove into Germany to check the records of every prison camp where former members of the SD were being held. He drew more blanks.

Before the war, Popov found, Salzer had worked for one of Jebsen's companies in Hamburg. Popov drove there. This time he was successful. He browbeat a former director of the company to tell him where Salzer was living under an assumed name. Popov trapped Salzer and, at pistol point, had the German drive the jeep to a woods outside town. Popov motioned Salzer to get out of the jeep and stand with his back to a tree. He fully intended to shoot Salzer but not until he found out what had happened to Jebsen. Abject with fear, Salzer sank to his knees and said repeatedly, between sobs, that he had only been following orders. At last he admitted that one of those orders was to execute Jebsen.

Popov was so overcome with revulsion for the man that instead of shooting him he beat him senseless with his fists and left him to recover there as he might. He saw his vengeance on Salzer as only a partial payment on his debt to Jebsen. In addition he sought out Jebsen's actress wife, Lore, and found her living a penurious life in Russian-occupied Germany. He arranged her passage to the Allied control zone, cleared her debts and helped secure her acting work in theaters there.

In addition to giving Popov his postwar honorary high rank in the army, the British expressed their appreciation of his wartime services in another way: he was awarded the Order of the British Empire. The ceremony took place, appropriately, in the cocktail bar of the Ritz.

Dusko's fondness for attractive young women never weakened. At the age of thirty-four he married an eighteen-year-old French girl and had a son by her. The marriage did not last. When he was approaching fifty he met a Swedish girl whose beauty bowled him over. She was also eighteen. He married her and took her to live at his estate in southern France. She bore him three sons and survived him as his well-off widow when he died in 1981 at the age of sixty-nine.

Popov's longtime spymaster, Ludovico von Karsthoff, suffered a singular fate. When Admiral Canaris was deposed as the Abwehr chief in

1944, his officers began jockeying frantically for favor with their new SD bosses. One of them, an officer named Wiegand, envied von Karsthoff's cozy life in Lisbon. In a deal involving documents brought to Lisbon by Popov, Wiegand outsmarted von Karsthoff, embarrassed him in the eyes of the Berlin superiors and replaced him. Von Karsthoff was transferred to Austria just in time to be in the path of the Soviet juggernaut when it rolled over the country. He was executed by the Russians.

A happier story is that of Wulf Schmidt—Tate. Having rejected the totalitarian regime of Nazism and embraced the freer life in Britain, he became quite Anglicized. Yet his spymaster, Major Ritter, never doubted his allegiance to the Nazi cause, even when Schmidt informed him that he had married an English girl worker on a farm in Hertfordshire and, later, announced that "I have just become the father of a seven-pound son." He continued exchanging messages with Ritter in Hamburg until May 2, 1945, only a few hours before the city fell to the Allies. Ritter's last message answered Schmidt's earlier question about a suitcase he had left at Hamburg in 1939 before his flight to England. Ritter assured him that the suitcase had been turned over to his sister after all dangerous documents in it had been destroyed.

After the war, Schmidt sought and was granted permission to stay in England. He was given British citizenship and a new identity. A subsequent report said of him that he "is now divorced from his wartime bride and leads a discreet and highly respectable life in what might fairly broadly be described as the legal profession."

When the end of the war made it no longer necessary for the British to keep Arthur Owens—Snow—in prison, he was released. Those in the know about him, however, were aware that, at his age and with his prison record against him, he would be unable to make a living. The authorities' sympathies were stirred by the memory that Owens had, after all, served Britain's interests well during those early times when he had become the first double agent. Also, he showed no resentment of his treatment. He was granted the sums he needed to sustain him through the rest of his life.

When last reported in these pages, Eddie Chapman—ZigZag—that safecracker turned German saboteur turned British double agent, was living in Norway and enjoying the substantial reward that his spymaster,

Baron Stefan von Groening, had secured for him in recognition of his bogus demolition exploits against the Allies. In Norway, Chapman lived well for months, serving the Abwehr as a consultant on sabotage methods. Then he again became restless. Von Groening agreed, in mid-1944, to put him back to work as a spy in Britain. As Masterman has described it: "News had trickled through to us of a mysterious figure at Oslo—a man speaking bad German in a rather loud high-pitched voice, clad in a salt-and-pepper suit, displaying two gold teeth and enjoying the amenities of a private yacht. This we thought must be ZigZag, and so it was." Masterman's image of ZigZag indulging himself on a "yacht" was a bit of an exaggeration. Chapman did live on a sailboat, which he used to hone his sailing skills in order to improve his chances if he had to engineer a sudden escape.

After giving Chapman a lengthy questionnaire, the Germans dropped him by parachute in Cambridgeshire, equipped with two wireless sets, cameras, £6,000 and a contract promising a princely reward for answers to the Abwehr's questions. These included reports on the damage caused by flying bombs, the locations of American air force stations, details of the radio location system by which Allied night fighter planes detected enemy aircraft and photographs of Britain's asdic gear for spotting submarines.

Alerted to ZigZag's arrival by Bletchley Park decrypts, the British were ready to receive him. He proved to be a rich source of information about the situation in Germany, the V-weapons, the disastrous destruction of cities by Allied bombing and the low morale of German submarine crews due to British anti-U-boat devices.

He plunged in to answering the Abwehr questions in the way the Twenty Committee wanted him to reply. However, a problem soon arose. With the money the Abwehr had lavished on him, he returned to boozing it up with his old cronies in the West End, spending long evenings at Smokey Joe's and the Shim Sham Club. And during these binges he couldn't restrain himself from bragging about the sources of his income. MI5 had to close down his case.

Ever irrepressible, Chapman continued to live well after the war. He opened a health farm that prospered, drove himself around the countryside in a Rolls-Royce and refused to let the Official Secrets Act stop him from publishing his memoirs. He married, had a daughter and four grandchildren and lived until December 1997.

Baron von Groening proved to be the most understanding of spymasters. Despite being deceived by Chapman throughout the war, he came to Britain to attend the wedding of Chapman's daughter.

After his great service in support of the D-Day deceptions, Roman Garby-Czerniawski—Brutus—encountered some personal trouble. On July 23, 1944, his house in London was damaged by a V-1 and his wife, "Moustique," suffered facial injuries that required plastic surgery. His British controllers took notice. Garby-Czerniawski had worked as a double agent without remuneration. Now, the controllers realized, he faced the costs of repairs to his house, the expenses of living in a hotel in the meantime and the medical bills for his wife's treatments. As with Snow, the British showed their appreciation for Brutus's secret contribution by extending him financial aid.

The liberation of France brought another problem for Brutus. The French began investigations and trials relating to those individuals who had cooperated with the Nazis during the war. Fearing that his pseudo-service as a spy for the Germans might be aired and endanger the double-cross system, B1A came to the decision to close down his case.

Garby-Czerniawski, postwar, settled down as an English resident, got remarried to an Englishwoman, raised a family, wrote his memoir and successfully ran his own printing firm.

His Interallié assistant and turncoat, Mathilde Carré, escaped German imprisonment and went to England, only to be arrested there and, again, sentenced to prison. She wrote her memoir, *I Was the Cat.*

Of the lesser agents, Jack Moe—Mutt—and the British impersonator of Jeff had come to the end of their repeated "invasions" of Norway and to the close of the Germans' interest in them. Postwar, Moe lived on in England while Tor Glad was released from his detention. He opted to live in Sweden.

Lily Sergueiew—Treasure—had her case brought to an abrupt close just over a week following D-Day. The decision came as the result of her controllers' egregious misreading of her volatile temperament. She had confided to her case officer, Mary Sherer, that she, Sergueiew, had it in her power to end, at any moment, the Germans' faith in her as a spy for them. At her last meetings in Lisbon with her German spymaster, Emil Klie-mann, he had given her a security check, a detail she could insert in a message that would warn him she had been compromised. Sherer pressed her to reveal what the check was, but Treasure put her off.

The whole secret turned on a hyphen—a hyphen she could insert be-tween two letters in the opening signal of a message. But since she had never made use of it, she saw no need now to give in to the British. One would have thought that by then they would have learned how quickly she could get her back up. But oh, no. Their understanding of her prickly character failed to go that far. One day Tar Robertson bustled in and, ac-cording to her accounting of the scene, immediately announced that be-cause of her intransigence on this point, she was no longer trustworthy and would transmit no more.

His subsequent words and actions made it clear he was bluffing in the hope of bending her to compliance. Not a chance. Sergueiew would have bitten off her tongue rather than let it tell him what he demanded. "Go away," she told him.

Treasure assured herself this was all just as well. She had achieved the task she had come to England to do. She was tired of the game. Besides, the Allies were now in France, and France would soon be needing her more than would these nasty Brits.

A day later, Sherer came to see her. It was evident that a strong affec-tion had developed between them. Mary made it clear that she'd had no choice but to go along with Robertson. Lily said she understood.

"Do you think you could look on me as a friend?" Mary asked.

Lily reassured her. "You are my friend."

At the end of that final talk, Sergueiew came to the decision to disclose the security check to Mary, knowing it would increase her stature in the eyes of her superiors.

Sergueiew, leaving off any signs of her sickness, enlisted in the French army and returned to France after Paris was liberated. While serving as an interpreter for an American unit resettling displaced persons, she met a genuine American officer, Major J. B. Collins, married him and, after the war, went to live on his farm in Cedar, Michigan.

She had completed French and English drafts of her book *Secret Service Rendered* before she died from kidney failure in 1950. Despite British efforts to prevent its publication, the French version came out in 1966 and the English one in 1968. Subsequently it was chosen by the editors of Time-Life books to be one of its series of "Classics of World War II."

Of Elvira Chaudoir/Bronx, as previously noted, no records are available in the National Archives. Britain's Security Service indicates they have scheduled the release of files on her but the scheduling comes too late for any of the material to be included here.

And what of Juan Pujol—Garbo, the greatest? In December 1944 an official of MI5 matched Garbo's Iron Cross with the award of a Medal of the British Empire. Anthony Cave Brown has pointed out that with this award Pujol became surely the only man in history able to wear both medals on the same dinner jacket.

When the war in Europe ended, MI5 still had one more task for Garbo: to use his prestige with the Germans to determine whether the Nazis planned any clandestine postwar activity. As Tomás Harris explained it: "Our main object was to get Garbo quickly to Madrid to make contact with his German masters as it was thought that he alone would be able to ascertain whether or not the Germans were proposing to carry on any form of underground organization in the postwar."

At the end of the hostilities, consequently, Pujol went to Spain to find out what he could from his former spymasters. First he found Karl Eric Kuehlanthal's associate Friedrich Knappe-Ratey, who was living under house arrest by the Spanish authorities. Friedrich told him how to find Kuehlanthal, who was in hiding in Ávila. When Pujol found Kuehlanthal, they had an emotional reunion. During their three-hour conversation, Pujol expressed his willingness to continue to operate for the Nazis if they should have any plans for the future. Kuehlanthal's response was reassuring. He felt bound to accept Germany's defeat and to abandon hope of rendering any further service. He planned to remain in hiding for fear that if the Spanish found him, they would send him back to Germany.

The conversation yielded another reason why Kuehlanthal wanted to avoid that eventuality: one of his grandparents had been of Jewish origin. That was why he was in Spain. He had come there during the Spanish Civil War after having to abandon his commercial career in Germany. The good connections he had made in Spain had enabled him to secure his wartime job with the Abwehr.

Returning to London to submit his report, Pujol had to decide what he himself would do with his postwar life. British friends wished to have him stay in the United Kingdom and offered him employment with an insurance company. His choice, though, was to start a new life in South America. MI5 gave him a gratuity of £15,000 to start him on his way. He decided upon Venezuela. Settled there, he lived quietly, in anonymity. "I wanted to be forgotten," he wrote later, "to pass unnoticed and to be untraceable."

History, though, included one more glorious chapter in Pujol's history. He remained in his Venezuelan seclusion for thirty-six years. Then in 1984 Nigel West, nom de plume for English writer Rupert Allason, proved him not to be untraceable. West hunted him down and induced him to return to England. He was met with a hero's welcome. The Duke of Edinburgh received him at Buckingham Palace and expressed personal thanks for all that Pujol had accomplished. After a heart-lifting round of reunions with friends and former colleagues, he returned to Caracas. He learned about oil field operations and worked at Shell's head office in Caracas. Later he opened up a gift shop in the commercial center of Caracas and died there in 1988.

And what of the masterminds who guided and controlled the double agents? LCS chief John Bevan kept the organization alive by holding a dinner for members each year at his club. He himself returned to a quiet but prosperous business life and became a Privy Councillor.

Stewart Menzies, august head of British intelligence, sequestered himself in his country home until the Cold War heated up and Winston Churchill returned to 10 Downing Street. Churchill summoned him to resume his old job, which he held until the scandal about Kim Philby broke into the news. As the man who had appointed Philby to his wartime post, Menzies had his reputation severely blackened by the disclosure that Philby, all unbeknownst to Menzies, had used his position at the center of British intelligence to spy for Communist Russia. Menzies was compelled to tender his resignation and once again retire. He died in 1968 before his leading role in the secret war could be revealed and a good measure of his stature restored.

As the war approached its end, Dudley Clarke closeted himself at the "A" Force headquarters building that the outfit had shared with a Cairo brothel. There he composed his history of the organization. On his last page he wrote that "the pounding of typewriters once more gave place to the squeals of illicit pleasure." In 1948, he published a book of memoirs, *Seven Assignments,* but it dealt only with his prewar experiences. He sought permission to write a book on wartime deceptions but was turned down. Clarke founded an "A" Force Association and kept in contact with his former colleagues until his death in 1974.

Tar Robertson continued his service with MI5 into the Cold War years, taking on as one of his responsibilities that of presiding over the new equivalent of the Twenty Committee. He died in 1994.

John Masterman resumed his academic life at Oxford, became provost of Worcester College and a university vice-chancellor. He received his knighthood in 1959. Masterman also returned to writing books. His account of Oxford life, *To Teach the Senators Wisdom,* was published in 1952, and his second detective novel, *The Case of the Four Friends,* in 1956.

Much could be said, much could be claimed, in a final assessment of the results of the double agents' efforts. Perhaps it is best to leave the summary to an up-close expert. Here is how U.S. general Omar Bradley expressed it:

> [Operation Fortitude] was responsible for containing a mini-mum of twenty enemy divisions in the Pas de Calais during the first crucial months of the invasion. The enemy was led to be-lieve—and reacted to—a long inventory of opportune untruths, the largest, most effective and decisive of which was that [the Nor-mandy invasion] itself was only the prelude to a major invasion in the Pas de Calais area. . . . Best testimony to the effectiveness with which this information influenced the enemy's command decisions is the historic record of the enemy's committing his forces piecemeal—paralyzed into indecision in Normandy by the convic-tion that he had more to fear from Calais.

CAST OF PRINCIPAL CHARACTERS

Arnim, Hans-Jürgen von. German general assigned to help Erwin Rommel defeat the Allies in North Africa.

Auchinleck, Claude. British general in charge, for a time, of Middle Eastern forces opposing Rommel in North Africa.

Bevan, John. British officer put in charge of the London Controlling Section (LCS), responsible for planning deceptions.

Canaris, Wilhelm. German admiral, head of the Abwehr secret service, whose secret anti-Nazi beliefs led to his dismissal and eventual execution.

Caroli, Gösta (Summer). Swedish mechanic recruited by the Abwehr but who became, for a time, a British double agent.

Chapman, Edward (ZigZag). Convicted British criminal who became a pretend spy and demolition expert for the Abwehr.

Chaudoir, Elvira (Bronx). Peruvian diplomat's daughter who became a British double agent and was highly regarded by the Abwehr.

Clark, Mark. U.S. general in charge of the Allies' Seventh Army in the Italian campaign.

Clarke, Dudley W. British officer, head of "A" Force, who planned many Middle Eastern deception programs.

Eisenhower, Dwight D. American general in command of Allied forces in North Africa and then of the Supreme Headquarters, Allied Expeditionary Force.

Gaertner, Friedl (Gelatine). Austrian woman turned anti-Nazi who became a double agent in Dusko Popov's triumvirate.

Garby-Czerniawski, Roman (Brutus). Polish Air Force officer who was imprisoned by the Germans as a leader of the French Resistance and who "escaped" to become a British double agent.

Glad, Tor (Jeff). Norwegian Abwehr recruit who served as a British double agent until his Nazi past was revealed.

Groening, Stefan von. Abwehr spymaster in charge of Eddie Chapman case.

Harris, Tomás. British case officer handling the Juan Pujol case.

Jebsen, Johann "Johnny" (Artist). Anti-Nazi German member of Abwehr who became a confederate of Popov and a double agent for the British.

Karsthoff, Ludovico von. Abwehr spymaster in Lisbon who handled Popov and other agents.

Kliemann, Emil. Abwehr officer assigned as spymaster for Lily Sergueiew (Treasure).

Kuehlanthal, Karl Eric. Abwehr spymaster in Madrid to whom Juan Pujol was assigned.

Levi, Renato (Cheese). Italian who established the Abwehr Italy link with Cairo that was actually run by the British.

Masterman, John Cecil. Oxford don and novelist who was chosen to chair the Twenty Committee.

McCarthy, Sam (Biscuit). Reformed British wastrel who became a trusted subordinate to double agent Owens.

Metcalfe, Dickie (Balloon). Ex-army officer who supplied technical information as a subagent to Dusko Popov.

Moe, Helge "Jack" (Mutt). Norwegian trained by the Abwehr as a spy and saboteur but who became instead a valuable agent for the British.

Montagu, Ewen. London barrister who became the Royal Navy's representative to the Twenty Committee and cocreator of "The Man Who Never Was" deception.

Montgomery, Bernard. British general in charge of the Eighth Army who used deception to beat Erwin Rommel at El Alamein.

Nicossof, Paul. "Notional" spy created by the British in Cairo to report to German spymasters in Italy.

Owens, Arthur George (Snow). Welsh businessman whose travels to the Continent led the Abwehr to recruit him as a spy but who became Britain's first double agent.

Patton, George S. U.S. general in charge of the largely notional First U.S. Army Group (FUSAG) in England and then of the real Third Army in France.

Popov, Dusan "Dusko" (Tricycle). Yugoslav businessman sought as a spy for Germany who pretended to agree but instead joined the British double agents.

Pujol Garcia, Juan (Garbo). Spaniard whose will to bring down Nazi Fascism drove him to volunteer as a British double agent and become foremost among them.

Ritter, Nikolaus. Spymaster in charge of Owens, Schmidt and other double agents.

Robertson, Thomas A. "Tar." Officer in charge of B1A section of MI5, which oversaw the running of British double agents.

Rundstedt, Gerd von. German field marshal whose varied assignments included command of German defenses against the Allies' Normandy invasion.

Schmidt, Wulf (Tate). Young Nazi and Abwehr recruit who, turned by the British, became a convert to democracy and a trusted double agent.

Sergueiew, Natalia "Lily" (Treasure). Russian-French woman who volunteered to be an Abwehr spy while intending to work against the Germans as a double agent.

Wavell, Archibald. British commander-in-chief in the Middle East and then in the Far East who was a strong believer in and advocate of military deception.

Williams, Gwilym (G.W.). Believed by the Germans to be an anti-British Welsh nationalist but who served as a double agent with Owens and, later, on his own.

ACKNOWLEDGMENTS

As one of the fortunate veterans of World War II who has survived into my octogenarian years retaining a reasonable degree of my wits and energies, I need to express my appreciation to several indispensable aids in the research and writing of this book. Foremost is Patricia, my wife of fifty-seven years, who shouldered many extra burdens to allow me the time to concentrate on the task. She has also been my chief consultant and critic.

I'm deeply indebted to my English friends John Gallehawk, Mike Reed and Doro Sharpley for their ever-willing help, and to my professional researcher, David List, who provided expert guidance in dealing with Britain's National Archives and other sources.

And once again I'm most fortunate in having had the wise counsel of Richard Curtis, my literary agent. I've welcomed the creative suggestions of Tina Brown as my editor at New American Library.

Of my many sources, I've looked to Martin Gilbert's history, *The Second World War,* to help me keep my chronological and factual bearings in the shifting tides of the war. My quotes from Winston Churchill are largely excerpted from the prime minister's magisterial six-volume *The Second World War.*

The main sources for my particular story have been Britain's National Archives at Kew. During the last few years, many of the files relating to the double agents have been declassified. It has been my privilege to examine several thousands of these documents.

My bibliography makes clear that I have also benefitted from the works of many other writers on the subject. Sir John Masterman's *The Double-Cross System* and Roger Hesketh's *Fortitude* began as reports that each of them wrote at the war's end, when the details of what had been done were still fresh in their memories. For nearly three decades their books were denied publication by Britain's Official Secrets Act. For a researcher, both give indispensable testimony—the one of the work of the Twenty Committee, the other of the agents' role in the deceptions for the Normandy landings.

Other general sources I found to be of special value include Ralph Bennett's *Behind the Battle*; Anthony Cave Brown's monumental but sometimes untrustworthy *Bodyguard of Lies*; Charles Cruikshank's *Deception in World War II*; James Gannon's *Stealing Secrets, Telling Lies*; Thaddeus Holt's *The Deceivers*; Michael Howard's *Strategic Deception in the Second World War;* Ewen Montagu's *Beyond Top Secret Ultra;* and Jeffrey Richardson's *A Century of Spies*.

Of the many books dealing with the vital support given the double agents by Allied codebreakers, the ones I most depended on were *British Intelligence in the Second World War* by F. H. Hinsley et al, *The Ultra Secret* by F. W. Winterbotham, and my own 2003 book on the subject, *Codebreakers' Victory*.

Sources for accounts of specific double agents and events include the above as well as more specific sources as indicated in the following summary.

Chapter 1: The Most Delicious Irony: Details of the various double agents are drawn primarily from the KV 2 and WO 169 series of National Archives files.

Chapter 2: Masterminds of the Double Cross: Main sources are Masterman and Montagu. The "thinly disguised novel" is Sefton Delmer's *The Counterfeit Spy*.

Chapter 3: Ultra, the Double Agents' Indispensable Ally: The codebreakers' contribution to the double agents' successes, especially their ability to carry out deceptions, are drawn primarily from my book *Code-breakers' Victory*.

Chapter 4: In the Beginning, Snow: KV 2/444 to 453. Material on Gwilym Williams is mainly from KV 2/468.

Chapter 5: Tricycle, the Abwehr's Yugoslav Socialite: Sources include KV 2/862, 3 and 5; Popov's own glamorized memoir, *Spy/Counterspy;* and Russell Miller's *Codename Tricycle*.

Chapter 6: Tate, Convert from Nazism: KV 2/61 and 62; and Chapter 4 of the book *Spy!* by Richard Deacon and Nigel West.

Chapter 7: ZigZag, the Most Daring: KV 2/461 and 2; and Chapman's own memoir, *The Eddie Chapman Story*.

Chapter 8: Code Name Brutus: KV 2/72–3; Garby-Czerniawski's own memoir, *The Big Network*, and Hugo Bleicher's *Colonel Henri's Story*.

Chapter 9: Treasure, First Violin in the Deception Orchestra: K/464–466, plus Sergueiew's own memoir, *Secret Service Rendered*.

Chapter 10: Garbo, the Greatest: KV 2/39–42; KV 2/63–71; KV 4/191; WO 208/4374; *Operation Garbo,* a collaboration by Pujol and Nigel West; *Garbo: The Spy Who Saved D-Day,* in which Mark Seaman supplies an introduction to Tomás Harris's postwar report on the Garbo case; and Delmer's "novelized" version, *The Counterfeit Spy.*

Chapter 11: Mutt, Jeff and Other Lesser Agents: KV 2/1067 on Moe; KV 2/1068 on Glad; although, as noted in the text, no Archives files are available on Chaudoir, her story was known to and reported by Masterman et al; KV 4/268 on G.W.'s rebirth; and Masterman on Rainbow and Hamlet.

Chapter 12: Tricycle's American Misadventure: Popov's memoir; Miller's *Tricycle*; Thomas Troy's attack on Popov's credibility, *The British Assault on*

J. Edgar Hoover: The Tricycle Case; and B. Bruce-Brigg's rebuttal, *Another Ride on Tricycle.*

Chapter 13: Trickery in the Middle East: KV 2/1133; KV 4/197; KV 4/234; WO 169/24804; WO 169/24847–24849; plus Cruikshank, Howard, David Mure's *Master of Deception* and *The Rommel Papers,* edited by Liddell Hart. The identification of Renato Levi as Cheese is my own deduction from the Archives files. Probably for protection of the individuals, actual names have been whited out in the files, although many of them have become known by other means. In the files for Cheese, the attempt was made to remove all identifying references, but there were slipups that made the identification possible. My identification is confirmed in Holt's *The Deceivers.*

Chapter 14: For Operation Torch, Strategic Deceptions: KV 2/39–42; KV 2/1067-8; KV 4/62; Cruikshank and Howard.

Chapter 15: Anywhere but Sicily: KV 2/234; KV 2/1133; KV 4/234; and WO 169/24848. The Operation Mincemeat account is a summation of Montagu's *The Man Who Never Was.* The Currer-Briggs anecdote is from Michael Smith's *Station X.*

Chapter 16: Prelude to Fortitude: Significant Bletchley Park decrypts from Hinsley et al; accounts of main pre-D-Day deceptions from Cruikshank, Gannon, Howard and Mure.

Chapter 17: Double Cross in Jeopardy: Cave Brown, Hesketh, Masterman et al. The doubts about Brutus, from KV 2/72. The problem with Mrs. Garbo, from KV 4/191.

Chapter 18: The "Grand Strategic Deception": Since Roger Hesketh was in charge of the D-Day deceptions, his long and detailed report in *Fortitude* is the main source of the summation here. Other sources, from Bennett to Volkman, were of value.

Chapter 19: Deceptions Beyond D-Day: Masterman for deceptions regarding V-weapons and U-boats; Dr. R.V. Jones's *Most Secret War* for V-weapon countermeasures; Cave Brown for Goodwood and Cobra; Harclerode for the catastrophe at Arnhem; and my *Codebreakers' Victory* for the intelligence failures of the Battle of the Bulge.

Chapter 20: The Final Reckoning: Miller for Popov's postwar search; Hesketh for Fortitude South II; journalist Oliver J. Campbell for details of Garbo's last years; and Cave Brown for the Bradley quote.

Andrew, Christopher, ed. *Codebreaking and Signals Intelligence.* London: Frank Cass, 1986.

Beesly, Patrick. *Very Special Intelligence: The Story of the Admiralty's Operational Intelligence Centre, 1939–1945.* New York: Doubleday, 1978.

Bendeck, Whitney Talley. "The Art of Deception: Dueling Intelligence Organizations in World War II." Master's thesis, Florida State University, 2004.

Bennett, Ralph. *Behind the Battle: Intelligence in the War with Germany, 1939–1945.* Rev. ed. London: Pimlico, 1999.

Bleicher, Hugo. *Colonel Henri's Story.* Translated by Ian Colvin. London: Kimber, 1954.

Boyd, Carl. *Hitler's Japanese Confidant: General Ōshima Hiroshi and Magic Intelligence, 1941–1945.* Lawrence: University Press of Kansas, 1993.

Bruce-Briggs, B. *Another Ride on Tricycle.* London: *Intelligence and National Security,* Vol. 7, No. 2, Frank Cass, 1992.

Cave Brown, Anthony. *Bodyguard of Lies: The Extraordinary True Story Behind D-Day.* New York: Harper & Row, 1975.

Churchill, Winston S. *The Second World War.* 6 vols. New York: Houghton Mifflin, 1948–53.

Cruikshank, Charles. *Deception in World War II.* Oxford: Oxford University Press, 1979.

Deacon, Richard, with Nigel West. *Spy!* London: British Broadcasting Corporation, 1980.

Delmer, Sefton. *The Counterfeit Spy.* New York: Harper & Row, 1971.

Farago, Ladislas. *The Game of the Foxes: The Untold Story of German Espionage in the United States and Great Britain During World War II.* New York: McKay, 1971.

Gannon, James. *Stealing Secrets, Telling Lies: How Spies and Codebreakers Helped Shape the Twentieth Century.* Washington, D.C.: Brassey's, 2001.

Garby-Czerniawski, Roman. *The Big Network.* London: George Ronald, 1961.

Gilbert, Martin. *The Second World War: A Complete History.* New York: Henry Holt, 1989.

Harclerode, Peter. *Arnhem: A Tragedy of Errors.* London: Caxton, 2000.

Harris, Tomás. *Garbo: The Spy Who Saved D-Day.* Introduction by Mark Seaman. Toronto: The Dundurn Group, 2000.

Haufler, Hervie. *Codebreakers' Victory: How the Allied Cryptographers Won World War II.* New York: New American Library, 2003.

Hesketh, Roger. *Fortitude: The D-Day Deception Campaign.* Woodstock and New York: The Overlook Press, 2002.

Hinsley, F. H., E. E. Thomas, C. F. G. Ransom and R. C. Knight. *British Intelligence in the Second World War.* Vols. I–III. London: Her Majesty's Stationery Office, 1975–1990.

Holt, Thaddeus. *The Deceivers: Allied Military Deception in the Second World War.* New York: Scribner, 2004.

Howard, Michael. *Strategic Deception in the Second World War.* New York: W. W. Norton, 1990.

Hughes, Terry and John Costello. *The Battle of the Atlantic: The First Complete Account of the Origins and Outcome of the Longest and Most Crucial Campaign of World War II.* New York: Dial, 1977.

Jones, R. V. *Most Secret War: British Scientific Intelligence 1939–1945.* London: Hamish Hamilton, 1978.

———. *Reflections on Intelligence.* London: Heinemann, 1989.

Kahn, David. *The Codebreakers: The Comprehensive History of Secret*

Communication from Ancient Times to the Internet. Rev. ed. New York: Scribner, 1996.

————. *Hitler's Spies: German Military Intelligence in World War II.* New York: Macmillan, 1978.

Keegan, John. *The Second World War.* New York: Viking, 1990.

Kesselring, Albert. *A Soldier's Record.* Westport, CT: Greenwood Press, 1981.

Liddell Hart, B. H. *The German Generals Talk.* New York: William Morrow, 1948.

————, ed. *The Rommel Papers.* With the assistance of Lucie-Marie Rommel, Manfred Rommel and General Fritz Bayerlein. Translated by Paul Findley. New York: Harcourt Brace, 1953.

Masterman, John C. *The Double-Cross System in the War of 1939 to 1945.* New Haven: Yale University Press, 1972.

Miller, Robert A. *August 1944: The Campaign for France.* Navato, CA: Presidio Press, 1988.

Miller, Russell. *Codename Tricycle.* London: Secker & Warburg, 2004.

Montagu, Ewen. *The Man Who Never Was.* New York: J. B. Lippincott, 1958.

————. *Beyond Top Secret Ultra.* New York: Coward, McCann & Geoghagen, 1978.

Mure, David. *Master of Deception.* London: Kimber, 1980.

Overy, Richard. *Russia's War.* New York: Penguin, 1997.

Owen, Frank. *The Eddie Chapman Story.* London: Allan Wingate, 1953.

Popov, Dusko. *Spy/Counterspy.* New York: Grosset & Dunlop, 1974.

Richardson, Jeffrey T. *A Century of Spies: Intelligence in the Twentieth Century.* New York: Oxford University Press, 1995.

Sergueiew, Lily. *Secret Service Rendered.* London: Kimber, 1968.

Smith, Michael. *Station X: The Codebreakers of Bletchley Park.* London: Macmillan, 1999.

————. *Foley: The Spy Who Saved 10,000 Jews.* London: Hodder and Stoughton, 1999.

Stephenson, William. *A Man Called Intrepid.* New York: Harcourt Brace Jovanovich, 1976.

Summers, Anthony. *Official and Confidential: The Secret Life of J. Edgar Hoover.* New York: G. P. Putnam, 1993.

Troy, Thomas F. "The British Assault on J. Edgar Hoover: The Tricycle Case." *International Journal of Intelligence and Counterintelligence* 3, no. 2 (1989).

Volkman, Ernest. *Spies: The Secret Agents Who Changed the Course of History.* New York: John Wiley & Sons, 1997.

West, Nigel (Rupert Allason). *Counterfeit Spies: Genuine or Bogus? An Astonishing Investigation into Secret Agents of the Second World War.* London: St. Ermin's Press, 1988.

——— with Juan Pujol. *Operation Garbo: The Personal Story of the Most Successful Double Agent of World War II.* New York: Random House, 1985.

Winterbotham, F. W. *The Ultra Secret.* New York: Harper & Row, 1974.